D0914025

IN THE BLOOD

IN THE BLOOD

BATTLES TO SUCCEED IN CANADA'S FAMILY BUSINESSES

GORDON PITTS

Doubleday Canada

Doubleday Canada and colophon are trademarks.

Canadian Cataloguing in Publication Data

Pitts, Gordon
      In the blood : battles to succeed in Canada's family businesses
Includes index.

ISBN 0-385-25829-1

1. Family-owned business enterprises — Canada.   2. Family-owned business enterprises — Canada — Succession.   I. Title.
HD62.25.P576 2000   658'.045   C99-932213-3

Jacket and text design by Susan Thomas/Digital Zone
Printed and bound in the USA

Published in Canada by
Doubleday Canada, a division of
Random House of Canada Limited
105 Bond Street
Toronto, Ontario
M5B 1Y3

Three-circle model on page 243 reprinted by permission of Harvard Business School Press. From *Generation to Generation: Life Cycles of the Family Business* by Kelin E. Gersick, John A. Davis, Marion McCollom Hampton, and Ivan Lansberg. Boston, MA 1997, pp. 6. Copyright © 1997 by the President and Fellows of Harvard College; all rights reserved.

BVG   10   9   8   7   6   5   4   3   2   1

To Mom, Gayle, and Jayne,
my family business partners

CONTENTS

PREFACE

ONE DAY IN THE MID-1970S, I told my father I wanted to join the family business. That business was a dairy farm in eastern Ontario that consisted of 300 acres, about fifty head of purebred Holstein cows, and a dozen cottages on a lake, which my father rented out largely to American tourists each summer. At twenty-six, I did not have the obvious credentials to be a dairy farmer — my degrees were in history and journalism — but I was the only son and I worried that the hundred-year-old farm and its fine dairy herd would slip out of the family. And I genuinely liked working with the cattle, and looked forward to improving the business in partnership with my father.

My father, an emotional man, was enthusiastic about the idea, until I outlined my grand plan: I would come in as a junior partner, and over about ten years I would gradually buy the farm. More important, he would move toward the side-lines, allowing me to assume the dominant decision-making authority. I didn't see it at the time, but this schedule was distressing to my father, who had rarely shared decision-making with anyone.

We never again talked about my joining the business. The grand plan wasn't actually discarded: it was just left in the corner to wither away and gradually die. I know now that my father couldn't have eased himself out of the picture. I went on to a career in journalism, moving from job to job. Dad sold the milk quota and the purebred cattle, ran some beef cattle on the old farm, and rented the rest of the land. After he died in 1984, my family sold the farm. I still have the farm signs that my father had ordered: JAMES A. PITTS & SON, PUREBRED HOLSTEINS.

When I see those signs — and think of my father's dreams, which they embody — the guilt still tears me up. At the same time, I am somewhat relieved that my father and I never had to work together. We could not have got along. He would never have relinquished his authority, and I would have raged out of control, frustrated and confused.

Memories of the farm, and of my stillborn partnership with my father, stuck with me through every stage of writing this book, which examines the family business in Canada. I would be sitting in some office with some young heir, who would be complaining about a parent's unwillingness to give up control, and I would find myself nodding my head, a bit too enthusiastically at times. "Right," I would think. "I was there too, I know how you feel."

There are other inspirations for this book. In the early 1990s, I interviewed Harrison and Wallace McCain, back in the days when the two brothers who ran McCain Foods were still speaking to each other. I found them engaging, interesting men who seemed to have worked things out in their sibling partnership. Their ugly split, which came a couple of years after I interviewed them, taught me that things in a family business are never exactly what they seem. Below the surface, emotions are simmering.

Another inspiration came during a freelance consulting assignment for the Ontario government, which I undertook in the early 1990s when I was between newspaper jobs. I got to know a young man named Peter Cuddy, whose father had built a tremendously successful turkey-breeding operation in southwestern Ontario. The Cuddys were getting into Europe and they were interested in research I was doing on the European Union and the collapse of trade barriers in that part of the world.

Several years later I ran into Peter again. By this time he was gone from the family company, which had disintegrated into armed camps, with three brothers, including Peter, arrayed against their father, Alfred McInroy "Mac" Cuddy. I was struck by the sadness that Peter seemed to carry around with him, and by his regret that he, his father, and his siblings just couldn't get the succession thing right.

A couple of years ago I decided to do something about these percolating thoughts and write a book about family businesses. It would not be an academic work, but rather a piece of journalism — stories about real people in difficult situations. During the research many survivors of family businesses opened up to me about their fears and hopes. I was surprised how much people would tell a complete stranger about themselves, their parents, and their siblings. I think my interviews became a kind of therapy for them.

The complexity of these relationships came home to me one afternoon in Strathroy, Ontario, when I sat down with Mac Cuddy, Peter's father, one of the most cantankerous, frustrating, and engaging people I've ever met. We both agreed afterward that we had got along famously. And why not? For me it was like talking again to my own frustrating and always interesting father.

I have had a lot of help in making this book happen. First, I thank the families who gave so much of their time and of themselves. Many of these people believed in this project as much as I did. Peter Cuddy has been an inspiration, even though he didn't always know it. Geoff Smith, president of Ellis-Don Construction Ltd. in London, Ontario, was remarkably helpful. Philippe and Nan-b de Gaspé Beaubien of the Business Families Foundation were supportive. And there are many more whom I would like to single out — Penny Omnès; David, Barney, and Bob Bentall; Glen Price; Rick Chaplin; Joan Fisk; the late Peter Wilson; Eric Molson; the late Fred Mitchell ... the list goes on.

I must also thank Douglas Goold, editor of *Report on Business*, for his unwavering support. My senior editorial colleagues Cathryn Motherwell and Michael Babad were patient with my comings and goings. Above all, this book belongs to the team that has worked on *Report on Business*'s Managing and Enterprise pages: principal editors S.R. Slobodian and Paul Vieira and reporters Elizabeth Church, Dawn Walton, Wendy Stueck, John Heinzl, and Margot Gibb-Clark. Thanks also to Gayle MacDonald for her constant support, and to Janet McFarland for urging me to write this book. Ann Gibbon, Dave Pyette, Greg Keenan, and Paul Waldie were great listeners. Outside *The Globe and Mail*, Hugh Larratt-Smith and Barbara Moses fed me ideas and inspiration. My editor, Kathryn Exner, and my agent, Dean Cooke, gave valuable support.

Across the country, a number of people helped in important ways — in Toronto, Min Mah, in Saskatoon, James Parker, and in Calgary, David Scobie and Ken Taylor, to name a few. My wife Elaine and daughters Martha and Katie deserve medals for their patience. I may not be leaving my children a family business, but I hope to help them find the same joy in their working lives as I did in writing this book.

INTRODUCTION

UNHAPPY FAMILIES

P ETER CUDDY AND GEOFF SMITH are friends. Both are smart young
businessmen with good educations — Peter with his University of
Western Ontario MBA, and Geoff with a law degree from that same university, which is located in their hometown of London. Both are in their early
forties and are raising young families who ski and ride horseback and play
soccer. Peter and Geoff are perched at what should be the peak of their working lives. What's more, both are from gilded families, the sons of two of the
leading businessmen in that southwestern Ontario city, self-made men who
built great businesses during the economic boom after the Second World War.
Their fathers are hard-driving, profane, self-styled entrepreneurs who pushed
their companies and their families hard but built something fine, visionary,
and lasting.

Peter's father, six-foot four-inch Mac Cuddy, is a giant in Canada's poultry
business, the man who supplies the Chicken McNuggets on the menus of every
McDonald's restaurant in this country. Geoff's dad, Don Smith, is the founder
of Ellis-Don Construction Ltd., the company that spearheaded the building of
Toronto's Skydome, Atlanta's Olympic village, and scores of other building
projects, including sections of the Canary Wharf megaproject in London,
England. In London, Ontario, a city of 350,000, the Cuddys and Smiths are
members of the city's business élite.

At this point in their lives, it might be expected that Geoff Smith and Peter Cuddy would now be helping guide their family companies into the twenty-first century. But only one of them is. Geoff Smith, a tightly wired lawyer with a direct way of talking, is the second-generation president and largest shareholder of his family's company. His father Don, at seventy-five, is retired and looking after his personal investments at a downtown office, far from the suburban headquarters of Ellis-Don. It hasn't been smooth, but the succession is complete. Meanwhile, Geoff's pal Peter Cuddy has been embroiled in a long-running legal battle with his family's company, Cuddy International Corp., which is controlled by his ailing seventy-eight-year-old father. He has been banished from his father's business, along with two of his brothers, who are now building their own lives as entrepreneurs. The family is now split between two camps, three brothers on one side, their father on the other. "This is the greatest struggle I've ever had to go through personally," a teary-eyed Peter told a press conference in 1997 when he launched a lawsuit against Cuddy International. "My father and I are close friends. To bring an action like this ... is really gut-wrenching." And such a waste of time, money, and people's lives.

Is Geoff Smith complacent about succeeding where his friend has failed so tragically? Hardly. The fact that he and his six brothers and sisters have inherited the family business amounts to nothing more than a stroke of luck. By the mid-1990s, Geoff, then Ellis-Don's president, had given up any hope of replacing his father in an orderly succession. Convinced his father was freezing him out, he quit Ellis-Don and bought a small business. He became estranged from his dad, who was on the verge of selling ownership control to a group led by company managers. But that deal suddenly collapsed, and in an eleventh-hour showdown at the family cottage on Lake Huron, Geoff and his siblings agreed to buy it from their father. Now everyone is pulling together, but it was nip and tuck for a while.

Does Geoff Smith have some words of wisdom to pass along to his friend Peter Cuddy and to other young heirs in similar situations? Not really. "The problem with family companies," he says ruefully, "is that even if there was a model, even if there was one set of rules that everyone should follow, given the very essence of family companies, nobody would follow them. I'm glad we found the path that worked for us, but I couldn't get up on any pedestal and say this is what everyone should follow." In essence, the Smith formula for happy business families is nothing more than this: Be patient, be willing to forget words that were spoken and actions that were taken in the heat of the moment, don't try to force things too much, and just hope for the best.

Ah, the mystery of the family business. So many people own them, work in them, and support them as customers or clients, but no one seems to agree on what makes them tick. Until very recently the academic world shied away from studying them. Family business is such a murky field that the *Harvard Business Review*, in a recent case study of a fictional family succession crisis, asked four experts to prescribe solutions as to who should inherit an imaginary company: they provided three different versions of how the succession should unfold. No wonder real-life family business leaders have problems. Much of what happens in a family company is based not on sound management practice, but rather on feelings that have been simmering for years. There often seems to be nothing scientific about the management of a family company. Much of what goes on is rooted in emotion, and succession is the most emotional issue of all. Business professors hate this kind of situation; psychiatrists thrive on it.

The Cuddys and the Smiths exemplify the family business paradoxes — the affection and the contempt, the love and the hate. These are families that talk about their businesses in almost mystical terms. They speak of values and legacies and dynasties and missions. Despite all this passion — or maybe because of it — they have found it difficult to take their companies from the first to the second generation. And even when a company is successfully transferred, later generations are notoriously bad at making it thrive or even survive. Consider all the hoary old clichés about the fate of family businesses over three generations: "rags to riches to rags" and "shirtsleeves to shirtsleeves." Unfortunately, the clichés are accurate. "Keeping a family business alive is perhaps the toughest management job on earth," writes John L. Ward, the American dean of family business academics, in the first sentence of his classic 1987 book, *Keeping the Family Business Healthy*.

There is lots of evidence of how tough that job is in contemporary Canada, in the stories of men and women who built their companies in the booming postwar era and have found it devilishly difficult to pass them on successfully. Their struggles have been the fodder for many a newspaper story, to the point that "family business" today is almost synonymous with "feuding business." Besides the Cuddys, the high-profile battling clans have included the Steinbergs of supermarket fame, the Billeses, who built Canadian Tire, the Bentalls, whose office towers form the core of downtown Vancouver, and the meat-packing Mitchells, the biggest private employers in Saskatoon. Then, of course, there are the ultimate warring brothers, Harrison and Wallace McCain of Florenceville, New Brunswick, who made all the right moves in creating a multinational frozen-food giant, McCain Foods Ltd., but couldn't agree on who would succeed them. Goodbye Wallace, hello lawsuits. All these large companies, built by very smart people, were torn apart by jealousy and suspicion. "Most families fight," shrugs Jimmy Pattison, who runs a multibillion-dollar conglomerate from Vancouver. "If the owners don't fight, the wives fight or the children or the cousins do." Pattison, pointedly, has kept his children out of senior corporate management; he is also notoriously reticent about who will inherit his vast collection of assets.

The travails of family businesses are not unique to Canada. Perhaps the most warring business family of all is Italy's Guccis, the makers of luxury fashion accessories. Fistfights regularly broke out during family meetings; members were constantly at each other's throats. In the final indignity, Maurizio Gucci, the last heir, sold the company to Arab investors in 1993, only to be shot to death in 1995 on his way upstairs to his Rome office. His ex-wife Patrizia Reggiani was later sentenced to twenty-nine years in prison for hiring the hitman. She had been nervous that her children would lose their birthright if Maurizio remarried.

The United States has witnessed some very public family spats. In recent years the fate of that country's second-largest family business, Koch Industries, has been bitterly contested by two factions of the secretive Koch brothers — company owners Charles and David on one side, and non-owners Billy and Fred on the other. In late 1998 a Kansas jury rejected Billy and Fred's contention that they had been cheated out of US$1.1 billion when they sold their interests to their brothers in 1985. Billy, who is now fifty-eight, is prepared to keep on fighting this war. The brothers' father, Fred Koch, saw the problem coming, and in a letter to his offspring in 1936 beseeched his small children to "be kind and generous to one another."

The story of the Haft family, once owners of the Dart drugstore empire based in Washington, D.C., would almost be comic if it wasn't so desperate. Let's see now, how did that go? Father and founder Herbert Haft rejects son Robert's ambitions to take over the company. Herbert's wife Gloria supports her son's campaign. Herbert then fires Robert and Gloria and forms an alliance with younger son Ronald. Herbert starts to suspect that Ronald is on a power trip, and each takes legal action against the other. In time, Herbert divorces Gloria. While the family is busy feuding, part of the business goes bankrupt and the family is forced to give up power. These days, young Robert is selling vitamins on the Internet and Herbert has set up a competing Web site. Herbert Haft concludes: "You're a product of how you're raised by your parents." For better or worse, apparently.

A successful business is often the best thing that can happen to a family — and the worst. As evidenced by the Hafts and the Koches, the successful companies are the ones that become nests of intrigue, jealousy, and bitterness. Companies that founder are rarely worth fighting for or shedding tears over. But once family discord takes hold in prosperous firms, bitterness, jealousy, and intrigue can easily distract once-focused owners and managers from the real job of raising sales and maximizing profits. Some families hang together despite the pressures — the ones that plan well or are united by such a strong culture or sense of family that they can't be entirely beaten down. The unlucky ones split apart, or slip into deadly decline as the next generation fails to maintain the dynasty. Many companies avoid the rough stuff but wither away through the incompetence of later generations. Timothy Eaton, who founded his namesake department store chain in the 1860s, was a smart and scrappy entrepreneur; the retail empire he built was so impressive that it took three more generations to destroy it.

These issues of survival and success are not limited to large companies. They preoccupy the garage owner down the street, the farmer on the rural route, and the Korean Canadian running the corner milk store. Big or small, these businesses' futures hinge on the highly charged relationships between family members. That's what makes family businesses so difficult to sustain — they're about more than just business. They're about fathers and sons, mothers and daughters, uncles and aunts and cousins. The talk around the boardroom table becomes the grist of conversation around the dinner table at night, and the other way around. The "business" is always with you when you live in a business family; the "family" is always with you when you work in a family business.

Every situation is complicated, and no family is spared some degree of pain. They will try to tell you otherwise — the McCains were in denial for years — but these businesses are often touched by tragedy and dispair. The Blackburns, the media family of London, Ontario, were cursed by the suicide of one heir and then by the sudden fatal heart attack of Martha Blackburn, who had moved smartly into a leadership position. But for pathos nothing matches the story of the Mitchells of Saskatoon, a prosperous meat-packing family dogged by suicide, illness, constant feuding, and sudden death. Fred Mitchell, the gentle pork entrepreneur of Saskatoon, died as a result of a fluke complication during a minor surgical procedure, leaving a wife, three small children, and a mother he had not spoken with in two years. This is surely one of the saddest stories in Canadian business. A few months before his death, Fred insisted he didn't hate his mother, Johanna, his sister Camille, and his brother Charles, from whom he was bitterly and irrevocably estranged. "I love them and I wish them all the best," he had said.

Why should we worry about family businesses, except to cluck sympathetically at their particular horrors? Because they are arguably the most important economic units in Canada. Their success or failure carries profound significance for our communities, careers, and social well-being. When business families feud or fail, towns and cities hang in the balance. The death of Eaton's as a family firm underlines this point: at the end, the department store chain had 13,000 employees of its own, but generated many thousands more jobs among its suppliers. Chances are very good that in your lifetime you will have worked for a family business, or owned one, or have a close family member who does. A 1999 survey of 750 family businesses by Deloitte Touche estimates that in Canada, this form of enterprise employs 4.7 million full-time and 1.3 million part-time workers. Total revenues of family companies are estimated at more than $1.3 trillion — and may be even higher, depending on how one defines "family business." Some sectors have been dominated by family empires. The broadcast media from west to east encompasses the Allards, Shaws, and at one time the Griffiths in Alberta and British Columbia; the Aspers and Craigs in Manitoba; the Rogers, Slaights, and Waterses in Toronto; and the de Gaspé Beaubiens, Greenbergs, and Chagnons in Quebec — and that's just the beginning. Newspapers? Even with the passing of the Southams from the scene, there are the Thomsons, the Péladeaus, the Irvings, and the several Toronto families that control the Torstar empire. Take a look at the meat and frozen food sections at your local supermarket. Various McCains run Maple Leaf Foods and McCain Foods, the Mitchells have their Mitchell's Gourmet brand pork, and the Cuddys sell turkey and chicken.

The future of family businesses is particularly critical at this stage in Canada's economic development. Entrepreneurial clans were the driving force behind many of the successful Canadian businesses that were built in the postwar era, when the economy was moving beyond its farming base and building its momentum as an industrial force. But the entrepreneurs who established these great companies between the 1940s and the 1970s are getting old and are passing from the scene. Often there are plans to transfer these companies to the next generation, but can these handoffs be accomplished with minimal pain and disruption? This generational bequest marks the largest transfer of assets in Canadian history. Families that do it badly may be forced to sell their companies to outsiders, or even break them up and dispose of the chunks.

Recent studies underline the challenge about to confront North American family companies. The survey by Deloitte Touche indicates that more than half will lose their leaders through retirement over the next ten years, and more than three-quarters within the next fifteen years. Yet most of these companies have not established a process for choosing a successor. The same survey indicates that most Canadian family businesses are highly dependent on their top executives and are vulnerable if that key individual dies or becomes disabled. There is a leadership crisis on the horizon, it warns. "Whether the family business is sold to a third party or passed on to the next generation, the upheaval caused by leadership change will be unstoppable. There is an urgency therefore for family businesses to put in place the planning that will secure their future."

A massive 1997 U.S. survey by Arthur Andersen and MassMutual echoed these concerns. It found that almost 43 percent of family-owned businesses would change hands within the next five years — a dramatic passing of the torch, considering that "the average CEO tenure at a family-owned business is as much as six times longer than at a typical non-family public company."

The Deloitte Touche survey uses a precise definition of family business: a company with revenues of more than $1 million a year that is not publicly traded and is not a partnership or a sole proprietorship. In other words, it is owned by a family. It estimates that there are 123,000 such companies in Canada, of which about 66 percent are still being run by the first generation. Interestingly, almost half of these companies say it is not important to keep the business in the family (although this figure may decrease as the founders grow older and more interested in preserving their legacies). It could be argued that most companies in their early stages are family businesses — a member of a family starts the business, and other family members work in it. Other observers question whether a company can really qualify as a family business until the founder designates a successor, at which time it moves from the entrepreneurial to the family phase. But Jess Chua, a professor of finance at the University of Calgary, has trouble with this definition too: it would eliminate the ethnic restaurants that are operated by family workers, but whose owners don't necessarily see them surviving into the next generation. He and fellow researchers Jim Chrisman and Pramodita Sharma are proposing another definition: a family business is one whose vision is shaped and/or pursued by a dominant coalition controlled by a family or a small number of families. So take your pick of definitions — the observations in this book apply in any case.

As any parent knows, keeping the family structure intact is hard enough these days without the intrusion of a demanding business. And business is hard enough in the twenty-first century without family dynamics playing a complicating role. The typical family company lived a somewhat sheltered life in the immediate postwar era thanks to the trade barriers that governments had erected around our borders. The Canada–U.S. Free Trade Agreement of 1989 and the North American Free Trade Agreement changed that. And the challenges of the new century are particularly severe — globalization, free trade, fickle consumers, the Internet, and on-line commerce. Many companies are dealing with these economic challenges while trying to handle a difficult family transition. The McCains have had to confront free trade, and the pork-packing Mitchells have had to deal with economic and business pressures to consolidate the meat-packing industry. The MacPherson/Dix/McDonald family of Burnaby, British Columbia, is striving to become a world player in bearings distribution just as matriarch Wendy McDonald is approaching retirement. The challenge for many family successors is to regenerate the company in the next generation. Edgar Bronfman Jr. is attempting to do just this by diversifying his third-generation family business, Seagram Inc., beyond liquor and into entertainment and multimedia.

An article in the Fall 1997 issue of *Sloan Management Review* highlights the challenge. Nancy Drozdow and Vincent Carroll, both consultants at the Center for Applied Research at the University of Pennsylvania's Wharton School, point out that family businesses are particularly vulnerable when trying to cope with rapid economic, competitive, and industry change. "While the members of a founding family can draw on their powerful feelings of loyalty and love to sustain the business in its early years, the same family ties can inhibit change when later generations inherit the business. The family business system, once a source of innovation and creativity, can sustain a profound conservatism."

The same authors worry that the strategic needs of companies and the life cycles of families are often out of sync. The succession process unfolds too slowly or in the wrong way after the death of the founder or as children join the business. But the world outside does not change slowly. "As competition rages and the need for decisive action is paramount, planning for or making a leadership or ownership change can destabilize both players and the firm, exacerbating an already anxiety-filled process."

Amid the broad sweep of the economy, should we really care about the death of family businesses? Surely, when one company dies another nimble, innovative competitor rises to take its place. Life goes on. It's part of the organic nature of business — what the economist Joseph Schumpeter captured in his theories of "creative destruction." The family business has had to contend with a double-edged reputation in North American business life. On one level, it symbolizes a traditional craftsmanship and quality that has been lost in an age of shoddy mass production. To say "I bought this at a small family business" is to suggest that the bread, or the furniture, or the wine was made with care and is somehow better. Defenders of family business say these companies are institutions in which strong values and beliefs can still flourish, as an extension of the founding family's own values. They often lack the layered hierarchy of big public companies; they practise teamwork at all levels; and they can afford to take a long-term perspective instead of being ruled by quarterly financial statements. There is a mythology that family business is somehow better for people — a belief that in many cases is justified. Fred Mitchell, the late owner of Mitchell Gourmet Foods of Saskatoon, tried to carry on the people-oriented approach instilled by his founder-grandfather, Fred Mendel. One manager of Oshawa Group, the supermarket company built and finally sold by Toronto's Wolfe family, said: "It was a family company. When you joined the company, you joined the family. It was paternalistic in the positive sense." At their best, the family members put in long hours and extremely hard work, pushed to greatness by pride and loyalty and tradition. At their worst, of course, they are the most loathsome kind of parasites, profiting gloriously from others' hard work.

Management theorist Peter Drucker argues that in this age of the new economy, making family succession work is in the public interest. He points out that the growth dynamics in the economy are quickly shifting from the industrial giants to medium-sized businesses, which tend to be owner controlled and owner managed. He feels that any effort to foster entrepreneurship should include encouraging family-managed businesses and making possible their continuation.

However, his book *Managing in a Time of Great Change* also contains a stern warning for family companies, as he describes the conditions under which success and succession can happen. "Both the business and the family will survive and do well if the family serves the business. Neither will do well if the business is run to serve the family. The controlling word in 'family management business' is not 'family.' It has to be 'business.'"

Family business detractors say that owners quite naturally put their personal interests ahead of the company and its employees, particularly after the hard-driving, passionate founder departs from the scene. Companies become stores of personal wealth to be plundered, not organisms to be fed and watered. People who establish businesses are hailed as innovative entrepreneurs, but the moment they designate a family successor, the rot sets in, according to the critics. This leads to the much quoted "lucky sperm club" theory — that any hope for great talent in the next generation is a high-risk game of reproductive craps. The critics point to the Eaton "boys": rich men who raised horses, drove race cars, built gaudy mansions, and took high-profile political appointments while their venerable retail company was in disarray. The anti–family business argument goes like this: surely it is better if these companies die or are sold to someone else. The alternative is for them to deteriorate under the stewardship of heirs who lack the brains or the fire to succeed.

"But what a waste," counters Philippe de Gaspé Beaubien, the charmingly hard-nosed builder of Telemedia, a Montreal-based media empire, which he

and his wife Nan-b have now passed on to their three children. De Gaspé
Beaubien, one of Canada's most forceful advocates of family enterprise, argues
that the decline of all these family companies is destroying wealth, jobs, and
tremendous productive potential. He doesn't believe in perpetuating incompetence; rather, he argues that in a global economy we can't afford to simply let
family businesses go down the drain without a struggle. His contribution to
that struggle is a new foundation that aims to teach family enterprise the tricks
of survival and succession. He says that other parts of the world, while facing
the same business challenges, are more successful in exploiting the strengths of
family businesses. "Look at Asia, look at the networks of families in business
there — it's the foundation of their economies. They have a strength, they don't
throw the baby out with the bathwater every generation; they build on each
generation and there is momentum and growth."

Conservative estimates are that somewhere between 65 and 80 percent of
the world's businesses are controlled by families. In many countries these businesses are just as fragile as in Canada. Yet those that survive — that move into
the second, third, and fourth generations — are often among the world's most
powerful, successful, and innovative corporations. There is ample proof that
family companies can be flexible — that they cannot automatically be equated
with second and third generation dry rot. The Rothschild banking network,
the Ford Motor Co., the chemical giant DuPont, the Fiat car business — all
were under family control for decades, even centuries, and emerged as highly
successful multinationals.

And some cultures simply do the family business thing better than others. The
southern Europeans seem especially immune to family upheaval, perhaps because
of (or some would say despite) a tradition of primogeniture that automatically
makes the oldest son or oldest male descendant the successor. Primogeniture
makes generational transfers rather neat and tidy, if inequitable. Consider the
Berettas of Gardone Val Tompia, Italy, who have been making and selling high-
quality firearms for close to five centuries. *The Wall Street Journal* recently
described the company's ability to adapt and change through thirteen generations of family ownership and management. The company argues that it can
make daring, even quixotic, investments because it answers only to the current
"padrone" and a close circle of mainly male relatives. No clumsy independent
board of directors or public shareholders. *The Journal* reports that "succession
follows a father-to-son line and the Berettas have had an extraordinarily lucky
run. Over 13 generations, virtually every padrone has produced an heir with the
leadership gene." One of the rare exceptions to the family succession rules
occurred in the ascent of the latest family leader, the mustachioed Ugo Beretta.

The two Beretta brothers who ran the company before him produced no heirs and thus turned to Ugo, the son of their sister, who actually took the Beretta name instead of his own father's name.

Family businesses remain the backbone of the European economy, particularly in the south of the continent, *The Wall Street Journal* says, and these companies tend to flourish as long as their horizons don't change. But in Europe, where old market barriers have been tumbling, many family firms are now linking with partners or going public to secure their place in a tougher, pan-European marketplace. Beretta too may have to go this route at some point. But for the moment it is operating in one of the "few sectors in which being a family-owned and run company isn't a problem," says Claudio Corbetta, a management strategy professor at the Milan business school Luigi Bocconi. In firearms, "it's important to identify the product with one last name. Buyers see it as a guarantee."

In Asia the postwar period has seen the rise of perhaps even stronger family businesses. Many Chinese fled from mainland China in the early decades of the twentieth century and established multinational Chinese families; these families now operate throughout Southeast Asia — in Hong Kong, Taiwan, Thailand, and Singapore — and to some extent in North America. Strongly influenced by their perilous flights into exile, these business founders operated on the assumption that you only trust your own kin. "Although family-controlled business empires are encountered in the United States or Europe, the scale and scope of modern overseas Chinese family businesses are unprecedented. Kinship ties are extremely important and family control over firms is the rule," write economist Murray Weidenbaum and consultant Samuel Hughes in their 1995 book, *The Bamboo Network*. Yet even these highly disciplined companies are not immune to failure once they move beyond two generations. There is a Chinese proverb: "Wealth doesn't last more than three generations."

In North America, ideas about fairness and equality have consigned the concept of primogeniture to the trash heap in many family companies, although some still quietly practise that creed. Women, as elsewhere in the workforce, no longer timidly accept their male counterparts' self-proclaimed natural right to rule. Daughters are beginning to fight for their right to lead, although these champions are still in the minority. More female family members are taking key roles: Martha Billes has finally triumphed over her siblings to become the major shareholder of Canadian Tire Corp. Joan Fisk heads Tiger Brand of Cambridge, Ontario, a mid-sized garment maker now in its fifth generation. For fifty years Wendy McDonald has presided over BC Bearing Engineers Ltd., a distributor of industrial bearings, ever since her late husband plunged his airplane into the Pacific Ocean. But in all cases these women have faced resistance of one kind or another from men who still believe they have the God-given right to rule in the family company.

For nonfamily managers, the outlook is also more encouraging. Many families have come to understand that their job is to direct the wealth and ownership of their inherited assets while leaving actual management to nonfamily professionals. This is a hard decision to make, often because pride and responsibility get caught up with issues of succession. "If the old man could establish the company and take it to great heights, why not me?" many a child has asked. "By not managing the company, am I somehow surrendering my duty and natural role?" For male heirs particularly, giving up management often seems like emasculation, or an abrogation of duties. But the families that succeed move beyond this hangup.

At the other extreme, some successful entrepreneurs don't get hung up on this idea of the "family business" at all. In their view they are simply creating wealth, and they will buy and dispose of companies in a way that maximizes this wealth. Surely, Peter Munk doesn't get all teary-eyed at the thought that he might sell out his interest in his Barrick gold-mining company. Nor does Jimmy Pattison get too emotional over his stable of assorted companies, including a major billboard business, a supermarket chain, and the Ripley's Believe It or Not amusement chain. These are "wealth players." They lack loyalty to any community, any workforce, even a company name. But even wealth transactions can be hard on the emotions. When an entrepreneur sells a business that the family grew up in, it can be jarring, particularly for the children who have enjoyed nice jobs as a result of the parent's risk taking. Take Ted Turner, the emotional roller coaster who built Turner Broadcasting and the cable news giant CNN. The week he sold out to Time Warner, he met his family for a quiet Sunday dinner at a restaurant. When son Teddy, an employee of Turner Broadcasting, asked about his future in the new organization, his father gently advised him: "You're toast." By selling out, Turner was probably being kind to Teddy and his other children. He was turning the business into a potful of wealth, which in time they will be able to deploy as they wish. And he may have been protecting them from a potentially nasty succession fight some day.

Vancouver's Jimmy Pattison takes a particularly hard-nosed attitude toward the idea of family business. He started his business career working in a car dealership in Vancouver. He stayed ten years and eventually was offered half-ownership of the business for nothing. His partner was to be a member of the founding family, "a good guy," Pattison remembers. But Pattison walked away and went into business for himself. According to him, "a family business constrains top talent" by pushing family members ahead of other, more talented people. "It's an accident of birth — you might get a good kid or not," he says. "Over a long period of time, it is unlikely the proper talent is in the family." Pattison won't talk about his own succession. He has one son working in his vast constellation of businesses, as the manager of an aquarium in Orlando, Florida. "He reports to a president," Pattison points out. In fact, his three children have never worked in the management of the parent company. He would discourage such activity because "other good people will leave you."

The tensions in family enterprises are often invisible to the outside world and even to the company's nonfamily managers and employees. Family companies are usually privately owned and often lack the cathartic forums of board meetings or annual meetings. Troubles burst forth violently and unexpectedly, occasionally in messy lawsuits. Consider the drama that was played out in Florenceville, New Brunswick, at the headquarters of food-processing giant McCain Foods Ltd. For years the McCain brothers had presented to the world the image of a hard-working team; privately, however, they were jostling for succession. In 1990, in a second-floor executive office with a view of the broad St. John River, Harrison and his younger brother Wallace, who had built the company over thirty years, talked with me about strategies in Europe, free trade in North America, and how they had taken a small potato business and turned it into a multinational food conglomerate. At this point in their lives, the brothers were still on speaking terms. Few people outside Harrison's office were aware of the jealousy and resentment seething beneath the surface. Everything seemed amicable until the brothers, then in their early sixties, were asked who would succeed them in the business.

Immediately the temperature in the office plunged to the deep-freeze level of the winter day outside. "Talk to Wallace there," Harrison replied icily. Wallace in turn pointed to Harrison: "He's in charge." Asked if he was worried about succession, Harrison said cagily, "We're talking about a lot of people now. We've got to be careful." And what about Michael, Wallace's younger son, who at thirty-one was already running the U.S. operations? Harrison didn't want to talk any more about the subject, but when asked if Michael was interested in the business, Wallace replied, "Very."

In hindsight, it should have been clear that even then the McCain brothers were deeply divided over succession. Amid phenomenal success, and soaring sales and profits, they were on the verge of tearing themselves apart. The rest is history. This disagreement turned into a public brawl as Wallace sought to install his son as the family's next-generation successor. Harrison fought young Michael's ascent, and in response tried to remove Wallace from the company. There were court fights, stormy board meetings, and spectacular headlines, and ultimately Wallace was exiled from his beloved Florenceville. Wallace, Michael, and Wallace's other son Scott eventually took over Maple Leaf Foods, the giant Toronto meat packer — a company they could run without Harrison's interference. As the 1990s ended, the brothers were rarely speaking to each other, even though Wallace stubbornly remained part owner and a member of the board of McCain Foods, which his brother was running with the help of family loyalists and professional managers. Harrison has designated another nephew, Allison, son of a deceased brother, as his successor.

Since that meeting with the McCain brothers, I have crossed the country talking to families about their companies, how they work and how they are preparing for succession. I have tried to be more alert to the emotions below the surface. Yet some of the stories I hear are happy, even joyous — of people who love each other and love working together. The Smiths of Ellis-Don found accommodation and compromise at a time when it appeared they might be casualties of the generational wars. Dave Wilson and the late Peter Wilson were Nova Scotia brothers who continued a seven-generation family business without public discord. The Price family of Acme, Alberta, are pulling together to develop a second-generation integrated meat operation that takes beef and pork from the farm right to retail outlets. And the Molsons, now entering their seventh generation as beer makers, are one of the world's most enduring business dynasties.

What is clear from all these stories is that people in family companies are not all bad or good — they are just real people, often confused and stuck in impossible roles. It's not just a question of the so-called "lucky sperm club" — the simplistic concept that leadership is a high-odds gamble as we head down the generational road. Certainly, there are children who lack the drive of their fathers, and daughters who are frustrated by their less capable brothers' unwillingness to share power. In other roles at other times, these people can be quite competent and well-adjusted. It is just that the family business places such responsibility on children, who in their hearts of hearts might rather be doing something else. The quarrels that emerge from these ill-fitting roles are often not waged over large issues. They're the product of a thousand slights — patterns that began at an early age and have persisted into adulthood. That is what makes these stories so evocative — it could be your family or my family. These are roles that we all play, and the stories are therefore close to the heart.

ONE

THE CUDDYS —
FATHERS AND SONS

The Cuddys, of Cuddy International, from left to right: Peter, Robert, Douglas, patriarch Alfred (Mac), Bruce, and Brian.

"YOU MUST THINK I'M A TOUGH SON OF A BITCH. Not really. I'm resolute." This is the closest Alfred McInroy (Mac) Cuddy ever gets to introspection. He is sitting in his book-lined study in a century-old yellow-brick farmhouse just outside Strathroy, Ontario, a neat farming community in southwestern Ontario. He bought the house as a young man in 1950, as part of the hundred-acre farm that would launch him on a remarkable entrepreneurial career. Fifty years later, Mac Cuddy, the turkey king of Canada, is at once defiant and bewildered: the agile body that made him a top athlete and a passionate horseman is now tortured and bent by multiple sclerosis. But his most painful affliction is the quarrel that has alienated him from three of his five sons and weakened his company, Cuddy International Corp. "It's cost us a lot of money and a lot of respect ... and it's depressing. It's not easy to live with." What makes it even more painful is that he knows he is somehow responsible for what has happened, even though he can't quite grasp what he might have done differently.

Sitting among his books and photographs, Mac Cuddy, at eighty, is the lion in winter — a handsome, opinionated, charming, unapologetic old coot who refuses to accept his own mortality, despite the illness that is clawing away at his six-foot, four-inch frame. He is wracked with pain and contradictions. He loves his estranged sons, Peter, Bruce, and Brian, but he doesn't entirely trust them. Bruce and Brian, in particular, are great entrepreneurs, but in his mind they possess fatal flaws that have forced him to drive them from the business. He has opinions on everything and everybody — on his daughter Barbara's husband, on his son's wives, on all his top managers — and he's willing to share them on a moment's notice with a reporter he's known for only two hours.

Bruce, the oldest son, and now a business competitor to Mac, is tough and hard-headed, his father says, but he's too greedy. Brian is "Bruce's attaché, he falls in line behind him." Peter is "the most naïve forty-year-old I have ever known," but highly intelligent. Robert, the head of the Cuddy Foods division, just likes to be stroked and praised, Mac says. He should be in sales instead of management. (In fact, Robert would leave the management of Cuddy Foods a few weeks after this interview was conducted.) And Douglas, who heads Cuddy's transport division, is "a good guy but he wants to be loved by everybody."

Above all, Mac still wants to be in control, of his business and his family and of everything he surveys. Today he is talking about a possible resolution to the split that has been damaging his family and his company for almost a decade and triggered firings, lawsuits, and volumes of angry words. He has hired a Toronto lawyer who is an expert in dispute resolution to act as a mediator. Somehow, miraculously, he has remained on speaking terms with most of his children, although his relationship with Bruce, his oldest son and former heir apparent, remains badly fractured. He is supporting his youngest child Peter's credit line for a new snack food business, even though Peter once launched (and then dropped) a lawsuit against the family business. But he is almost crudely adamant that his banished sons will never again work in the family business. "They don't have to be in the business. I think it could be as good or better a business without them. I have a trite saying that 'you can hire better than you can sire.'" His sons would love to be back in the company, he boasts. "I think they all respect me still, but in different fashions. I talk to Brian almost every day, I talk to Robert every day, I talk to them all except Bruce."

Asked if there is any possibility of a rapprochement with his father, Bruce Cuddy, speaking by phone from North Carolina, drawls a short and definitive answer: "No chance at all." Bruce, who has lived in the southern United States for thirty years, says the barriers are too solid and the issues too complex. "He runs *our* company the way *he* wants to," says Mac Cuddy's oldest child. Later he describes his father as "an older gentleman who obviously doesn't know what's going on."

At first glance the Cuddys look like a storybook family — a tall, handsome father with five tall, handsome sons and one attractive, talented daughter. All of the sons have worked in the business, and all passionately share the same interests as their father. The business, nurtured in the rich farm country of southwestern Ontario, is the breeding, growing, and processing of poultry; the family hobby is raising and racing fine horses. But shared interests are not enough to keep a family together when power, jealousy, and human frailty enter the picture. The company is Cuddy International Corp., the largest turkey breeding and hatching company in Canada, a $350-million-plus a year business (and that's down from sales of more than $500 million in the early 1990s). And Cuddy's is about more than turkeys — for eighteen years it has held the lucrative contract to supply chicken products for McDonald's Restaurants in Canada. All those McNuggets, McChickens, and chicken fajitas tumble off the chicken-processing lines at Cuddy's London factory. Cuddy International owns turkey and chicken breeding, hatching, and processing operations in the United States and has been a significant exporter to Europe. The whole empire is owned entirely by the Cuddy family — just over 50 percent by Mac and the rest split equally among his sons, although the father still firmly controls the voting rights.

What happened to the Cuddys that was so awful, so contentious, that the family today sits in two armed camps? In fact, Cuddy's is a textbook case of all the things that can go wrong with a family company. You've got it all — the domineering, controlling, and ageing father who will not leave; the failure to develop a rational succession plan; the untrained, wilful children who have never worked anywhere else; and the failure to attract and support talented managers from outside. Personal family issues have intruded on the family business, poisoning the air. Outside advisers have been brought aboard to advise but then nothing has been followed through. Senior executives have been hired and then disposed of. Between 1994 and 1999, Cuddy International had five CEOs, including Mac Cuddy himself. Once a thriving, growing business, Cuddy International has suffered from the feud; it has experienced lapses of leadership and has been distracted from its strategic needs. Lack of discipline and continuity, combined with a depressed North American turkey market, have exacted a heavy toll.

One family friend remarks that the only family rivaling the Cuddys in its dysfunctionality is the Royal Family. "The Cuddy situation is an extreme case of family company dysfunctionality," agrees one former senior manager with Cuddy International. "It's the epitome of it. At some point, there is a great story to be told about it ... for students of family companies, if only to say how bad things can get." As is so often the case, the saga begins with a rags-to-riches story of a brilliant and single-minded entrepreneur who created a great company, but then couldn't manage it — and who later would fail miserably at building a satisfying and enduring relationship with all his children.

The defining moment in the Cuddy feud took place in a small meeting room at the Toronto law firm of Aylesworth Thompson Phelan O'Brien, on the thirtieth floor of the South Tower of Toronto's Royal Bank Plaza, on a Monday morning in early December of 1997. The room was packed with reporters and photographers — a standing-room-only crowd. The subject of all this curiosity, Peter Cuddy, sat red-eyed, unsmiling, and nervous at one end of the conference table, beside his lawyer. "I yearn for happier days when we all worked together as a family," he told the assembled throng. "This is the most painful choice I ever made."

Peter Cuddy, a boyish-looking thirty-nine-year-old, was announcing to the world that he was suing Cuddy International, his own family's turkey-breeding and poultry-processing company, in which he himself owned shares. He was breaking an inviolate rule in family feuds by carrying his dispute into the courts and bringing it under public scrutiny. He made it clear he was bringing the suit more in sadness than in anger. "I last spoke to my father two weeks ago. We had spoken of allegations ... My father I always considered a very close friend." The real war, he would explain later, was with the professional managers who had taken over the firm and were running it for his ageing, ailing father. He was making his claim as an oppressed shareholder in a company that would not provide him with the financial information he was demanding. Despite his close friendship with his dad, he was alleging that company funds were being misspent and misallocated by his father, by one of his brothers who worked in the company, and by other officers and directors. In all, he was asking for $11.5 million in damages.

There were various allegations: that his father took an interest-free loan from the company that was not authorized; that Mac engaged in business deals that put his personal interests ahead of the company's; and that the company paid for various personal services. Peter cited, for example, that Cuddy International and its affiliates paid for Mac's personal horticulturist to be flown to the father's beachfront property in Florida and to his second wife Patricia's summer cottage on Georgian Bay. The statement of claim also accused his father of directing the Cuddy companies to provide his wife Patricia with a 450 SEL Mercedes-Benz.

Peter also raised concerns about a junk bond issue the company had floated in New York, which he said was pegged at an interest rate much higher than could be obtained on the open market. Most important, he said, among its conditions was that the debt would have to be repaid in full if there was a change in control. This amounted, he said, to an expensive "poison pill" to prevent himself and his two insurgent brothers from ever taking control of the family business. He alleged that because of the high cost of the junk bonds, the company had become financially unstable, teetering on the brink of financial collapse. The company would vigorously contest this charge.

In his court action, Peter said he was supported by his older brothers Brian and Bruce, although they were not a party to the action. In fact, the company would later argue that Peter was serving as a kind of a proxy for his brothers. The suit followed several attempts by the three sons to take over Cuddy International, all of which had been rebuffed by Mac Cuddy. Arrayed against Bruce, Brian, and Peter were their father and, to a lesser extent, one brother — Robert, who ran the Cuddy Foods processing operations. Douglas, a former truck driver who operated the transportation side of the business, had taken a more neutral stance.

Through all this, Peter insisted that he still sought his father's support and love. He said his father had always maintained that the roles of family member and shareholder should be mutually exclusive. Here, he was clearly compartmentalizing his roles as loving son and aggrieved shareholder. He admitted that his wife Kate, who owned her own interior design business in London, Ontario, had asked him to end the court action because of the divisions it could cause. "This is the greatest struggle I've ever had to go through personally," Peter said. "My father and I are close friends. To bring an action like this ... is really gut-wrenching. I'm doing it for all the shareholders involved."

Peter said in an affidavit that his father had been pressuring him to drop the action, and that his stepmother Patricia had called his wife Kate twice, telling her that Peter was "a slimy, evil son of a bitch" and a "fucking bastard." According to Peter's statement, "These remarks upset my wife greatly and led her to urge me to abandon the application solely out of fear for the financial consequences it would cause for us and our three small children."

In her own affidavit, Patricia VanOmen Cuddy, Mac Cuddy's wife of ten years, insisted that she had not attempted to intimidate Peter. "I like Peter Cuddy's wife Kate and felt compassion for her. I called her the day that I learned of the notice out of a concern for her and what might happen. I told her what Peter was up to was dangerous and that I understood that the charges he was making would not stand. I told her Peter might be sued and that she and her children might lose everything."

Patricia Cuddy's comments were not far off the mark: the lawsuit was doomed. The company fired back a series of affidavits and counterallegations. Within a few weeks, Peter had withdrawn his action. The judge ruled that he would have to pay full legal costs. He and his lawyer were then sued for defamation by his father's company and its then president Peter Widdrington for comments made at the press conference and in a press release.

Talking in a London coffee shop two weeks later, Peter Cuddy admitted that it was probably all over between him and the family company. He had left his investor relations job with a London company and was pouring his energy into his own entrepreneurial venture — a new line of "healthy" snack foods marketed under the label Cuddy Plantation. He was seeking closure from the whole incident. Incredibly, he was still talking to his father; even more incredibly, Mac Cuddy had found him a new lawyer and was helping with his legal bills. In essence, Mac was helping Peter defend himself against a lawsuit filed by Mac's company. It's the sort of thing that happens in the Cuddy family.

Mac Cuddy grew up on a hardscrabble farm in Kerwood, near London in western Ontario. His mother, the former Hattie McInroy, was a teetotaller with a staunch Scots Presbyterian background. His father Alf was a handsome farmer with a bit of a roguish air. Alf Cuddy's passion was horses, and to a lesser extent farming. Known around town as "Squire Cuddy," he gadded about the country roads in his sulky. That love of horseflesh was passed on to young Mac; from his mother he inherited a driving ambition and an unflinching work ethic.

Urged on by his mother, young Mac started exhibiting farm animals at local fairs, becoming particularly enthusiastic about turkeys. His son Peter recounts that his father would take great care in making sure his birds "feathered" properly. He also started experimenting with the physiology and genetics of turkeys to develop better specimens, and he spent hours working with light to enhance egg production. Using kerosene lanterns, he could manipulate the turkeys' perception of daylight — and consequently the seasons — to stimulate egg production throughout the year. He likes to say today that feathers were in his blood.

At Strathroy District Collegiate Institute, Mac was a smart and athletic student, winning a scholarship to Ontario Agricultural College in Guelph, which he attended from 1939 to 1941. He threw himself into track and field, basketball, boxing, and the officers' training corps. At one point he needed to rent a tuxedo for a prom. Showing his entrepreneurial prowess early, he bought a radio and raffled it for a dollar a ticket. By the end of the week he had enough money to rent a tuxedo, take his date to dinner, and recoup his radio purchase.

By all accounts he was a very good student — so good he was offered a scholarship in landscape architecture at Harvard University. But he decided instead to enlist and fight the war in Europe. Mac was shipped off to England, anticipating

front-line duty. Instead, his athletic skills qualified him as the physical education instructor for the Canadian troops based at Aldershot, England. There he
met Dilys Scott, a young English ambulance driver. They were married in
Aldershot on February 3, 1945. After the armistice the couple settled into the
Cuddy household at Kerwood. It was a hard experience for the war bride from
London. Dilys was often homesick for family and friends, but she hung in. Their
first child, Bruce, was born in 1946.

Mac might have resumed his academic studies, but he had promised his
wife's parents that he would find gainful employment. So he took a day job
with the Veteran's Land Office, helping former military personnel resettle on
farms around Lambton and Middlesex counties. By night he worked at raising turkeys in the Cuddy barn. He hated the land office job, even though he
could do most of the work out of the Cuddy homestead. He recalls, "I always
had stomach problems; I felt like hell." When he went for a physical exami-
nation, the doctor told him there was nothing wrong with his body, but, he
noted, "I don't think you like your job."

Through all the frustration, Mac says he never entirely lost hope. "I can't
think of any time in my life when I didn't think that I'd be successful. I had a
sense that I could make things better." He was keeping an eye out for farms to
purchase. One of these was an attractive homestead just outside Strathroy. The
Douglas farm, at the time owned by a widow, sported a century-old brick farmhouse, a small tenant house, a three-storey red barn, a chicken-brooding house,
1,500 turkeys, and a hundred acres of land, but it was starting to look
rundown. In 1950 a feed store manager in Strathroy tipped him off that Mrs.
Douglas was finally planning to sell the farm. Mac visited her and they settled
on $10,000 as the sale price. He forked over his life savings of $3,000 and
borrowed the rest, bolstered by a credit guarantee from an uncle.

Mac still marvels at how poor he was in those days. When he and Dilys
moved to the new farm, the moving company mistakenly carried their handful of furniture into the tiny, insul-brick tenant's house, not realizing it was
intended for the big brick farmhouse nearby. Dilys, from whom he would later
divorce, was a great support to him in those early days. "She was the right
woman at the right time, I tell you," Mac says.

The business began in the big, three-storey, Pennsylvania-style red barn. Day-
old turkey poults occupied the top floor, while Mac raised heavy commercial
turkeys on the second. There were horses on the ground floor along with equipment and feed. The turkey-growing area contained "porches" — wooden and
metal cages that kept the birds off the ground so that they wouldn't peck at their
own feces. This pecking was dangerous because it led to black head disease, a

factor in high turkey mortality. Within months of buying the property, Mac had painted the words CUDDY TURKEY FARMS across the side of the barn.

In those early years, Mac Cuddy showed the trait that would prove to be both his strength and his curse: he was a perfectionist who quickly lost patience with people and circumstances that didn't live up to his ideal. To supply his turkey-growing operation, he bought day-old poults from hatcheries around the area. But he was never pleased with the stock. So Cuddy Farms started hatching its own poults in two old duck incubators. It was an important step in creating the kind of integrated operation Mac dreamed about — a vast assembly line of eggs, poults, and ultimately turkey meat. And Cuddy Farms, he hoped, would capture the value added at every level.

In his business dealings Mac Cuddy always assumed that whatever it was, he could do it better himself. But he found one exception. In 1952 he attended a turkey growers' convention in Atlantic City, where he met a California geneticist and turkey breeder named George Nicholas. The Nicholas organization, through its progressive methods, was revolutionizing the breeding of the fowl in North America. Mac Cuddy realized that this was someone from whom he could learn. It was the beginning of a powerful alliance, in which George Nicholas contributed the breeding stock and expertise and Mac Cuddy the marketing of turkey poults and eggs.

The two men were like family, talking constantly on the phone about market conditions, ideal bird weight, and turkey health, with Mac in London and George three hours behind in California. The Nicholases — George and his wife — were frequent house guests at the Cuddys. With George as his guide, Mac developed artifical insemination procedures that allowed the proliferation of fine breeding stock. He also refined the use of light to adjust the breeding and hatching of poults. Mac still considers George one of the most important positive influences on his life. George was the master breeder who supplied the grandparent stock for commercial breeders, or "multipliers," such as Cuddy Farms, which turned out the eggs and the young poults. Mac became George's best client in North America.

In response to postwar affluence and the rising demand for turkey meat, markets were opening for eggs and poults. In the 1960s and 1970s, Mac Cuddy vastly increased his business every year, partly through new technology and smart marketing but also through timely takeovers. Mac diversified into poultry processing by taking a stake in a London company called Riverside Poultry. He came in as a partner but later bought out his co-owners — a pattern that would repeat itself. He hated partnerships, one insider suggests. He needed to run the whole thing. He would get into bed with other businessmen, grow frustrated, and buy them out. In time, his ambitions would extend beyond Ontario, and Cuddy Farms — later known as Cuddy International — would develop operations in Michigan, Ohio, and North and South Carolina, and then Europe.

While establishing his business, Mac built a reputation as a horse breeder and harness-racing champion. "I've always had them — horses have played an important role in my life," Mac says today, agonizing over the fact his health has forced him to distance himself from the equine world. He also raised one daughter and five strapping boys; the sons grew up in the poultry business, working in the company as children and then as young men. Mac has always denied that he was keen to have the boys follow in his footsteps. "The children were always involved but I didn't point them in any one direction. They just grew in these directions. I never said 'this is for you,' I never said that in my life." He also maintains that he had no dreams of a legacy or dynasty — he just wanted to be "a good citizen who made a contribution."

This, of course, is a classic case of entrepreneurial denial. In fact, observers say he orchestrated events so that the sons would want to and have to join the company. They were so highly compensated, and so obligated to Mac, that they couldn't leave. As they grew up, these headstrong young men were chained to the company. At the same time, Mac never seemed to consider them good enough to follow in his footsteps. He often expressed contempt toward the women they married, which he could not keep to himself. He was a conflicted man, ambitious for his children yet also scornful of their abilities. It is said that he rarely complimented Bruce, the son most like him. Bruce, and to some extent the other sons, desperately tried to match him in smarts and wilfulness. They became inveterate gamblers, taking chances in business and in life. When they failed — and they sometimes did — Mac would bail them out. If they were weak, he would surround them with capable people. It was a dangerous pattern that hurt the company and damaged the relationships within this fragile family.

The oldest son, Bruce Cuddy, walked in his father's footsteps. In 1970 he graduated from the University of Guelph — the former Ontario Agricultural College, Mac Cuddy's alma mater. Bruce needed a job, so his father found him one: he sent the young man to North Carolina to run the family's U.S. operations. There was no question that he was inexperienced. Yet the U.S. business became phenomenally successful, and Bruce's ambition and arrogance swelled. The Carolinas, with their mild weather and low land and labour costs, had emerged as one of North America's turkey hotspots, just as Mac had expected. And U.S. consumers loved their turkey more than their Canadian counterparts did. Bruce's operation was practically autonomous from the family's London head office. Based in Marshville, North Carolina, he was a swaggering local celebrity who lived the high life, was a good buddy of right-wing politician Jesse Helms, and expressed unbridled contempt of the socialistic, government-dominated society back home. "I'm just enough of a renegade to do whatever I want," Bruce told the *Financial Post* in 1991. "That's the greatest thing about the U.S." That year he was elected president of the 4,000-member U.S. National Turkey Association, the first non-American to serve in that role. He sat on a posse of agribusiness committees. He also became a cattleman with a fine herd of Simmental beef cattle.

For many people Bruce Cuddy was the smartest poultry man in North America — but that was not his father's view. As he grew older, Mac Cuddy was not convinced that his son had what it took to run the growing international company. Or, some say, he was afraid that his son might be too good a successor.

The other sons gradually joined the company, mainly because Mac created places for them. Brian, with his agricultural diploma from the University of Guelph, wanted to be a farmer, but that wasn't Mac's idea. So Brian came into the company as a manager at Strathroy Foods, the vegetable-processing business that was controlled by the Cuddys. Robert, who went to the University of Western Ontario, joined Cuddy Foods just as his father began to crank up the food-processing part of the business. Robert, in fact, deserves much of the credit for snaring the valuable McDonald's chicken contract in the early 1980s. Peter, a history graduate and a sensitive young man, worked in various positions, never rising terribly high. Observers say he might have done very well as an academic or a writer, but he too was chained to the business. The lifestyle and the weight of family tradition and expectations wouldn't let him go.

Peter recalls that when he graduated with his bachelor's degree in 1981, the head of the history department at Western approached him about pursuing graduate studies. Peter was highly tempted and went to Mac with the idea. Mac said that if he really wanted to, that was fine; he would financially support his studies. "But," Peter recalls, "he said, 'Why don't you come work for me? Let's work together.' Those words ring in my ear — they meant a great deal because I was invited to join." So Peter joined Cuddy Farms, a decision that he now admits was probably a mistake. He entered the company as a trainee in the hatchery, at first toe clipping and debeaking poults, then moving into other roles, usually in the marketing and corporate development fields. Peter says none of the sons ever discussed with their father going off and doing something else. It was implicit that they would join the company.

Douglas's career is another example of how Mac manipulated his sons, say people who know the Cuddy family. A high-school dropout, he loved the life of a truck driver; eventually he was hauling goods across Canada in his own eighteen-wheeler. He worked on his own for about a decade, building a small company. Mac brought him closer to the fold as a contract trucker, carrying turkey eggs between Texas and Ontario. After Douglas got married, Mac bought his business and set up a transportation division with the young man as president. Douglas never seemed to resent this interference. Mac says today that he had no choice but to buy Douglas's company; his son had suffered a back injury. And, Mac adds, the trucking operations were important if the Cuddy companies were to ensure prompt delivery of the company's young poults across North America.

While Mac was pulling his sons into the company, there were divisions at home. Dilys Cuddy had been a great help to her ambitious husband during the business's formative years. At home in Strathroy, she would make her legendary turkey pies in the family kitchen and sell them to local customers. But Mac demanded the same perfection in his personal life as he did in business. Dilys buckled under the pressure and the verbal barrage. She was "a victim of uncompromising perfectionism, that you could never do enough to please him," says a family friend. Finally, in the mid-1970s, she divorced Mac. It was hard on the boys. Peter, still a teenager, felt terribly torn. Although Mac and Dilys would show up at the boys' weddings, things were never the same. Dilys later remarried; she died of cancer in 1988.

Barbara, the second-oldest child, was one Cuddy sibling who avoided being sucked into the vortex of turkeys and takeovers. When still a young woman, she told her father she wanted nothing to do with the business. The relationship was further strained by Mac's intense dislike of Barbara's husband, a designer whom she met as an eighteen-year-old studying at the Ontario College of Art in Toronto. Mac, in fact, refused to give his daughter's hand in marriage. For many years Barbara, now an artist living near Montreal with her family, kept a safe distance from the Cuddy clan and its great obsession, the company. But after Dilys Cuddy died, Mac made a real effort to connect with his estranged daughter, and the two have grown closer.

Mac Cuddy moved into the U.S. market, forging a partnership with another turkey entrepreneur, Jay VanOmen, who operated Central Farms of Zeeland, Michigan. As was his pattern, Mac eventually bought out his partner. VanOmen retired and moved to Arizona with his younger wife, a slim, attractive former flight attendant named Patricia, but he kept in touch with Mac. When

VanOmen died, Mac started paying calls on Patricia, who was about twenty-five years younger than he was. In 1987 the two married, and Patricia VanOmen moved into the Cuddy home.

The divorce, and death of their mother, and their father's remarriage, may have been more damaging to the children than they will ever acknowledge. The mother often acts as an important buffer between a wilful entrepreneur and his children. The overriding priority for mothers is often family harmony, not the family firm. Had Dilys stayed married to Mac, and had she lived longer, she might have kept the family from disintegrating. Mac, on the other hand, says that Dilys would never have got involved in the business issues — she didn't like the pressure. His second wife has found it understandably difficult to cope with the pitched battles. "Stepmother is a tough mantle to assume," he admits. Mac says Patricia often advises him to step away from his conflicted relationships with his children, but he insists that he has to walk in his own shoes.

It was not that Mac Cuddy didn't think about succession — he just didn't deal with the issue in any concerted way. "Dad would always say, 'Guys, this is your company, you've got to treat it like that and run it like an owner,'" Peter recalls. Yet the idea that ownership and management could somehow be separated was never discussed explicitly. There was always the implication that Bruce would eventually succeed Mac as president and CEO. Mac was also intent on keeping the sons close to each other and to him. At one point he moved the family business headquarters into larger space in London so that he could provide offices for all the boys, including Bruce. Of course, Bruce was rarely there.

Cuddy watchers say that a number of factors precipitated the all-out warfare. Three of the sons were particularly ambitious — Bruce in the United States, Robert at Cuddy Foods, and Brian at the Cuddy Farms division. "Each business unit operated under the leadership of a family member as a quasi-autonomous business, usually with separate bankers and separate auditors," chief financial officer Robert Clark later observed. Compounding the problem, these men were moving into their forties — a time of life when old patterns are usually too established to change. The brothers needed to be trained in professional management, as Cuddy International evolved into a mid-sized multinational facing complex strategic challenges. But it was too late for that kind of training and discipline. And some of the sons felt that it was time for Mac to move over and give them complete control.

To complicate matters, external challenges were beginning to mount. Cuddy's had been on a trajectory of constant, impressive expansion. But in the late 1980s, the business plateaued, and then turned downward for a few years. In the United States, after years of explosive growth Cuddy International experienced some actual losses. Mac Cuddy had always tiptoed close to the line in terms of keeping within his bank loan covenants. Now he started to stray across that line. Documents filed by the company show that Cuddy International suffered four separate debt crises in the early to mid 1990s. At times it was in breach of its loan covenants and had fully drawn down its operating lines of credit. People close to the company say that bankers were starting to dictate conditions — namely, more outside directors and a stronger team of nonfamily managers. The new directors that were appointed were not convinced that the sons had the right stuff to run the company.

Mac's version is slightly different. He says that all the moves — the outside directors, the passing over of Bruce as his successor — were his own calls. He wanted a majority of outside directors on the board to end the incestuousness that was plaguing directors' meetings. His sons were treating the meetings more as shareholders' meetings, pursuing their own interests as owners or potential owners. Not enough attention was being devoted to a strategic vision for the company. He admits that the company was always highly leveraged, but also insists that the banks were not calling the shots — *he* was.

Bruce was talented, he acknowledges, but his attention was diverted from the company. The younger man had become chief operating officer in 1989, with Mac retaining the role of chairman and CEO. But there was constant tension. Mac says that Bruce never acted like the operating chief of the entire company: he was obsessed with the U.S. operations and his own incessant deal making back in North Carolina. At lot of that deal making was being done on Bruce's personal account, Mac says, which made him angry. "Bruce would come for board meetings and stay in our guest room here, but he'd be on the phone to Carolina for two hours every night, and first thing in the morning. I finally said, 'You should stay in the hotel in London instead of this house.' He just couldn't divorce himself [from North Carolina]. I said, 'You're the operating officer of the whole company, not just North Carolina.' Bruce never adjusted to the idea of being COO of whole company. He was a wheeler dealer." Asked if Bruce wasn't simply trying to match his wheeling-dealing father, Mac admits that probably he was. "I think Bruce and Brian are like me and Peter would like to be like me. What the hell's so great about me?" But he adds that there was an important difference between his own actions and Bruce's — he was more careful in separating his personal interests from those of the company.

He insists that Bruce just got "too damn greedy, trying to emulate his old man. He is an entrepreneur, no doubt about it." By coincidence, Bruce also labels his father as "greedy." Told that Mac used that same adjective to describe his actions, Bruce replies that his own greed must have been a good thing because it built Cuddy into a significant U.S. player. "I put food in his mouth," he says. He adds that, "for twenty years, we talked every day, ten times a day, and suddenly it stopped." But why did it stop? Is it possible there was room for only one Mac Cuddy in the company? "I'm probably like him," Bruce concedes, adding that "it's all genetics." It takes a turkey breeder to know.

In the early 1990s, Mac Cuddy was talking about retiring as CEO. He was newly remarried and the sons and other managers were taking on increasing roles. He was also not well. He first started to feel a tingling in his hands, which he largely ignored. Then he suffered a riding accident in the late 1980s — he fell while he was out on the family's traditional Thanksgiving Day hunt. Badly hurt, he was laid up for more than two months. It was clear that something serious was wrong with his body, and it turned out to be multiple sclerosis.

Bruce was waiting in the wings. "We believed it was a matter of time when Bruce would be anointed as CEO," Peter recalls. "There was never any question." But Bruce's independent streak was working against him. At one point his father wanted Bruce to relocate to London from North Carolina; Bruce resisted, arguing that an international company such as Cuddy's could be managed from anywhere. Mac was adamant that Cuddy's was a Canadian company so its COO should be located in Canada. In the middle of this clash, an article about the company appeared in a national magazine. According to Peter, it depicted Bruce Cuddy as "a big macho, cowboy-boot wearing, tough-talking guy .... [The author] put him in a light that made Dad feel inadequate. I think Dad felt that he was a bit overwhelmed by Bruce."

Pressed by key board members, Mac reopened the issue of succession. The board set up an executive search committee and hired the headhunting firm Caldwell Partners of Toronto to find a new president and CEO. Thus, Bruce would have to apply for the job he had always thought would be his birthright. In November 1993, in a shocking move, Mac turned the company over to a new president and CEO, a professional manager named Peter Green, who had no experience inside Cuddy or the industry. The move effectively sidelined Bruce and his ally Brian. Green, born in Britain, had extensive experience in family businesses and had served as president of the Canadian subsidiary of Alcatel, the French telecommunications company. Mac felt that he would be able to establish the strategic direction and the management discipline that would allow the company to go public within the next five years. That outcome would put Cuddy International on firmer financial ground though it would also dilute family ownership. Others felt that the old man's real purpose in hiring Green was to find someone to solve the family's internal problems.

Sources say that Green came into Cuddy with an open mind about the family and about the skills of the sons. He couldn't help but be impressed and somewhat intimidated by this band of charming, Hollywood-handsome giants. Yet he was immediately undermined when Mac decided to disperse about 50 percent of the common shares of the company to his sons, with 9.9 percent going to each of the five. (Mac retained a majority of the voting shares.) It created an untenable position for Green, who had to command five key employees who were also major shareholders. Even worse, at least three of the sons felt he was out to get them.

In a speech to a board meeting in 1994, Mac tried to appease his sons. Quoted in an affidavit filed by the company in response to Peter Cuddy's lawsuit, he acknowledged the lack of family harmony: "I carried a lot of baggage as being both a father and the CEO of this company. Some of you carried a lot of baggage as being sons and brothers and divisional presidents. I'm not sure if it was realistic for us to assume we could reconcile all of this and speak as one ... I don't know if we will ever achieve family harmony and be unified. But [Cuddy International] will be unified because it will have only one leader — Peter Green. Peter has often told me that he hasn't learned how to walk on water yet. I don't expect him to. I just expect him to lead this company, maximize shareholder wealth and rekindle our strategic awareness, vision and action.

"Having the name Cuddy should not and will not provide any divine rights with respect to management position or authority. I expect Peter to evaluate Cuddy family management in the same manner as if the names were Brown or Smith and he has complete authority to do what needs to be done."

Robert Cuddy, who ran Cuddy Foods, now says that the brothers always felt conflicting pressures from being both shareholders and employees of the company. He insists that he always took the approach of trying to be a good employee first, and a shareholder second. That attitude allowed him to maintain a career inside Cuddy International, even when he was working under nonfamily managers. "But one of my brothers thought the company was his first, and not the family's and not the employees'," he says, in a clear reference to Bruce.

At one point, Mac hired an American consultant to work on both strategic planning and the relationship between himself and the children. In 1993 Cavas Gobhai, a Boston-based expert in innovation strategy, led a weekend retreat of the father and sons, plus a couple of company managers and a family lawyer, at the rustic Benmiller Inn near Goderich, Ontario. From all accounts, the weekend degenerated into a bitch session, with the sons coming down hard on Mac for his real and perceived inadequacies. Gobhai had impressive credentials, particularly in his work with the U.S. investment bank Drexel Burnham and its controversial junk bond guru Mike Milken. But he told one of the Cuddy sons that there was nothing he could do — this was the most divided family he had ever worked with. Says Peter Cuddy, "It wasn't so much a family meeting about succession planning as it was to air our differences and realize how deep the differences were. It was a bad two days."

Mac Cuddy left the meeting feeling like a fighter who had been pummelled for fifteen rounds and lost the match. He had always maintained an open-door policy in the company head office in London. After the Benmiller confrontation, he walked into his office Monday morning and closed the door. It was a signal of how he felt about his sons and the prospects of healing.

Meanwhile, Peter Green, the new president, was becoming more aware of how far things had slid out of control. An affidavit by chief financial officer Robert Clark, filed in response to Peter Cuddy's 1997 lawsuit, said that the company had learned of financial discrepancies in the U.S. operations in early 1993 and had commissioned a forensic audit of the company's finances. The investigators reported that Bruce had improperly obtained $6.2 million in extra payments from the Canadian parent company, Clark's affidavit said. The affidavit also alleged that a contract had been altered to mask the payments. There were problems on other fronts. The court documents also stated that Bruce and Brian had sought Green's support for buying hatchery operations in France. Green had told them not to proceed until a real business case had been established. But in early 1994, the affidavit said, a series of faxes turned up at head office showing that Bruce, Brian, and two Cuddy employees had incorporated a French company and had run up costs of $220,000. It was discovered that the brothers were working toward the purchase of a French hatchery. They also incurred expenses of $500,000 in clearing customer claims from a disease outbreak in France. These allegations, on top of all the other tensions, spelled the end of the line for Bruce, who was dismissed in June 1994.

Peter Cuddy acknowledges that his older brother ran the U.S. company as a personal fiefdom, making decisions and investments on his own. But, Peter argues, you have to understand how the family did business. Mac wanted his sons to run their operations just as he had — with a willingness to take risks and deal with the consequences afterward. "That's the way that we were told [by our father] to do things, it was suggested to us that 'this was your company, operate it as such.'

"We were always taught to be entrepreneurial. The French issue was an entreprenerial opportunity but Dad didn't see it as an opportunity. He thought it was more problems than it was worth. To Bruce and Brian's credit, they recognized that France would be the centre of the poultry industry in Europe in the coming years." But Peter acknowledges that they made one fatal error. "When Dad said no, it should have been no, but they went ahead and did it."

Bruce realizes that he was portrayed as being out of control. He won't comment on the allegations directly but does say, "I had a bad habit. I'm not real polished. I like calling a spade a spade. I like dealing with my friends, and I don't like too much pomp and ceremony." He says he was characterized as the bad guy in the company. "But to tell you the truth, you had to see it to believe it."

The real problem was that the company was changing. It was no longer in an entrepreneurial phase, as it had been during Mac's formative years as owner — or even during his sons' apprenticeship. Growth was slowing down; the market was maturing. There were now professional managers in charge, and outside directors were watching the unfolding situation. Managers — even family managers — could no longer operate as free agents without keeping senior management closely informed. Company sales at one point had crested $500 million, and the employees now numbered more than 4,000. The company required discipline and strict financial controls, and it needed to operate by the rules. As Bruce himself says now, the company ceased to be "fun." The brothers were out of step with the new Cuddy International.

Peter Cuddy, the youngest son, felt this new wave coming. He was later in joining the company and was the most frustrated by the lack of advancement. As he applied for assignments and promotions, he was told he was not qualified, that he did not have the skill sets. In his view, the board and top outside managers were inherently prejudiced against family members and were blocking his chances. At one point in 1993 he got a call from one of Cuddy's lawyers saying it was time for Peter to do something else with his career. The lawyer sent over a document — basically a termination agreement — for Peter to sign.

Bruce, who was still in the company at that time, leaped to Peter's defence and got his younger brother reinstated. But Peter Cuddy realized that the writing was on the wall. His father was no longer his defender and advocate. "It suddenly occurred to me that my best and closest friend had other motives and other plans, and they may not be in my best interests." A few months later, Peter negotiated a severance package by which the company would finance his MBA studies at the University of Western Ontario. According to court documents, between 1994 and 1997 Cuddy International continued to pay his salary and benefits, as well as tuition, for total payments of more than $400,000. Yet even as he left, Peter always felt he would come back to Cuddy International, armed with the skills he was deemed to lack.

Peter Green himself was not long for the company. Mac simply wouldn't get out of his hair. Green was turning the company's finances around, largely by disposing of certain noncore assets, particularly in the United States. But he never felt he had free rein to be the CEO. Mac, for his part, was frustrated by Green's modus operandi, which was very much that of a professional manager. His new recruit did not have a feel for the business or its people, Mac says now. Also, Green was lobbying for Mac to remove himself entirely from the company and take a real retirement. That clearly was not going to happen. By mutual agreement, Green left in April 1995; he was replaced by one of his own recruits. Mac, in explaining Green's departure, says, "I picked the wrong guy. He's a bureaucrat. Between him and me, there was no chemistry, absolutely none."

A former manager in the company says that the underlying problem was that Mac Cuddy had built a great company but could no longer manage what it had become. "He was a great entrepreneur but he didn't have the training to run a complex company. The boys got out of hand, they were never trained, never properly directed from a young age. As the sons moved into middle age, things started to go wrong between them and their father and between them and the company. At the end of the day, it was hard to say it was anybody's fault. I don't think I can say it is — it was inevitable probably."

Peter Green will not comment on the Cuddy affair. But from his experience in several family companies, he is convinced that the biggest challenge in family businesses is the patriarch who lingers too long. By age sixty, he argues, entrepreneurs should simply state that they are going to retire, and provide a timetable for their total retreat. And by retirement, Green means they should have no executive functions at all. The bosses should say, "I will have somebody in place. It might be a son or a daughter, or a nonfamily manager." Unfortunately, many of them cannot let go of the consuming passion of their lives.

Mac's explanation of what went wrong is laced with contradictions. He now believes that the sons should have worked outside the company when they were younger, but he is vague on how that might have improved matters. The old man is sceptical that they could have received better training than they did at Cuddy International. And he is both bitter and forgiving in his attitude toward Bruce. Mac wonders if the riding accident that removed him from operations left Bruce with too much latitude. But basically, his argument is that Bruce simply got too greedy and ruthless, and had to be passed over. He avoids any suggestion that by allowing his oldest son so much independence and so little career planning — and then denying him the leadership role he craved — Mac had helped create this condition.

After Peter Green left, the war continued to rage at Cuddy International.

Bruce, flush with a financial settlement from Cuddy International, was forging his own small U.S. turkey-breeding business, with operations in North Carolina and Kansas. In some cases the turkey-hatching eggs he was supplying were winning contracts in competition with his father's company. After Green's departure, the three insurgent brothers — Bruce, Brian, and Peter — launched several efforts to buy out the company, but their advances either were spurned or never took shape. At one point they felt they had swayed Cuddy International's new president, Stan Smyth, to their point of view. Smyth would later deny this. Smyth too resigned as president after just five months on the job.

Mac, in his mid-seventies, had to move in as temporary CEO, running things for a few months. Then a couple of board members stepped into the breach. But the company's new U.S. bondholders required a single CEO, so in early 1996 director Peter Widdrington assumed the role. A hard-nosed professional manager now in his sixties, the former chairman of John Labatt Ltd. was seen as a caretaker to keep the company afloat until a managerial succession plan could be developed. The three Cuddy sons, meanwhile, saw Widdrington as yet another obstacle in their attempts to assume what they saw as their rightful place. "Dad used to say you had to have feathers in the blood to run this operation," Peter Cuddy recalls. That was clearly no longer the case.

Widdrington stayed for three years, but he was not working full-time at Cuddy International and kept a low profile in the poultry industry. The top day-to-day manager was Kathy Houde, a tough and capable vice-president who zealously protected Mac and the company from media intrusion. The company was not the growth engine it had once been. Sales had slipped since the glory days of the early 1990s, and in some years there were losses. The turkey market had slumped, particularly in the United States, and Cuddy International now began to convert more of its turkey hatcheries into chicken operations.

The sons drifted a bit. Brian was president of a small agrifoods company for a time, but it too suffered financial difficulties, and he left. He had also been helping Bruce in his U.S. business. After completing his MBA, Peter found a job as an investor relations specialist with Emco Ltd., a building products company in London. Then came his shareholder's suit against Cuddy International, which he promptly withdrew. He parted company with Emco and, with his father's backing, established a company that developed healthy freeze-dried snacks. In late 1999, he said his legal disputes with Cuddy International had been settled. And he continued to harbour the faint hope that the three estranged sons would come back to the family company in some capacity, perhaps as owners.

But in the final analysis, would Mac transfer ownership to the rebellious faction of his family? On Mac's death, his slightly more than 50 percent ownership share, part of a family trust, is to be divided among the five sons and daughter Barbara. But what about voting control? Peter was confident the sons will get the voting interest too: "I don't think for a moment my father is going to go to his grave saying 'You guys will never control this company.' I don't think that for a moment."

Bruce, meanwhile, has other things on his mind: he is working flat out to try to establish his own turkey egg operation. Would he come back to Canada? "Shit, no. Canada has nothing for me," he says. He explains that he gave up his Canadian citizenship when he was fired at Cuddy International in 1994. Now, he's looking forward to getting his own two sons to work in his small company. The older one, at twenty-five, is a trader for Archer Daniels Midland, the big agriculture commodity company. It's good training, Bruce observes, for a family company.

Resting in a soft chair in his farmhouse study, Mac Cuddy is pondering the same kinds of issues. He admits that the designation of his voting shares after he dies is a tough call. "It's a very difficult awkward situation ... I just don't know, I don't know. Mortality is something that never crossed my mind, even with my lack of mobility, and yet I know it will happen. In the meantime, I just have to use all the resolve I have and come to grips with these issues and put them all to bed."

Mac Cuddy is showing that he'll never really learn. Peter Widdrington is leaving the company, and Mac couldn't be more pleased. The patriarch says he is frustrated by Widdrington's deliberate decision-making, which he believes comes from a large-corporation mentality. "I know people are going to say that Mac Cuddy is tough to work for, that he interferes, and they are probably right," Mac says. This time, he says, the board's selection committee will have to find a CEO who has a chemistry with the company and with its employees and — most importantly — with its majority owner. Some of the sons, he admits, don't get along with Widdrington, and he hopes that the executive's departure will help heal wounds.

In the end, Mac Cuddy replaced Widdrington with a committee of senior managers, including Kathy Houde, who took over Robert Cuddy's position as the head of Cuddy Foods. Robert, at forty-five, left the company to buy a franchise outlet of the East Side Mario's restaurant chain. Robert said that after twenty-five years with Cuddy Foods, he needed a change of life, and that he had become frustrated by the corporate politics. While he had been loyal to his father, he felt frozen out by the nonfamily senior managers. "I also see a potential conflict when Dad passes on," he added ominously.

Within a couple of months of Robert's leaving, Douglas Cuddy was also out of the company, sent packing when the new team closed down Cuddy International's trucking operations. Douglas was looking for new opportunities, his brother Robert said. With Douglas's departure, all five Cuddy brothers were now gone from the family firm.

Cuddy International's exit from the transport business was part of an effort to shore up the firm's finances. In July 1999, Moody's Investor Service, the U.S. bond rating agency, downgraded the company's senior unsecured notes, noting that the outlook for the company was negative. In its report, Moody's observed that the company's financial numbers had weakened, reducing its comfort level in covering interest payments. The situation reflected "adverse market conditions" in the U.S. turkey market and narrower profit margins as the firm moved increasingly from turkey eggs to lower-margin chicken eggs.

Moody's also expressed concern over the revolving door of senior management. "The CEO, president of Cuddy Foods, [chief financial officer] and some members of the board of directors have all recently departed or will leave soon. This creates a vacuum in leadership at a time when the company needs to address its operational needs. The company has a chance to reorient itself with new management but the transition could take time."

Among the Cuddys, only Mac remains with the firm. So why didn't he simply sell out to his sons when he had the chance? The lion is suddenly reflective. "That wasn't really in the cards. They wouldn't have ended up with it." Besides, he says, "I didn't want to sell the damn thing, I still don't. What the hell am I going to do? My horses are gone, I don't have any hobbies. I can't play golf in this condition, I never did. My hobby is work and the people that go with that element."

TWO

THE BATAS —
MOTHERS AND FATHERS

The Batas — Sonja and Thomas Sr.

I T IS A SWELTERING JUNE DAY IN 1998 at York University in the northern outskirts of Toronto. Graduation Day is unfolding in an enormous tent in the centre of the campus. A few protesters have congregated around the tent entrance and are handing out pamphlets excoriating the policies of the Bata Shoe Organization in the Third World. BATA: PAY YOUR WORKERS A LIVING WAGE, the leaflets demand. Except for this small bit of unpleasantness, it is a day of celebration for Bata Shoe — Thomas Bata Sr., its octogenarian builder and honorary chairman, is being granted an honorary degree.

The "old man," as he is affectionately known by his employees, is tired and limping a bit. He fell skiing a few months ago at St. Moritz and has just come off a long flight from Indonesia. But at eighty-four, tanned and silver-haired, he is his usual undaunted self, cheerfully playing his role as the human face of the global shoe manufacturing and retailing empire. As the ceremony unfolds, his wife, Sonja Bata, a cool and steely beauty at seventy-two, is wandering around with a video camera, occasionally whispering instructions to a company photographer. It is yet another grandstand performance by Canadian business's longest-running and most resilient husband-and-wife team.

Mr. Bata's speech is funny and warm, if a little light on profundity. Nobody seems to mind his off-the-cuff approach. In response to an effusive introduction, he cracks a joke: "At times of deepest depression, I will recall what a great fellow I really am." His final words to the graduating class: "Be flexible, keep up your education, and be careful to operate in an ethical way — and have fun."

But to outside observers, including some of Tom Bata's closest friends, there is not a lot of flexibility and fun back at the Bata Shoe Organization. The world's largest shoemaker and shoe retailer has been drifting for more than a decade; it lacks drive, consistent leadership, and a sense of what the twenty-first century holds for it. There is evidence of a severe succession crisis. At the reception afterward, as the Bata family and university dignitaries gather to honour the patriarch, there is one notable absentee: son Thomas G. Bata, often referred to as Tom Jr. The heir who is no longer apparent has exiled himself to Europe. Although still a director of the Bata parent company, he is no longer involved in the day-to-day management of the shoe empire.

Bata Shoe is a not-so-shining case study of two strong and charismatic parents and one able son who, they finally determined, did not quite measure up. Tom Bata Sr. will argue fervently that the company remains strong and that its succession problems are only a blip on the screen. Yet he appears to be a conflicted patriarch caught between a very strong wife and a son who has found it hard to function in the same space as his dyamic, domineering parents. Throughout most of the 1990s, outside managers came and went; eventually the company was placed in the hands of a team made up largely of loyal but uninspiring long-term executives. All this at a time when Bata's business model was under merciliess attack from global shoe brands.

Some Bata-watchers called it the lost decade, a period when the organization's deepening succession crisis paralyzed its ability to solve major strategic problems. Mr. Bata Sr., interviewed in the company's low-slung, modernistic headquarters in Toronto's Don Mills area, is not so critical. "I'm sure there was a temporary loss of momentum," he says. "It's not the only time it's happened, and not only for family companies. I hope now we are back in momentum. I'm confident there are lots of changes coming."

Thomas Bata Sr., as honorary chairman, still plays a highly influential role — both symbolic and operational — at Bata Ltd., the core operating company. At his age, other entrepreneurs would be taking long afternoon naps or going golfing. But Tom Bata has never been the napping type, nor does he enjoy the laid-back pace of golfing — not when there are dignitaries to entertain or shoe stores that could be visited. He denies that the succession issue is any big concern, or that he is disappointed that no Bata family member is prominent in the management of the company. "Yes, I want the family [involved]. But look, if it isn't well led and profitable, it cannot survive. So the question is: have we created a structure where there are all the strengths of a public company and good private companies which will carry us on into the next two generations? I hope so, but our responsibility is not just for the family but for the people working in the whole organization. We've got to be damn sure that it's sound."

Mr. Bata insists that the company, because of its size and complexity, has got to be run just like a public company, with a strong parent-company board on which independent directors form the majority. That, he says, is what he has achieved in his more than fifty years at the helm. The legal owners of Bata Shoe are three family trusts, two of them based in Bermuda and another in Switzerland. The trustees were appointed originally by his mother and himself when they set up the structure many years ago. Mr. Bata himself is a trustee, as are other "trusted people and members of the Bata family." The trusts, along with the board itself, have the responsibility of appointing new directors. It is not a hollow board of family members, or even friends of the family, the honorary chairman insists.

The company, which as recently as fifteen years ago employed 85,000 people, has been shrinking. It's down to 52,000 employees in 69 countries. But it's still a giant, with a network of over 5,000 company-owned retail stores, 100,000 dealers, 52 shoe-manufacturing plants, and 9 tanneries around the world. Bata Shoe likes to say it is the world's largest footwear manufacturing and marketing organization, serving over one million customers each business day. Sales are not reported but are believed to be in the range of $3 billion a year. Yet Bata has been perceived as losing market share to shrewder marketers such as Nike, Reebok, ECCO, and the like. Mr. Bata argues that the decline is overstated and that while Bata may have lost market share in athletic shoes, it is unassailable as the world's major overall shoe brand. He argues that it is supreme in all significant international markets except the United States, where it was forced to unload a disastrous investment in a shoe store chain. Its critics, meanwhile, argue that while it may still be shoemaker to the world, it mainly serves a market in which margins are low and merchandise is cheaply priced.

However severe the decline, it has been a comedown for the proud company, which was founded a century ago by Thomas Bata Sr.'s father, Tomas. Its birthplace was Zlin in what is now the Czech Republic, a town the Batas once ruled as quasi-feudal chiefs. The son Thomas grew up in the business and was considered the heir, although he always found it difficult to live up to the legend of his father. In his autobiography, *Bata: Shoemaker to the World*, published in 1990, in a passage that presaged his own son's challenges, Thomas Bata Sr. described the enormous weight on his young shoulders: "Being the only son of a legendary father can be a mixed blessing. On the minus side, there is an enormous weight of expectations, along with a sometimes frustrating struggle to acquire one's own identity, away from a parent's shadow. When the son is successful, he is perceived as a chip off the old block; when he makes a mistake, he is perceived not to measure up to the father's standards."

In many ways Bata was not just a family business — it was a way of life, a laboratory for industrial organization and social engineering. Zlin was a pure company town where strict rules were imposed on residents' morality and civic duties. (Drinking was not allowed in the city at certain periods of Bata rule.) It was a total culture, not just a business culture, and it was in certain ways highly idealistic and egalitarian. The Bata Shoe Organization established one of the world's first business schools, the Bata School for Young Men, recruiting bright young Czechs of all backgrounds and sending them out into the world like missionaries to spread the gospel of shoemaking and social progress. Bata was centralized in product development and innovation at its Czech base; yet it became highly decentralized in manufacturing and sales, which were directed by local management in the regions where the Batas set up shop.

The guiding philosophy of the Bata Shoe Organization was contained in Tomas Bata's "moral testament," which was found among the papers in his safe when he died. It said essentially that the business he had created was not to be considered simply as a source of personal profit but rather as a vehicle of public trust. "We were motivated by the knowledge that our enterprise was providing an entire region with new previously unknown advantages, that its growth was contributing to the wealth and the education of the nation," Tomas Bata wrote.

Sam Blyth, the Toronto travel entrepreneur who is the former husband of Thomas Bata Sr.'s daughter Rosemarie, says that members of the family came to share the company's mission, even as it extended into the third generation. "The mission goes largely to issues of creating employment and security and opportunity for tens of thousands of employees around the world, as opposed to enriching the shareholders ... Some goals were set down by [my former father-in-law] but many were established by his father Tomas. That vision was frequently referred to in family meetings."

Thomas Bata Sr.'s life changed profoundly in July 1932, when his father Tomas died in a plane crash while flying from Zlin to the company's new factory in Switzerland. Succession was fast and clearly laid out. Tomas's younger brother, the idealistic and emotional Jan Bata, was to take over as CEO, with the tacit understanding that he was merely holding the fort until the next generation, young Thomas, then eighteen, was ready. In Czechoslovakia, marriages were often late and having children was often delayed, so it was quite common for younger brothers to bridge the generations — even when accidents did not snuff out their siblings' lives so precipitously.

In the late 1930s the Nazis were steamrolling across central Europe and the Bata empire appeared to be in mortal danger. Young Thomas, now in his mid-twenties, was determined to move the company beyond the reach of expansion-minded Nazi Germany. After exploring for a new site, he packed up the company and moved to Canada. The plan was to build a new company town, to be called Batawa, on the Trent River one hundred miles east of Toronto. One hundred Czech shoemakers and managers joined him.

The Second World War destroyed Bata's international network and infrastructure. Then the Communists came to power in Czechoslovakia and nationalized the company. After the war, young Thomas threw himself into rebuilding the Bata organization from its then-headquarters in London, England, and its operational centre in Batawa. But a huge distraction arose — his uncle Jan challenged Thomas's right of ownership over the worldwide Bata assets. Jan was a controversial figure, a utopian dreamer who some have accused of being a Nazi sympathizer. Both he and his nephew were very strong personalities, and they inspired divided loyalties among emigré Czechs. In many communities and within many families, there was a faction that was pro-Jan and another that was pro-Thomas.

In country after country, the two Batas engaged in legal warfare over who controlled the company's assets. Gradually, young Thomas won the war, but it was not until the 1960s that the final embers of the legal battle burned themselves out, giving Thomas Bata Sr., by then a middle-aged man, control of the worldwide organization. This victory was powerful evidence of Thomas Bata Sr.'s stubbornness and persistence — two strengths that served him well but have also been a hindrance in recent years as the company has required change. He has also benefited from an energy that leaves younger men in the dust. Despite his great wealth and sophistication, he feels he is essentially a shoemaker — it is his life. It is said that he has occasionally dismissed would-be recruits because "they aren't shoe men."

He had found a willing soulmate in Sonja Wettstein, the daughter of a Swiss lawyer and longtime Bata confidant. He'd met Sonja before the Second World War when he was a callow fifteen-year-old and she was a toddler. Their families were close. Dr. Wettstein was a business adviser of the older Tomas Bata. In fact, it was he who set up the family trusts that now own the company. When they met again at the end of the war, Tom was a busy thirty-one-year-old rebuilding his family company, and nineteen-year-old Sonja was studying architecture in Zurich. "She always said that she was going to be the world's best architect," he recalls. But she gave up the dream to marry Thomas and help build a new Bata Shoe Organization from Canada.

As a former architecture student, Sonja was fascinated with shoe styles and store design but did not immerse herself in the details of business and finance. She tirelessly accompanied her husband on his tours of far-flung operations. Mr. Bata's autobiography is plastered with photographs of meetings with local retailers, company officials, and dignitaries; Tom is always in the foreground and Sonja, Zelig-like, in the background with her icy smile and perfect couture. In all their trips to Bata's far-flung outposts, she couldn't dampen her husband's obsession with the business. One manager recalls a trip to Iran with Tom and Sonja. Ms. Bata and some of the managers were keen to head off to see the antiquities of ancient Persia; Tom Sr. stole away to find a local shoe store.

Sonja couldn't be the world's greatest architect, but she strived to be the greatest shoe magnate's wife. There was another aspect to her work, her husband says. "Having grown up in Switzerland, in a family of philosophical breadth, she had a feeling of responsibility of looking at the Third World and at the opportunities it presented. Although she had no formal position, she began to exert influence on the organization, in asking for conferences, seminars, and design sessions ... We tended to listen to her and now she's on the board. She is part of the decision-making group and I am sort of, shall we say, the elder stateman, sitting around and being present."

For years after it moved to Canada, the company was dominated by the old emigré Czech hands, who were well drilled in the Bata culture. They were great shoe people but often resistant to change and evolution. Many had been recruited by the Bata company while in their early teens and had never worked a day outside the organization. They created a company that for a time thrived by being so decentralized — its national companies were almost self-governed, and there was little trade between the far-flung units. The Bata organization provided the expertise and technology, nurtured by its core of loyal Czechs; local managers did the rest. This collection of quasi-independent, self-sufficient companies was an ideal structure for a world still divided by steep national trade barriers, but as tariffs fell through the 1980s and 1990s, it became an obsolete way to do business.

Working at Bata head office meant belonging to a highly conservative culture in which "Mr. and Mrs. Bata" ruled. When the president entered the room, and often when his voice was heard over the office intercom, the staff stood up. However, as time passed the original core of Czech managers began to shrink; they were replaced by a new generation of executives, many of them recruited from Bata operations in Italy, the Netherlands, Germany, and India.

Yet something was lost when the head office moved from Czechoslovakia to Canada, says Georgina Wyman, the Czech-born former federal civil servant who as a Bata executive spearheaded the company's return to Czechoslovakia in the 1990s. The Bata organization had become separated from its heartland, says Wyman, who recently returned to Bata after a stint with a life insurance company. It lost that ready supply of dedicated and loyal Czech managers and employees, as well as the environment from which they sprang. In a sense, it became less of a total culture and more of a family business; lost was the strong loyalty and identity that had held the company together. If there was a common thread to this untidy collection of country companies, it was Thomas Bata Sr., who ruled like a patriarch, staying in constant touch with his country managers and maintaining a whirlwind schedule of overseas travel. This gave birth to an organizational paradox. "Bata was a decentralized organization, but a highly centrally controlled decentralized organization," recalls Gerhard Jannsen, a former Bata senior executive and later a director of rival ECCO, the Danish shoe company.

There is certainly a Bata way of doing things — from shoemaking to human resources — that does not vary greatly from country to country. Also, the head office in Toronto does contain a small product-development area, and there is increasing communication among country companies. Even so, there is always the feeling that Bata has never exploited its international potential and the muscle it could put behind its brand.

"Bata was trying to run a company for the 1990s with an organization of the 1930s," Jannsen says. As barriers to trade were relaxed, powerful global brands began to emerge. Some players, such as Nike and Adidas, became brand managers rather than manufacturers. Manufacturing was contracted out to low-cost operators around the world, and shoes were shifted easily from market to market. In fact, Bata became a manufacturer for some other people's global brands. Meanwhile it stuck to its collection of local companies, each with its own production and retail infrastructure. Says Jannsen, "Bata is a federation of companies, not a global organization. There is no global shoe line, all companies do their own shoes, there is no centralizing in brands and marketing approach."

As the company evolved, the Batas were building a family. Thomas George Bata — known as Tom Jr. — was born in Zurich in 1948. Three daughters followed — Christine in 1953, Monica in 1955, and Rosemarie in 1960. Since this was a traditional European family, young Tom was groomed to eventually run the company. It was clear that the daughters were not to be considered. "It was always said, 'The girls never showed any interest,'" says one former Bata manager. "It's implicit in a European patriarchy that women do not fit into management." Asked why his daughters were not prepared for management positions in the company, Mr. Bata says simply that "the girls started getting married and started producing families. That was not really an option."

Interviewed in August 1998 about his daughters' careers, he explained: "Monica has been running businesses of a small entrepreneurial character out of Paris. Christine works with her husband in an international trading business. Rosemarie has had bad luck with her marriage [to Sam Blyth] and now she's got a job. I forget the name of the company but she started last week full time." (The employer was an advertising agency.) However, all three daughters serve on various boards of Bata regional companies.

Tom Jr. was given the best training money could buy. He was sent to an English boarding school at age six to replicate his own father's boyhood experiences. After graduating in science from the University of Toronto, he spent two years working with a rival shoe company in Argentina to learn the business. Then he enrolled at Harvard for an MBA. As expected, the chosen heir joined the Bata organization, moving lock-step through the ranks. He worked for Bata companies in Switzerland and France for nine years, then came back to Toronto to move through a number of corporate jobs. It was widely believed in the organization that he would eventually become the CEO. It just was a matter of time.

That time finally arrived in 1984, when Thomas Sr. decided to step aside at age seventy, allowing Tom Jr., then thirty-six, to take over as president and CEO of Bata Ltd., the main operating company. "They studied and carefully planned the transition," says Sam Blyth. "They relied on family and outside resources [for guidance]. It was treated with a degree of objectivity by Tom Sr., who as with anything else in his way, was analytical about it." Despite the careful planning, within a decade Tom Jr. would be out of that job.

In his autobiography, Thomas Bata Sr. put his finger on precisely what went wrong. He wrote of his son attending a seminar on family companies in which the "father comes back" syndrome was discussed. "In other words the old man, having retired, can't stand having nothing to do, besides which he believes his successor is a fool. Result: he keeps turning up in the office and tries to start running the show all over again. The ideal remedy, the seminar agreed, was to buy Father a small business to keep him occupied. One chap, for instance, had a father who loved horses, so the family bought him a stud farm and thereby got him off the son's back.

"In my own case, I am happy to say, no such dramatic measures were required. When I decided, a few weeks before my seventieth birthday, that the time was right for me to vacate the chief executive's chair, I didn't have the slightest doubt about my son's ability to step into my shoes. Tom was by then a mature executive with an excellent educational background and years of managerial experience, both within and outside our organization."

The lesson here is to never write your memoirs prematurely. The fact is, the Bata parents never really let go of their dominant roles in the company. Bata Shoe contained not just one but two outsized personalities, and neither ever dreamed of surrendering the huge space they occupied. Inside the company, managers had to constantly skate around both Tom Jr. and his father to get things done. One former manager points out that Tom Jr., while not a compelling leader, did possess a certain managerial drive. But he was also an introvert — he needed space, perhaps in understandable reaction to his gregarious father. Even when he made necessary changes, he often did not — or, perhaps, could not — put enough money or people into them, the former manager says, and that was particularly the case with critical marketing resources.

While Tom Jr. was running the company, his parents were energetically pursuing their personal projects, including the dramatic return of the family to Czechoslovakia following the collapse of the Iron Curtain. The Batas came back to reclaim their traditional place as the country's shoemakers, but the event was more symbolic than substantive. The family re-established a retail presence in their native country, but the manufacturing infrastructure had been so badly damaged by years of Communist rule and would be so costly to rebuild, that the project was not zealously pursued by the family's managers. Today, the Czech Republic produces only a small quantity of Bata shoes.

Still, the return packed an enormous emotional wallop. Sam Blyth recalls taking Rosemarie to Zlin in 1985, even before *perestroika* and the family's return. They checked into the Hotel Moscow, which had been the Bata company guest house in an earlier era. When Blyth presented his wife's passport at the desk, the clerk was quick to notice Rosemarie's last name: "Are you part of the family that lived here?" she was asked. On being assured that was the case, the clerk burst into tears. The hotel immediately fixed up the couple with a guide, a former Bata employee, to escort them around the city much like visiting royalty. The guide took them through the factories, prefacing his descriptions with the phrase, "As a Bata employee, I ..." When Blyth pointed out that he was not in fact a Bata employee anymore, the man responded, "I will always be a Bata employee."

Meanwhile, Sonja, with customary singlemindedness, was becoming increasingly involved in the business, as well as the driving force behind the acclaimed Bata Shoe Museum, which occupies a prime location on Toronto's Bloor Street. As Tom Sr. grew older and began to lose a step, Sonja, a half-generation younger, emerged as an inside player in her own right, first informally and then as a member of the parent company's board. Until then, Bata Shoe had been a patriarchy. Now there was a capable and strong-willed woman in its midst. It got so that Tom Sr. often found himself in the middle, mediating between Tom Jr. and Sonja, both of whom expected to exert more authority.

One former manager says that Sonja does not hold sway on every issue in the company. Some say she tends to flit around like a butterfly, which can hamper her effectiveness. But she chooses her battles carefully and at times demonstrates intense focus on issues that interest her. "She has a laser-beam kind of mentality," another former manager says.

According to some Bata watchers, the issue that finally fractured the family consensus was Tom Jr.'s desire to take public some of the company's operations. Merrill Lynch, the investment banker, studied the possibility of a public offering by the company in 1993. Tom Jr. was also convinced that some Bata regional operations might sell shares on their own. Bata branch companies often sold shares to local investors, mainly to satisfy country laws demanding domestic ownership. Sonja never liked the idea of going public, insiders say. She was proud that Bata was the world's largest privately owned shoe organization. But Tom Jr. felt that the high share-price multiples in Asian stock markets in the early 1990s could reap hundreds of millions of dollars. That money could then be channelled into regions, such as North America and Europe, where the company was facing intense competition. "It became a major collision at the board level," one observer recalls. "In hindsight, Tom Jr. might have had the right approach."

But he lost the battle with Sonja and others on the board, and resigned from the company's senior management. By this time Tom Jr. was tired of fighting the same old battles, and he appeared to welcome the chance to do his own thing. He felt blocked in his goals, both in unlocking the value of the company through the stock markets and in building a new organizational structure. One of his ideas had been to divide the Bata organization into three large units — the developed world, emerging nations, and certain special situations — each with an entrepreneurial leader. While remaining a board member, Tom Jr. moved to Switzerland, first to work for the company and then to become a venture capitalist on his own. He was invited to be an executive-in-residence at the Institute for Management Development, an élite business school in Lausanne. In Europe he turned his intellectual attention to a subject he knew something about — family business. "I get involved in helping businesses, in developing their governance," he said in an interview in mid-1999, adding that he spends about 5 percent of his time on such matters. "It's a bit of a hobby."

The late Stanley Heath, the outside manager recruited to succeed young Tom, believed that the problem was that the younger man was never allowed to develop in his own space, and on his own time. "Young Tom is well put together, attractive, well-educated, intelligent, personable, easy to be with. He's not exactly the village idiot," Heath said. But the family did not allow him enough time to develop a career outside the family shoe business. His parents should have let him work in an unrelated industry to give him space, confidence, and seasoning. "That's close to the heart of the tragedy," said Heath. "If that had happened, I would have never been in the top job." He concluded: "It's tough for a son with such a dominant father to be anything else but a strong second place. He was not his own person."

Another former manager agrees, but adds: "If he had been a strong person, he wouldn't even have been in the company. If he told me to do something, the next day the old man was sure to contradict him. I felt Tom [Jr.] should have gone out and learned how to operate a normal business. He had to learn how to operate in an unprotected environment. [At Bata] there was always wealth around to make up for mistakes."

In retrospect, Tom Bata Sr. agrees that the chosen heir of a family organization should probably be allowed to join the company only after reaching a certain level in a totally different business. In fact, he says the intention had been for Tom Jr. to spend more time in Argentina, "but there was a little bit of a hurry to get him in here."

Tom Jr., for all his supposed limitations, did understand what was necessary to change Bata Shoe — a more concerted global marketing effort, a shift away from manufacturing, a stronger executive team. He recruited some top-notch people, and he closed some marginal operations. Yet he also made some questionable decisions; for example, he purchased a French shoe chain that actually competed with Bata. If he had had just a touch of his father's magnetic personality, some observers feel, he might have built a stronger power base. That being said, Howard Book, a Toronto psychiatrist who works with family firms, says that a vivid personality is often overrated in family companies. In fact, it is precisely what is *not* needed at certain stages of a company's life cycle. A charismatic founder may be required in the early years, but as the company gets larger a professional manager like Tom Bata Jr. is often the essential ingredient. The danger is that the culture of the company is already conditioned to glorify charisma, and this puts a more cerebral successor at a disadvantage as he tries to establish himself. Dr. Book also sympathizes with the tremendous burden that comes with being the next generation of an old family company. "The successors feel the weight of history, the burden of ensuring this whole legacy doesn't end with them."

In the end, young Tom became a casualty of the one thing that his father did reasonably well. The old man had established a board dominated by independent directors, and he persuaded some strong people to sit on it. Of course, the board was ultimately beholden to Mr. Bata — who wields considerable influence through his trustee role — but the personalities gave it a rare independence of mind. The chairman was Frans van den Hoven, the tough former chairman of Unilever, the Dutch-British consumer products giant. Van den Hoven and Sonja Bata eventually agreed that Tom Jr. should go. The company embarked on a search for a new president and latched on to Stan Heath, a veteran manager with RJR Nabisco. The announcement of his hiring came in July 1994. A new era had begun in the history of Bata Shoe — the era of the outside manager.

Stan Heath was a savvy and charming executive, an expatriate Brit with extensive international experience. But if Bata Shoe is a hard place for a son to work, it is even harder for outsiders. Heath developed a strategy to serve Bata in a new age. Certain businesses would have to be sold, including some of the sacred cows in Bata's European retailing. But the family just couldn't make the shift — it couldn't let go. Heath and his new team of managers ran up against the strong regional fiefdoms that effectively ruled the grass roots operations of the company. While the new leadership could craft a different direction for the company, it was difficult to implement in the face of local resistance.

The Bata organization comprises a large number of people of diverse ethnic groups who have known each other for decades. Many of them came up through the organization, moving from one local company to another, developing close personal bonds. The decentralized structure has allowed them to establish strong power bases, and this makes it a hard culture for outsiders to crack. At the top, Bata Shoe has operated as a highly formal culture. One manager recalls being recruited by the Bata organization to work under an executive whom he greatly respected. In the halls, the new recruit would call the executive by his first name. He was quickly taken aside and informed that inside Bata, he should address his higher-ranked colleague as "Mr." The young recruit decided that this was not the organization for him. The culture clash became even more pronounced in the Heath era, since some of the team he recruited were informal types, given to casual dress, slang, and, according to one Bata loyalist, "bad habits."

Says one manager, "I don't know if anyone could have done any better [than Heath]. But he perhaps underestimated the links between the family and some of the old guard and he underestimated the insidious behaviours of these people. The old man had a terrible habit of checking up on people. He would call country managers and say, 'How is Stan doing?'"

The regional bosses knew how to play Tom Sr.; while they were fiercely devoted to him, they also manipulated him. Heath probably should have cleaned house and established his own team of loyal regional managers. Others say he simply failed to understand the cultural and institutional barriers, take them into consideration, and work around them. He reported to van den Hoven and the board, but at times he seemed to ignore the views of the Batas, who were still the effective owners. Again, personality may have been a factor. "Stan was too low-key for that culture," says a source close to the company. "It needed someone to take the bull by the horns and an extroverted person who can make tough business decisions."

Mr. Bata Sr. was clearly not content to retreat from day-to-day operations. Peter Legg, who was recruited by Heath as senior vice-president of human resources, later alleged that the old man tried to direct the agenda for his department. In a 1996 lawsuit against the company, Legg said that Tom Sr. gave him, on more than one occasion, a document describing what should be the mission and operations of the human resources staff. Another time, Mr. Bata gave him handwritten instructions on what his priorities should be for the next six months, Legg said.

But the real problems started when the Heath team initiated a plan that involved closing some stores, selling some companies, and asking for concessions by lenders. Heath's group, in a review of Bata's European subsidiaries, had uncovered deepening losses in a number of operations. The critical decisions were to be made at a Bata board meeting in the Italian shoe-making centre of Padua in April 1995. According to company sources, Heath's proposals to close some businesses were accepted by the board. But after the Padua meeting, Tom Sr. reverted to form, Heath said. He began phoning managers in Europe who were most affected by the closings to gauge their views, and they reported these conversations back to Heath. Van den Hoven became aware there was a problem, but the chairman admitted he could not rein in the honorary chairman. After months of stalemate, Heath said he called a meeting with Mr. Bata, and asked how he could keep him better informed. But the patriarch didn't have an answer and the issue was left hanging. Five months after the Padua meeting, frustrated with his inability to get things done and sensing that he was being undermined, Heath quit.

Mr. Bata, however, tells a different story. He insists that after the Padua meeting, the board, and not just him, lost confidence in the strategy of the Heath team. The board had approved the closings, "subject to certain things happening," Mr. Bata says. "Those things didn't happen." He insists that some of the operations that the Heath team advocated closing had "good potential" but their management needed to be reinforced. Mr. Bata says too much has been made of the Heath issue. "If you take any large organization, at some particular moment there was some difference of opinion. One can go and analyze it.

At that particular time, the board felt that some of the people were not as good as they might have been."

Heath left the company to become the dean of business at Ryerson Polytechnic University in Toronto. Interviewed in the summer of 1998 — a year before he died of a heart attack — he seemed at ease with how things had turned out. He had recently held a reception to open the university's school of retailing. The venue? The Bata Shoe Museum. "It's hard not to be respectful of that amazing man," he said.

But he wondered whether the Batas cared that much about the losses in some of their regional companies. In public corporations, managers feel constant pressure from Bay Street or Wall Street to perform, and the slightest downward blip in profits can throw organizations into a frenzy. In a public company, there is a strong reaction to any change in bottom-line expectations. In wholly owned family businesses, the only shareholder is a family, whose agenda may not be entirely profit-driven. "My conclusion is that they [the Batas] were not that threatened by the losses," Heath said. They cared more about their reputation, he added, and how it would be affected by closing or selling companies, particularly in Europe where the company had its origins. Heath also observed that the Bata organization's decentralized structure meant that a local company could go under without seriously damaging the finances of the family.

In terms of strategy, Heath said the company should have outsourced large parts of its manufacturing, and concentrated more on marketing. "But just try telling a man whose company's mission starts with the statement, 'Bata, shoemaker to the world' that he should get out of manufacturing," he shrugged.

Mr. Bata says the problem with Stan Heath was his management recruits, who within the company earned the somewhat derisive nickname of "Heath's Dream Team." "They did not prove to be successful in their positions," the old man says. He argues that Heath, although a seasoned manager, had never done much recruiting in his old corporate jobs. And, he says tellingly, Heath "started with the premise that everyone inside [Bata Shoe] was no good."

In fact, there were some talented recruits who might have turned Bata around. George Heller, a savvy retailer who went on to become CEO of Hudson's Bay Co., was highly respected, but was passed over, perhaps because he lacked the necessary shoe industry credentials. Heller had been born in Czechoslovakia, and seemed to establish a rapport with Mr. Bata. But the older man once complained to Stan Heath that "he [Heller] doesn't know much about shoes." When Heath left, his team followed, and they were quickly replaced by company loyalists with long experience inside the organization. Rising to president was Rino Rizzo, a twenty-year Bata Shoe veteran and part of a strong cadre of Italian managers. This was not considered a team that would lead Bata into the twenty-first century with great vision and insight. They were an incremental group, not revolutionaries. For a time the Bata organization flirted with Adrian Bellamy, an aggressive manager from South Africa with a rich retail background. But after serving as executive chairman of Bata Ltd. for a short period, Bellamy also left the firm. "Bellamy was a bull in a china shop," Stan Heath said. "He wasn't going to piss around."

For a couple of years the company settled into a kind of stability after nearly a decade of tumult. The management team was running the company day to day, and the board was handling the broader issues, including the question of succession. Two family members sat on that board — Tom Jr. and Sonja. Van den Hoven had moved on, and the new chairman was Thomas Symons, a former university president and friend of Mr. Bata. The old man insisted that the board was at least as strong-minded as in van den Hoven's day. "Very often the honorary chairman's views don't prevail," he insists. On the issue of succession, he says, the board would call the shots, not him.

Despite Mr. Bata's reassuring words, the future of the company seemed very uncertain. It had been shaken by financial and management troubles in some of its key subsidiaries, including India, traditionally a strong market for the company. Mr. Bata insists, however, that the decentralized structure seemed to adapt well to the Asian financial crisis; the companies suffered little foreign exchange risk.

The unspoken question is, of course, what will happen when Tom Sr. dies? Will Tom Jr. come back in a more powerful role? "Tom Jr. is very capable," insists his former brother-in-law Sam Blyth. "He has a wide range of skills that made him very successful and could still make him successful." Tom Jr. is still a member of the board and chairman of the committee on governance and nomination, a key committee. But it is clear the older Bata does not see a natural role for his son. The father says only that "he is encouraged to find ways to expand in various directions."

Those directions became clearer in early 1999, when Tom Jr. announced that he was spearheading a bid to take over the financially troubled luxury shoe retailer Bally. He pointed out that he was operating independently of Bata Shoe and in alliance with other financial partners. Because upscale Bally did not operate in the same market segment as Bata Shoe, Tom Jr. did not feel he needed to relinquish his seat on the Bata parent-company board. Asked why he was taking a run at Bally, Tom Jr., answering his cell phone on a busy London street, replied, "How can one not look at Bally if you have a heritage in footwear?" The bid for Bally ultimately failed, and the Swiss shoe company was picked up by a U.S. conglomerate. But Tom Jr. had indicated that if he couldn't run Bata, he at least aspired to control some kind of company, preferably in the sector he knew so well. Meanwhile, some Bata watchers were saying that he still aspired to assert himself as a major player in the family company as his parents grew older and his father, in particular, grappled with health problems.

Shortly after the Bally bid was announced, Bata Shoe made another dramatic announcement. Jim Pantelidis, a respected retail executive who had worked many years for Petro-Canada, was moving into the role of chairman and CEO of Bata Ltd., the operating company of the Bata Shoe Organization. Once again, the Bata family and board were pinning their hopes on an outsider with no background in shoe marketing. Asked about Pantelidis's appointment, Tom Jr. was careful in his wording: "Clearly every business needs a strong CEO. It's a very positive situation for a person with his experience and expertise."

Pantelidis quickly showed that he was being given a fairly free hand in running Bata Ltd. In October 1999, he announced he was closing the factory in Batawa, Ontario, the company town that sixty years earlier had become the new home of the Bata organization after the Nazis had overrun Czechoslovakia. Pantelidis explained that the company had lost $32 million at the Batawa plant over the past decade, and could not afford to keep it running. Production from Batawa — the company's only Canadian plant — would be shifted to a Maryland factory and to overseas operations with cheaper labour costs.

The writing had been on the wall. The plant's workforce had declined in numbers to about 200 from more than 1,200 in the 1960s. Still, some Bata observers felt it would not be closed down as long as Thomas Bata Sr. was still alive. It was a tangible link to those hard yet ultimately triumphant years when the Bata Shoe Organization stayed alive against tremendous odds. The surviving "pioneers" who had accompanied Mr. Bata to Canada mourned the plant's closing, along with other longtime employees. Yet few of them seemed to blame Mr. Bata. "He's a good man with a good heart," eighty-three-year-old retiree Frank Rabel, a native of Zlin, told *The Globe and Mail.* "I guess things just didn't turn out."

Pantelidis's closing of Batawa indicated that he is willing to discard some of the company's sacred cows, and that Bata Shoe may be prepared finally to exploit its scope as an international organization. The company also announced a stronger commitment to its retail business, saying it would bolster its Canadian chain by 50 new stores, adding to its existing 250. But the question still remains whether Pantelidis can cope with the Byzantine politics and entrenched culture of the world's biggest shoemaker. As the twenty-first century dawns, the company clearly doesn't have a lot of time to get its act together. It desperately needs some marketing momentum. The jury is still out on whether it can continue as an independent entity. But Pantelidis's biggest challenge may still be the same as his predecessors' — managing the balancing act between the two Thomas Batas and Sonja, a vigorous seventy-three-year-old with strong convictions. "She could still emerge from being the power behind the throne to taking the throne herself," one Bata insider acknowledges.

THREE

WARNOCKS AND CHAPLINS — FATHERS AND DAUGHTERS

Top: Joan Fisk, president of Tiger Brand Knitting Co. Ltd.
Bottom: Jan Chaplin, vice-chair of auto parts maker Canadian General Tower

JIM WARNOCK WOKE UP HIS DAUGHTER Joan Fisk late one night at the family's ranchhouse retreat in the foothills of the Rockies. "I'm going to make you president," he told Joan, who was then thirty-six and the clothing designer for Tiger Brand Knitting Co. Ltd., the family garment-making company based in Cambridge, Ontario. "I said to him, 'You're nuts,'" his daughter recalls. Indeed, it was an extraordinarily daring choice, for Joan had no senior management experience. But more important, her slightly younger brothers, Jim Jr. and Andy Warnock, both worked in key supervisory roles and had legitimate claims to lead the 118-year-old business into its fifth generation. She felt that her brothers were bound to resent the choice — and unhappily she was right.

A decade later, Joan Fisk, a tall, elegant mother of two daughters, is still running the company, which has about 1,100 employees and annual sales of $80 to $100 million. But the transition from father to daughter has been painful. In particular, Jim Jr. yearned to be president. For a while he was openly bitter about his sister's ascendance. Andy, at forty-two, two years younger than Jim Jr., has made the transition more easily but not without having to negotiate some rough spots. Relations between the siblings are much better now, but they could hardly be called smooth. Joan has gained an important insight: "There is no such thing as a seamless transition."

Jim Warnock Sr., an irascible seventy-three-year-old, has never done what was expected of him, and his choice for a successor was no less individualistic. Today he seems to enjoy sitting back and watching his children work out their problems, with the help of his occasional "refereeing," as he calls it. He says he is more convinced than ever that he made the right choice for the future of the family company. "You can't make money in any business if you don't sell — and Joan is good at selling," he says, and then adds mischievously, "Joan can tell a lie as well as anybody."

In the industrial city of Cambridge, in southwestern Ontario, Tiger Brand is one of the few old-line manufacturing companies to have survived in an age when satellite equipment and Japanese cars have become the region's biggest manufacturing exports. Globalization has come to the world of the family company and has driven many established players out of business or into the arms of larger acquisitors. Issues of management and succession have become even more vital — the stakes and risks are that much higher. Making one bad choice can be the death of a company. These days, customers can be supplied just as easily from Guangdong, China, as from Cambridge, Ontario. There is no room for a company with narrow and unimaginative leadership.

Tiger Brand isn't the only family business in Cambridge to be facing these kinds of challenges. Canadian General Tower, a mid-sized auto parts concern with annual sales of $320 million, is another one. It is searching for its place in a global industry that has been consolidating rapidly. What's more, chairman Jim Chaplin, sixty-seven, and his brother and vice-chairman Gordon, fifty-nine, will not be running the vinyl parts maker too much longer. So who is going to succeed them? Will it be Jan Chaplin, Jim's thirty-nine-year-old daughter, or Rick, his forty-year-old son, or both, or neither?

The Chaplins and the Warnocks represent the new wave in family businesses. It used to be automatic that the oldest son would take over when the founder moved on. That's been the accepted way of doing things in countless companies — daughters have been cast aside. They have been provided (perhaps) with a tidy inheritance but have been given no actual say in running the shop. The principle of primogeniture raises the odds even higher against a flawless succession. Now, some entrepreneurs are moving away from the first-born-male model, perhaps spurred by the knowledge that when it comes to picking successors, they can't ignore any family member — indeed, any candidate — on the basis of gender. The world is tough enough without leaving some of your best potential owners and managers on the sidelines. "Management is not about gender," says Joan Fisk. "A brain is a brain. I may speak with a different tone of voice than my brothers but that's about it."

Sometimes the daughter of a founding entrepreneur is the only possible successor, which makes the choice somewhat more clear-cut. Tom Beck brought his only child Catherine into Noma Ltd., the Toronto-based electrical products business. But the family decided it wasn't that committed to owning a business anymore, so the Becks eventually sold the company. Frank Hasenfratz of Guelph moved one of his two daughters, Linda, into the presidency of his Linamar Inc. auto parts business, thereby sparking the exit of his top nonfamily executive. Calgary's Ron Southern is grooming daughters Linda and Nancy to run his sprawling Atco Ltd. empire, which has interests ranging from utilities to the Spruce Meadows Equestrian Centre.

But the Tiger Brand case is the most fascinating. It's the rare example of a male entrepreneur in a substantial mid-sized company promoting a daughter ahead of her brothers while they are still active in the business. Some daughter successors seem cowed or subdued by their larger-than-life fathers, but not Joan. The same pattern could well be repeated across town at Canadian General Tower, where Jan Chaplin has been elevated to vice-chair, putting her in position to replace her father Jim, currently chairman, when he retires in a couple of years. At this moment, she sits above brother Rick on the organization chart.

The Warnocks and the Chaplins are joined together in another unusual way. Twenty-five years ago, Jim Chaplin and Jim Warnock and their wives, Daisy Warnock and Janet Chaplin, decided to switch partners. Mr. Chaplin married Mrs. Warnock and Mr. Warnock took up with Mrs. Chaplin for a while. In the small city of Cambridge, it was a gigantic scandal; the local folks gasped at the city's most prominent families engaging in such liaisons. More than two decades later, the families are still close, although Mr. Warnock ended up marrying an outsider — a former Tiger Brand employee. Family members talk with each other all the time. Jim Chaplin refers to the Warnock children as "my children," even though the relationship is only by marriage. He obviously takes a caring interest in how their succession works out. "Jim Chaplin has mentored Joan Fisk," says a consultant who knows the two families. "They get together and talk."

As for the children of these two intertwined families, they have gone on with their lives, and shrug at the tortured relationships of their parents. "It was a seventies thing," says one of the kids. They are also aware that in the hothouse atmosphere of Cambridge, the private lives of the leading business families are public information. It's the price they pay. They'll never be able to escape the fact that their parents' marital merry-go-round was the hottest gossip in the city for a brief moment in the 1970s.

Then again, the Warnocks have always been high-profile, as befits any business family whose head office, factory outlet, and main plant occupy a sprawling block in downtown Cambridge. The company, which has three locations in Cambridge, has been part of the landscape since 1881, when it started up just across the river from what's now the head office. At that time it was known as the Galt Knitting Company and the city blocks around it formed downtown Galt. In 1973, Galt merged with two other towns, Hespeler and Preston, to form the present city of Cambridge. The city today seems rambling and unfocused, and the suburban Wal-Marts and the fast food joints have sucked a lot of energy and commerce away from the original downtown areas.

To get to Joan Fisk's office, you have to ascend a steep and narrow staircase to the third-floor loft of the company's main office building. Joan is attractive, with the cheekbones and bearing of a fashion model. Her office is vast, white, and airy and has a view of the old Galt downtown and the Grand River, which runs close by. These days she feels a bit harried. She has just gone through a high-level change management program that has triggered a restructuring of her brothers' roles in the business. Tiger Brand is an integrated company: it produces its own textiles, which it uses to manufacture its own knit and woven garments. It produces a range of casual wear — from socks to sweatshirts — which it sells to private labels such as the Gap, L.L. Bean, Nordstrom, and Eddie Bauer. But it has also developed its own Non-Fiction leisure clothing brand, the brainchild of Joan, who as a designer in the 1980s sold the concept to her then sceptical father. "Dad didn't think Non-Fiction would happen," she says. Recently, she has added a new brand, TBK, for teenagers and young adults. Currently, about half of Tiger Brand's sales are from its own brands, and the rest from private label customers.

At Tiger Brand, textiles and knitting have operated as separate entities under separate management, led by the two brothers. But now Jim Jr., who has been in charge of making textiles, is moving into the broader role of director of all manufacturing — he will supervise the process all the way from fabric production to finished clothing. Brother Andy, who has been in charge of garment making and once ran the company's now closed plant in Pincher Creek, Alberta, is assuming the job of executive vice-president in charge of all nonmanufacturing operations, including information technology and human resources. "You have to change people from their birthright roles, but it's hard to do," says Joan, who remains a designer and is in charge of sales and product development.

This is the kind of let's-shake-things-up attitude that convinced her father to appoint her president. Her brothers are extremely competent people, but their expertise is narrow. "I am more visionary, I'm from the marketing arm," she says with matter-of-fact confidence. Still, she admits it was always expected that the sons would rise to the top job — until that night in Alberta ten years ago, "I was just the designer," she explains.

When it is suggested he made a tough decision when he annointed Joan as his successor, Jim Warnock Sr. snorts: "I did like hell. I knew the thing was right so there was nothing tough about it ... If you know you want [a focus on] sales, you choose someone who knows sales." Still, he feels Joan needs to compromise at times. "Joan is within her right to argue back, but often she has to back off in terms of what can be done." He says his sons have a lot of technical knowledge, which gives them the credibility to stand their ground with their sister over matters of production and operations.

"You look at her as a girl but really she's a person," says Jim Sr., who manages to be both politically incorrect and, in his mind, progressive at the same time. "They're people — forget the sex." Some unhappiness on the part of his sons was inevitable, so he didn't sugar-coat the message when he chose Joan as his successor. He just told his sons what he was going to do. There wasn't any visible reaction although "probably they kicked the walls outside." But in the end, it didn't really matter — he had made up his mind.

For about five years, relations in the company's top ranks were frosty, but eventually everybody got over it, at least on the surface. In a 1997 interview, Jim Jr. told *The Globe and Mail*'s Gayle MacDonald that he had wanted to be president, but losing the position was not a crushing blow: "It would do more harm than is necessary in a family transition to start sulking about what you did and didn't get. We don't worry about who got what, but about making it work as it stands now."

What changed things were Joan's persistence, her brothers' willingness to face reality, and the competitive challenges facing Tiger Brand. To compete against Third World suppliers, the company has become ever more zealous about controlling costs and forging efficiencies. It has had to get its quality control procedures in order so that customers will not penalize it for mislabelling goods, delivering late, or incorrectly packaging its products. Getting the company's operations on track has required tremendous effort from all the children, and naturally it pushed the succession issue to the background. There are some who say that Jim Sr., the individualistic entrepreneur, might not have been able to accomplish that transformation, that the children with their complementary skills were better suited to the task.

When a company operates in an emerging market, the entrepreneurial style works very well. Bill Gates, for example, can set the rules for the personal computer industry because he essentially created the industry, at least on a mass consumption model. But in a mature industry, such as the one in which Tiger Brand operates, the advantage goes to those who can deliver more quickly, more efficiently, and more accurately. Quality — of processes and of logistics — becomes the defining point, and that usually requires a degree of professional management. At Tiger Brand, much of that expertise is being provided by the family members themselves.

Joan Fisk seems to sincerely respect her brothers' contributions to Tiger Brand: "I lead the product, but I need superior management in manufacturing and IT." She also believes the company was lucky to have someone like herself (i.e., with the marketing and design savvy) who could take it to the next level. "It was the luck of the draw that there was a skill set available. It's not always the case with the family business." She believes that for Tiger Brand to survive, it must develop its brand identity and its sales and stop depending on its traditional role as a manufacturer. It must move closer to the Nike model — that is, it must become a co-ordinator of production, not simply a producer itself.

Jim Chaplin, now married to the Warnock children's mother, has watched the evolution of Tiger Brand as a kind of inside outsider. He has been disappointed at times with his wife's children's apparent unwillingness to co-operate. He describes his old friend Jim Warnock Sr. as "a bona fide entrepreneur." One problem, he says, is that the members of the next generation want to be just like the old man, and the more they try, the more they collide with one another. "It's really nobody's fault, it's just the way it is. My advice at different times is just to deal with those [succession] issues so they don't use up their energy. They use a tremendous amount of energy and if they'd put it somewhere else, they'd do a lot better."

Still, a lot of that energy does seem to be directed the right way. Joan and her brothers have managed a rare feat — they still manufacture garments in Canada, at a time when so much of the action has shifted to the Third World, where costs are lower. Under Joan, they have built for Non-Fiction a niche in the cotton leisure wear market. Then there is that stellar lineup of private brand products. This has not been easy to achieve in high-cost Canada, even with the currency advantage vis-à-vis the United States. Tiger Brand has hung in though, thanks to its investment in cutting edge technology, quality, and systems.

Tiger Brand has been challenged before. The company has been reinvented a number of times, which testifies to the adaptability of the Warnock clan. Galt Knitting Co. was founded in the early 1880s by eight local entrepreneurs, one of whom was Adam Warnock, Jim Sr.'s great-grandfather. The syndicate took over a water-powered mill on the east side of the Grand River, opposite the present complex. The trademark Tiger Brand was acquired from a Quebec firm in the year the company was founded. By the dawn of the twentieth century, Adam Warnock was firmly in control of Galt Knitting, along with his two sons

Charles and James. He died in 1902, leaving his sons to build a relatively successful business over the next few decades. But the company, in those days primarily a maker of men's underwear, staggered during the Great Depression and had to be reorganized. After the Second World War, during which the company supplied underwear to the armed forces, poor Galt Knitting had difficulty adapting its products to changing times. Its main customers, including Eaton's, were pressuring it to produce more cheaply and efficiently. Its key winter underwear market was hurting, and in 1954, under then owner Edward G. Warnock, the firm slipped into voluntary liquidation.

Edward Warnock's only child, Jim, then in his late twenties, was determined not to see the company die. He salvaged three knitting machines, seven sewing machines, and the jobs of seven employees, and tried to make a go of it. "I just went to work and I carried Dad for twelve years," he says now. It wasn't easy, and he struggled at first. In December 1954, he recalls, the company's sales added up to a measly $999. The garment industry was going through a shakeup and some additional pieces of machinery became available at rock-bottom prices. Jim started buying up this distress-sale machinery. He says that the combination of new equipment and threadbare overheads nursed Tiger Brand back into the black. "I paid the full debt," he boasts. "The creditors didn't lose a cent."

"He naïvely thought he could turn the business into something and he made it happen," Joan says admiringly of her father. She sees Jim Sr. — affectionately nicknamed "The Tiger" — as that rare combination: an entrepreneurial personality who is at the same time a technically minded manufacturer. He just has a feel for the business. "The mill is in his genetic makeup," she says. He built the business against all odds. Tiger Brand became a major T-shirt manufacturer, and when that business came under import pressure, he diversified, moving the company into fashion outerware, including woven goods as well as knits.

But growing up in the Warnock family was no picnic, Joan says. The patriarch was a demanding parent who expected total obedience from his six children. Jim Sr. seemed to thrive on a certain degree of upheaval, which may explain why he seems so unruffled by the dissension he has brought upon his children.

Joan, like her brothers, attended school in Galt, then went to the University of Guelph, where she studied textiles and design. She joined the business in 1976, and in 1977, when she was twenty-five, she became the company's designer. In the early 1980s, she helped develop a line of inexpensive sweatshirt and T-shirt items sold under the Tiger Brand label; her biggest customer was the Cotton Ginny chain of stores. By 1984 she had introduced Non-Fiction, a co-ordinated line of children's, men's, and women's leisure wear. Joan loved the life, which consisted of regular visits to Paris to follow the fashion trends.

Although he was the prototypical driven enterpreneur, Jim Sr. was determined not to be a slave to the business for his entire life. As he grew older he actually wanted to pursue other interests, including his love of travel. Not for him the life of the perpetual interfering busybody. But he clearly didn't want to sell to outsiders either. He wanted the family in the business and the business in the family. "You never sell, you always buy," he chuckles, describing his business credo. "And what you buy, you make it work for you."

Jim Sr. was also going through personal changes. There was the breakup of his own marriage, and his former wife's marriage to his friend Jim Chaplin. Then he fell in love with a woman thirty-five years younger, a seamstress on the Tiger Brand factory floor. Jim Sr. and his wife, Manuella, now have a teenage daughter. "She is a good match for him," says Joan. "It's a good relationship."

Still, arranging the succession was difficult. There was not only the question of managerial transition; the transfer of ownership also had to evolve. The controlling block of shares, held by Jim Sr., would be split evenly among Joan and her two brothers. These three siblings agreed to buy out their three sisters, Ann, Martha, and Nancy, none of whom now works in the company. There is a buy-sell agreement that ensures, if one of the three shareholders wants out, that the shares will be sold to the other two children.

The ownership deal was pretty much wrapped up by 1996 when Jim Sr. and his youthful wife headed off for a holiday in Egypt. There were still some loose ends, but they could be dealt with when he got back. He and Manuella were travelling by taxi in the Egyptian city of El Alamein. The cab driver was driving insanely, Jim Sr. says, and there was a terrible collision. The driver and another man in the front seat were killed. Manuella was injured, and Jim was thrown from the car and into a gutter, badly hurt. He was rushed to hospital in Alexandria, and Joan travelled to Egypt to help bring her father home. She remembers three-and-a-half days of pure hell as she came up with the money to pay the hospital and get her father on a plane home. He underwent surgery in London, Ontario, and somehow became ill with a powerful bug that almost killed him. It was nip and tuck, but he survived, although he has trouble getting around. "I'm not quite as good on the tractor as I used to be," he admits.

Today, Jim Sr. tends to his personal investments and occasionally offers his advice on matters of strategy. His three children at Tiger Brand, he says, are "getting into constant trouble, and they think what's happening to them is terrible. I just give them three instances in which I was in worse trouble. I say, 'Stop crying and go with your feelings.'" He gets into Joan's hair on the directions she is taking the Non-Fiction line. He worries that the line is sometimes being pushed too far out. He knows his children are thinking *Will he just shut up?*

Of course, he won't. "The [Non-Fiction] line is great, it's what you do with the line that's important. [I say to them] 'Don't fuck it up.' There are a few things going wrong with it."

Jim Sr.'s accident and illness cut short the transition period at Tiger Brand. Joan would have liked to see her father hang around a bit longer. Also, there remains the question of who assumes voting control among the three children in the company. That hangs rather ominously over the relationship between Joan and her brothers. It would be possible, for example, for Andy and Jim Jr. to vote their combined shares against their sister, who is the company president. The lack of closure on this matter has caused Joan to wonder about her future role in the business. Meanwhile, her father dismisses the voting control issue as something that will work itself out. In the end, he says, the person who makes the best argument will win any vote. But isn't the lack of voting control in a three-way ownership split a recipe for disaster? "Living is a recipe for disaster," he says.

If she hangs in, Joan has some big plans for Tiger Brand. Her dream is to develop an organization that works much like a public company. That means installing a board of directors that will develop a serious governance structure. It also means building up professional management, recruiting more extensively from the outside. A number of key hires are being integrated into the company now. "You cannot run this company from ownership. You have to run the company from management. Ultimately, that will be our success." Her great hope is that Tiger Brand will eventually carry on without the management presence of the Warnock family, under a strong and professional nonfamily president. Her aim is to separate ownership and management, with the Warnocks taking the role of knowledgeable and informed proprietors. "That could be my biggest achievement. That might take five years, but I want to do it."

Her own successor is not yet an issue. She is married to Brian Fisk, a retail consultant. One of their two daughters is studying music in Boston, the other is finishing high school in Switzerland. Neither has shown a burning interest in getting involved in Tiger Brand.

As for the company itself, its role will change dramatically if Joan Fisk has her way. She wants to drive it farther into marketing, sales, and design — and to de-emphasize its roots in manufacturing and production. "It should be a facility that directs manufacturing but is not necessarily a manufacturer itself." And, she says, it should exert some product leadership and build its own brands. That will certainly mean more upheaval in Cambridge and at Tiger Brand. The company will employ fewer people in manufacturing in Canada. Joan says her father always had a strong sense of the company's role in the community. He would increase the size of his workforce at times just to provide local employment. There was a sense that the "family" extended beyond the walls of the knitting mill and encompassed all of the community. "You can do that if you're making a little bit of money, as in the 1960s when it was easy."

Joan still sees a vital social role for herself and the company. But at the same time, employing more people just to play a community role probably isn't in the cards anymore. As Tiger Brand responds to the economic pressures of the new century, it will become a very different kind of company, with a different kind of relationship to the region that first gave it water power, and then gave it its people, and still gives it its identity.

"There are some things I cannot do that Rick can do," says Jan Chaplin, at this moment a vice-president of auto parts maker Canadian General Tower. The two men seated beside her at the table erupt into thunderous laughter. "Get that down. Get it in quotes," says brother Rick. Their father, Jim Chaplin, is staring in mock disbelief. Jan Chaplin's father and brother are amused because they're not accustomed to a lot of humility from Rick's little sister. She's whip-smart and self-possessed and knows exactly where she wants to go — in other words, she's leadership material. She holds a European MBA and has a résumé that includes work on Bay Street with a financial services firm and with the Toronto Stock Exchange. At thirty-nine, she's a catch for any major company, particularly for her own family's company.

Chances are she'll get what she wants — a leadership role in the next generation of this five-generation company. Already she's the senior executive plotting the company's strategy. But the situation is not quite so simple. Her more easygoing brother Rick, an academic underachiever who swallowed his pride to get an MBA at thirty-eight, is recharged and ambitious for a more important job than his current title, assistant to the president. And father Jim, the company chairman for thirty years, is being cagy about when it all might happen. "Check back with us in two or three years," he seems to be saying.

The three Chaplins are assembled one rainy afternoon at Langdon Hall, an upscale spa and restaurant in a Victorian mansion on the rural outskirts of Cambridge. Jan lives with her husband and two children in another old restored manor house just across the fields. They've come to talk about the challenges they're facing as a family business — and about the always thorny issue of passing it on. Both Jan and Rick are quite open to advancing their careers with the help of favourable press articles. Jim, a handsome man with a trim nautical beard, slyly admits his reason for attending. He feels the session should give him a bit of insight into where his children's thinking lies. It's a conversation laced with laughter — the Chaplins clearly like each other and work well together — but punctuated with uncomfortable body language.

Jan makes it clear that the big issue is not whether she rises above Rick in the family organization, or vice versa. The two siblings came to an understanding in their early years with the company that if one of them succeeded, they would both triumph in how they were perceived within the organization. Jim Chaplin has his own perspective. "All families are dysfunctional. All we're talking about is how much. Whatever you can do to limit the dysfunction — and you can say all relationships have dysfunctional elements — you have a better chance of being successful."

Still, it's no secret that both Chaplin children are somewhat frustrated by the pace of change at Canadian General Tower. Jim and his brother, vice-chairman Gordon Chaplin, have been slow to relinquish ownership control, although they ceded senior management authority to outside professionals many years ago. CGT has not grown or diversified to the extent Jan expected when she joined the company in 1992. "Sure, they're impatient," says Jim. "That's exactly where they should be. If I'm a bit of a sea anchor, that's their problem. In my own way, I'll try not to be. Life being what it is, I'll get in their way from time to time."

CGT hasn't backed away from the new economic order of the twenty-first century. Jim Chaplin, the latest in a breed of committed Tories in the family, strongly backed the Free Trade Agreement of 1989 between Canada and the United States, as well as the North American Free Trade Agreement, which pulled Mexico into the deal. He smiles at the memory of his grandfather James Chaplin, who won a parliamentary seat as a federal Conservative in the Free Trade election of 1911 on the plank, "No truck or trade with the Yankees." There's a lot of truck and trade with the Yankees now. Canadian General Tower does almost all its business with U.S. customers, including the big auto makers, such as General Motors and Ford.

The company makes vinyl products, mostly vinyl trim for automobiles. When you sit down on the seat of a GM car, there's a chance your posterior might be rubbing against CGT's vinyl. The auto industry accounts for about 75 percent of the company's sales, with the rest coming from a few diverse niches: for example, the vinyl lining on swimming pools, the vinyl covers on school notebooks, and vinyl roofing. The Chaplins are specialists in a process called vinyl calendering, which involves taking both dry and wet vinyl materials, mixing them, and rolling them out into big flat sheets known as skins.

It's been a strong business over the years, but the auto industry has been going through a dramatic consolidation. The auto makers want to deal with fewer suppliers, and they want their leading suppliers to manufacture more of the car. Thus, the industry has seen the emergence of tier one suppliers, who produce entire subsections ready-made for assembly plants to pop into the vehicles in process. For example, entire seats are supplied by companies such as Lear and Magna. Below them on the supply chain are tier two and tier three companies, who seek to attach themselves to tier one operators instead of the car makers themselves.

The jockeying for position has triggered a massive wave of takeovers, mergers, and downsizing in the auto parts industry. "Basically, it was eat or be eaten," Jan Chaplin told *Globe and Mail* reporter Elizabeth Church in 1997. "We looked quite seriously at being eaten, but at the end of the day, we didn't want to do that." Instead, CGT has made three square deals — it picked up a Toledo, Ohio, vinyl parts operation in 1995 and two former Uniroyal plants in 1996. Even so, it remains a tier two and in some cases tier three player, although of a reasonable size with annual sales of more than $320 million. Some observers, including Jan, believe the company still has to find a merger partner or a strong ally in this sharply competitive world.

CGT's future is clouded for another reason: ownership in the company is being shuffled even ahead of any generational transition. The company has a complex ownership structure for a family business. Jim Chaplin and his brother Gordon together own just 51 percent, enough for a control position. The rest has been in the hands of a German industrial vinyl company, Renolit-Werke Gmbh, since 1980. The challenge is that both Gordon Chaplin and the German partner want to divest their shares. The Germans have lost their appetite for the auto parts industry, and they don't like to hold corporate investments in which they don't own 100 percent of the outfit. Also, Jim Chaplin forged the partnership with a particular managing director of Renolit, who has since retired. Relationships mean everything in business, and that relationship has ended.

Gordon Chaplin simply wants out. The brothers are bound by a restrictive shareholders' agreement that basically requires them to get along. But according to brother Jim, Gordon is more risk averse than he is, and nervous about having all his wealth tied up in one company. "He [Gordon] looks at the business and says 'the sucker can fail,'" Jim says. But Jim figures that if the brothers cashed in their shares they would be just as likely to lose money in any other business. Gordon has been heavily involved in community and conservation work and admits that his interests are different from his brother's. Neither of his two children is in the business, and the general climate in the industry suggests to him that it might be a good time to exit. "Yes, I have a different view to risk. I think it's a defensive view. [We have] a lot of bricks and mortar and machinery, but at my age do I want bricks and machinery, or would I rather have cash?" At fifty-eight, he says, "I'd like to be master now of my own world."

Canadian General Tower has its roots in an old wagon-wheel factory that the brothers' ancestor James Chaplin bought in 1916. Unfortunately, wagon wheels were on their way out; however, the Chaplins were able to adapt and move on. By the 1940s the company was making a variety of rubber products, including another future relic — the rubber baby panty used with cloth diapers. During the Second World War it actually made "rubbers" — prophylactics for the Russian army. CGT would ship them out in barrels, and according to family legend the Russian soldiers would fit the condoms on the end of their rifle barrels to keep their equipment dry.

The condoms were formed in a "secret room" in which women were not allowed because of the nature of the product and the suggestiveness of the production process. The condoms were shaped and fitted by an artificial phallus. On Friday afternoons, when workers were feeling a little giddy, some joker might grap the baseball bat in the corner, fit a few rubbers onto the end of it, pull them off, and throw the items onto the top layer of a Russia-bound barrel, writing "Canadian Small" on the barrel's exterior. Whether any Russian understood, was amused, or felt his masculinity challenged is not known.

By the 1950s, CGT had concluded that rubber was out and vinyl was the hot thing as a production material. At the same time, another generation of leadership was coming on. Young Jim Chaplin didn't automatically aspire to lead a vinyl company. After graduating from school, he worked for a Toronto advertising agency, and he liked that life. But the Chaplins were Tories, and Jim did have a hankering for politics. He came home to manage the local Conservative candidate's campaign in the breaththrough Diefenbaker win of 1957. Six years later his father died, and Jim was immediately pegged as the successor. His son Rick says his father would probably have preferred to be prime minister, but he was given little choice. Later on, Gordon joined, and according to their father's directions the shares were split evenly between the two brothers. (Actually, not quite evenly. Jim points out that he ended up with a slightly larger amount because of a miscalculation by a company lawyer. The brothers Chaplin have ribbed each other about it over the years.)

The fraternal partnership worked, some observers say, because Gordon had no great aspirations to lead the company — it was always Jim's baby. "It's okay with me for Jim to be chairman," Gordon says. "Working here has allowed me to do a lot in the community. His life has been more tied to the place." Jim was the senior manager; Gordon was the visible family face in the factory and a front man on environmental issues, which are a passion of his. According to

Jim, the company was big enough that "if you were wildly interested in something you could carve it off." He caused untold frustration for his more laid-back brother, but at end of the day they stuck together.

But the brothers' perspectives were similar in one important way: each had been intrigued by other businesses, and fascinated by other worlds, but had been sucked into the orbit of the family firm because it was expected of them. Their own experiences inspired them to write a company policy that should serve as a model for any organization: a family member has to work at least five years outside the company before getting a chance to come back in — no ifs, ands, or buts. It would give the children a chance to develop their own skills, space, and sense of worth. It was also a gesture of support for senior managers who were not from the family.

That set the course for Jim Chaplin's kids. He has four children in all — Diana is a singer and actress, and Elizabeth is a successful real estate agent in Whistler, B.C. Jan went off to university, a stint on Bay Street, and then an MBA at a European university, all before she even thought of taking a role at CGT. Rick had a rougher road — he was the classic drifting scion of a well-off family. He attended private Ridley College in St. Catharines, where his best subject was rowing. He took two shots at university, including two years at the University of Washington, where he was on the rowing team. Alas, no degree. He joined a management recruiting company in Kitchener, and after a stint there went off on his own as a recruiter. A marriage came and went, and he began to get fed up with the isolation of the recruiting racket. By the early 1990s, he was ready to come in from the cold — about the same time sister Jan was doing some consulting for CGT. Jim Chaplin jokes that his daughter "was gunning for a position but was prepared to do other things."

Jim and Gordon Chaplin had already taken some steps to prepare their children for life in a family business. They explored what roles the children might play and worked through some of the unresolved family issues. Gordon had met up with a high-profile family business consultant named David Bork at a Young Presidents' Organization gathering in Istanbul. Impressed with Bork's approach, the brothers hired him to conduct family meetings. "All the different agendas and hidden meanings were drawn out," Gordon says. "There had been a lot of things that had never reached the table. A lot of things were painful." Jim's divorce and remarriage, for example, were put on the table. And Gordon talked about his desire to bow out at some point. The Chaplins learned some communications skills. The family won't say how much Bork's services cost, but his fee at one point was $5,000 a day. Some sessions were held in Ontario, others at Bork's Aspen Institute in Colorado. And Bork was not the only consultant who worked with the group. In the end there was a feeling that the family dynamics would work: Rick and Jan were middle children, and middle children tend to get along.

Jan admits that her decision to join the company was based on "pure emotion." She had been close to her father in her late teens, and the two had discussed how some day she might run the company. When the possibility of entering the company was raised, she was in her late twenties and living in Bermuda, where her husband was in the insurance business. She felt a strong sense of obligation when she was asked to come back. She immediately took a senior position as a kind of chief administrative officer. Rick had the tougher adjustment: he started as an entry-level sales rep in the division that sold specialty products such as vinyl roofing and various kinds of liners for shower pans, ponds, and landfill. In 1993 the company tapped him to head a pilot program for manufacturing a new product for a new customer. The challenge was particularly acute in a company with a traditional culture. He knows now that "it was a project designed to fail" — and it did. His father agrees it was probably a bad call from the start.

Rick feels that he was left high and dry by certain managers, who tried to disassociate themselves from the venture, leaving the Chaplin kid on his own. "He was in an environment where everything that went wrong was [thought to be] Rick's doing," his sister says, shaking her head. In the end, Rick was told he would have to share leadership of the project with two supervisors, who were brought in from outside. It was a crushing defeat for the son of the chairman and chief shareholder — and very untypical for a family business, which does not usually devour its young.

Rick Chaplin today is philosophical. "Being a member of the family, sometimes it gets you in the door and sometimes it hurts you ... Lots of people were out to get me. Lots of people didn't help me one iota, whereas if I were another manager, and it was in their interests, they would work it out." His conclusion is that as a child or sibling of the owners, "you have to step up and excel time after time after time. You have to do better than anyone else or you stand out." Jan, never one to mince words, says the problem was with leadership in the organization. There has never been a mentor for potential managers like Rick. It's clearly something she would change if she were in charge.

For Rick, the message was clear — he had crashed against some kind of ceiling. It didn't help that he was a Chaplin. He had to do something fast if he was to have a future in the organization. And he wasn't any spring chicken. As he moved into his late thirties, he went through counselling sessions with David Bork and also with Jonathan Kovacheff, a Toronto consultant who blends governance expertise with a graduate degree in industrial psychology. Kovacheff's advice: "All roads lead to an MBA for Rick."

Rick went looking for an MBA school that suited his background. He felt he needed to remove himself entirely from the Canadian environment, and to get into a program that would emphasize international business. He landed at the University of Bath, in the old spa town in southwest England. His idea was to do well, develop some academic grounding for what he had already learned on the job, and come back fresh. He did reasonably well academically, but even more important, he was a leader among the MBA class. It shocked him when he was nominated for a national MBA competition and ended up being named Southwestern England MBA of the Year in an event co-sponsored by the *Independent* newspaper. During his internship back at his own family's company, Rick developed a strong mission. He began working on re-engineering and quality control projects. Some of these projects fell under the sponsorship of his own sister, Jan. He returned to Bath and wrote his thesis on re-engineering.

He is now back at the company as assistant to the president, Charlie Johnson. His new role is to drive re-engineering through the entire company. At the same time, he wants to re-establish himself as an heir apparent. "I'd like to be on the senior management team," he says. "I'd love to perform. It's a show-me thing now."

Jim Chaplin makes it clear that his own shares will be evenly divided between the two children. It is entirely possible that Gordon's shares will also be split between the two. So who gets voting control? It's hard to say at this point, Jim Chaplin says. And there is also the issue of the German partner's stake and where it will go. It's difficult to sell a 49 percent share in a private company.

Jim Chaplin says that since his own father's era, CGT has worked to develop a governance structure resembling that of any nonfamily company. For example, there is an independent board of directors, although it's packed with friends of the family. He admits that the current directors are basically there at his behest and do not play the same fiduciary role as directors in a public company. "You have to build a private company board on people you know," he explains.

Jim Chaplin feels he has succeeded in developing a strong professional management team. If his children want to take a more central role in management, that will be up to them. Company president Charles Johnson is an affable Kentuckian who has some experience in family companies in the United States. His role is that of a change agent, Jim Chaplin explains. "He's a Yank and his mentality is different than what we've got here. Now, all of our customers are American, so it's very useful to have an American running the company at this stage. We want him to take us to the next level — and then it's a succession issue."

The children insist they are not hung up on titles, but they do see a role for each other in the company. Jan argues that there is a real value in having family members in the operations side, although not necessarily as president. Personally, she would hope to play a role in helping CGT map its strategy, whether as a manager or as part of the ownership group. Her father agrees that some family participation in management can be valuable, if only to bring a bit of truth to the owners. If a family member is involved in senior management, more information is fed up to the owners, which is very helpful in making decisions.

But it is clear that on some issues, Jan and her father don't see eye to eye. Discussions between the two often become sharp albeit respectful. It is not just that succession has been slow to take shape. Jan is bothered that the company has not grown or diversified to the extent she had hoped. Above all, she is impatient with the lack of any medium to long term strategic planning. Too often, the company is simply reacting to events in the industry. It is a typical confrontation between an instinctive owner-manager who has built the company, and a new generation that has embraced a more professional business model. Children often return to the family company armed with an MBA and immediately encounter a resistant parent.

"This is an issue on which Jim and I are not aligned quite yet," Jan says tactfully. "Jim is a classic entrepreneur — the strategy is in his mind. He's been in the business for forty years so why would he need a strategic plan? [But] this is what I think is important in terms of getting the generations aligned .... My impatience would come from not addressing that issue, and my need for having a strategic plan that goes out a number of years is very very strong." Her father is hardly surprised by Jan's frustration. He has heard it all before. He insists that in years gone by he formulated five-year plans but "they haven't been worth rat shit." Still, he acknowledges that they did get people thinking about the strategic issues.

In his view, the problem with strategic planning is that the industry has gone through a period of upheaval. Any planning simply got blown out of the water — by the GM strike of 1996, or by measures that CGT had to take, or by things it refrained from doing. Jan admits there have been unseen events that have thrown the company's projections off path. But, she argues, that will be the norm for their industry as it continues to experience consolidation, technological challenges, and globalization. "We're going to have a lot of bombardments from all corners. It's planning for the unexpected that I want to focus on. It

could very well be that we'll have a [turbulent] year next year like this year —
I'd plan with that in mind, not for normal business as usual. I'd plan for what
happens if the economy goes flat, or if GM goes on strike again. You know, shit
happens, and we have to pull ourselves clear."

Would CGT, which operates in what is very much a man's world, be able to
accept a woman president, chairman, or CEO? Jim admits that the company
would historically be described as a boys' club. His generation always assumed
that a son would take the leadership mantle, but Jim says that outcome doesn't
occupy his mind very much now. "I'm not against it, of course," he quickly adds,
eyeing Rick across the table. But he would rather see Rick doing something he
wanted and being fulfilled rather than feeling he had to be "the big kahuna."
Rick says he doesn't foresee a problem working below Jan in the hierarchy. In
his last two assignments, she was the one who was driving the strategy.

Asked what the company will be like in ten years, Jim Chaplin says, perhaps
joking, that he may still be here. And how does he feel about selling out?
"You've got to be open to that. You could be in a business that needs to be sold.
The automotive thing changing like it is, I could imagine a situation where we
couldn't compete, or we couldn't get a look-in because we aren't integrated."

But he admits he would have a terrible time emotionally dealing with the
sale of the company, which he built from $10 million in annual sales to 1,100
employees and more than $300 million in revenues. "You can say it's wrong,
but I identify my success as a person with the success of the company. That's
just because I've been there so long and it's how I look at the world." Jan would
also be sad about selling, but more from a practical point of view. "There's a
lot of opportunity sitting there, $300 million in sales, and to leverage that into
greatness, that's what I see. I would cry too, but for the missed opportunities."

Six months after Jim and his children met with me at Langdon Hall, the
succession was starting to roll. Jan, pregnant with her third child, was
promoted to vice-chair, the same title as her Uncle Gordon. That move put her
in a position to replace her father as chair when, as projected, he retires in two
years. "Jim and Gord are on their way out," she assured me in a telephone
conversation. She was already planning on how she would shake up the "old
boys' club" of a board, using it to drive the company's performance to higher
levels. At both Tiger Brand and Canadian General Tower, two old-style patri-
archies linked by history, divorce, marriage, and friendship, the daughters are
moving up.

FOUR

THE MITCHELLS —
MOTHERS, SONS, AND WIVES

LuAn Mitchell and the late Fred Mitchell

L UAN MITCHELL KNEW IT WAS SILLY, but she had this phobia about surgery on late Friday afternoons. She shrugged off her fears — after all, this was the prestigious Stanford University Medical Center in Palo Alto, California. At 4:30 p.m., doctors would be performing a minor surgical procedure on her husband, Fred, who had received a heart-lung transplant at the centre eight years earlier and was back for his annual checkup. She watched as attendants wheeled her husband into the operating room. LuAn told herself "he was doing great" and that the operation was only to make a tiny adjustment to what had been a remarkably successful checkup.

But when he emerged from surgery four hours later, Fred was "in obvious crisis," LuAn recalls. At seven the next morning, October 17, 1998, Fred Mitchell, president, chairman, and CEO of Mitchell's Gourmet Foods Inc., died from complications stemming from the minor operation. It was a shocking turn in a family saga that had already been characterized by the bizarre and the tragic. The pork-processing entrepreneur from Saskatoon was dead at fifty-two, leaving behind his thirty-seven-year-old wife, three young children, and one of the most harrowing family disputes in the annals of Canadian business. His passing catapulted LuAn, a self-described "at-home mom" and former beauty queen, into the role of chair and controlling shareholder of one of Canada's largest meat-packing companies. "This company is our family tradition and in

large part what this family is all about," Ms. Mitchell said, signalling her determination to hold on to the company her husband's grandfather had founded
nearly sixty years before.

LuAn Mitchell did not try to contact Fred's ailing eighty-one-year-old
mother Johanna in California with the news of her son's death. Nor did she
phone Fred's brother Charles (Chip) or sister Camille, also living in California.
The three found out about Fred's passing when a friend called from Saskatoon
saying he had seen the news on television. None of them was invited to the
small family gathering at the cemetery in Saskatoon, although Chip did attend
the public memorial service with thousands of other mourners. Johanna was
too weak to travel in any case, and had only a year to live herself.

LuAn feels she doesn't have to apologize. She had a lot to deal with — "I was
not throwing a party" — and her in-laws had never tried much to reach out to
Fred and, particularly, to her. When Fred died, he had not talked to his mother
for more than two years. Yet, according to Fred's estranged sister Camille, her
mother cried for three weeks when she found out Fred had passed away.

"Fred was specific about what he wanted when he died, and I followed it
to the letter," says LuAn, who says she in fact phoned no one in the hours
immediately after Fred's death. "I had enough of a challenge dealing with three
tiny crushed children who had lost their father."

In its own sad way, Fred's passing was a fitting chapter in this whole affair —
a story that includes feuding, sickness, lawsuits, and suicide in addition to sudden
unexpected death. The Mitchell story provides a classic example of how personal
animosity and business life can intermingle to disastrous effect. It highlights the
problems that can arise when family members who are owners and active
managers (Fred) come against family members who are owners but not managers
(Johanna, Chip, and Camille), and how conflicting interests can rip a company
and a family apart. And there was another major complication: the appearance
of a significant outsider who was resented and mistrusted by the family. That inter-
loper was LuAn, Fred's beautiful new wife. Above all, the Mitchell saga shows
that for a family business to work well, the family has to work well. There must
be a way to communicate feelings and opinions. This was a family that, in the
end, could not interact except through lawsuits and allegations.

Yet at the time of Fred Mitchell's death, he was on a roll. After battling his
family for almost a decade, he had finally won back the Saskatoon meat-packing company that his grandfather had founded and in which he had laboured
for forty years. He had orchestrated an amazing turnaround for a company
that had been on its knees. Always liked by his employees, he had negotiated
a milestone labour contract that had put a lid on labour costs without the

rancour of a strike or a lockout. And it seemed, until that fateful Friday afternoon, that he had overcome his ill health.

Still, there was a weariness and sadness to the man. In an interview at the company's sprawling Saskatoon plant three months before his death, he insisted he was in fine shape, but his colour was unhealthy and he seemed tired. He and LuAn were wearing white industrial smocks with their first names sewn into the breast pockets. Fred's hair was thinning and slickly combed back; he spoke with a drawl; he constantly flashed a nervous on-and-off smile. He was a survivor of one of the most acrimonious family fights in Canadian business, and the scars were showing. Yet he occasionally spoke warmly of his mother and siblings: "I'm not angry at them, I love them and I wish them all the best. It just seems like there's not a desire to sit down and talk and try to resolve some of the problems."

Mitchell's Gourmet Foods Inc., formerly known as Intercontinental Packers, employs more than 1,300 people, which makes it the most important private sector employer in Saskatchewan. The company turns out sausages, bacon, wieners, and a host of pork products under the brands Mitchell's Gourmet Foods and Olympic, as well as numerous store labels. Its annual sales amount to more than $300 million a year, making it the second-largest wholly family-owned food company in Canada, behind McCain Foods Ltd. It is one of the largest meat packers in Canada, although it vastly trails the industry leader, Maple Leaf Foods Ltd. of Toronto, a public company controlled by one arm of the feuding McCain family.

In Saskatoon the family's influence doesn't begin and end with jobs and sausages. The company founder, Fred Mendel, left a cultural legacy with the Mendel Gallery, a splendid showplace of Canadian art. Johanna Mitchell, until her own death in November 1999, was the gallery's honorary chair, and her sister Eva, an artist who lives in Calgary, has two of her own paintings in the gallery, including a portrait of Fred Mendel. Yet this immensely tasteful family became the subject of an immensely tasteless *Dallas*-type potboiler that played out in newspaper headlines and coffee shop chatter for months. The Mitchell saga took on the unpleasant scent of tabloid trash. Just to add to the fascination, Fred's father and Johanna Mitchell's former husband was Cameron Mitchell, a handsome Hollywood supporting actor whose most familiar role was Buck in the 1960s TV western *High Chaparral*.

The facts read like the plot of an airport novel but to understand the story you have to start with the factory, one of Canada's largest slaughterhouses, a sprawling monument to meat built up piecemeal over the years into a maze of cutting and processing rooms. This plant — actually, a much smaller version — was bought in 1940 by Fred Mendel, an affluent German Jew whose family by the 1930s had built a network of ham, bacon, and sausage processing plants in Eastern Europe, mainly in the Balkans. Fred Mendel, who had fought for Germany in the First World War, was a very short, intense man, a lover of race-horses and fine art. In the 1930s he saw the Nazi threat coming, so he moved his family — wife Claire and daughters Eva and Johanna — out of Europe. They sailed from Cherbourg, France, to New York in 1939. Fred Mendel, fifty-two at the time, was not the classic poor refugee with a carpetbag full of dreams: he had close to $100,000 in his hands. While in New York, he heard of a place called Saskatchewan, where there were plenty of hogs and a quieter lifestyle — a perfect place to start over.

So he bought an idle abattoir on the southern fringes of Saskatoon, near where the South Saskatchewan River flows into a valley of small farms. The factory had once been run as a co-operative but had fallen into disuse. He handed over $5,000 to the co-op's lawyer, a man named Emmett Hall, who was grateful to get that kind of money in 1940 on the prairies. Hall, later a prominent jurist and considered the father of medicare in Canada, became a friend of the Mendels; however, not all Saskatooners were so charitable. Fred Mendel had trouble with the English language, and one banker laughed him off the premises. So he went across the street to another bank. Local sceptics said that the business, called Intercontinental Packers, would be gone in a year. But he did well selling his canned hams to Britain and the Allies during the war, and later to the recovering economies of Europe. Fred Mendel didn't sell any products in Canada until 1946. In Europe he had been known as the "canned ham man" for his distinctive methods of preserving meat, first devel-oped by his father Robert in the late nineteenth century. He brought all that knowledge and experience to his new country. Fred Mitchell said his grand-father never looked back on Europe and what he and others had lost. Asked by his grandson to talk about the Nazi scourge, he merely said, "Freddy, I cannot hate."

Meanwhile, his younger daughter Johanna made a life for herself. She had studied acting in Europe and was about to star as Titania in a Viennese produc-tion of *A Midsummer Night's Dream* when the Nazis marched on Austria. She fled before opening night. When she landed in New York she took some drama classes to help improve her English. A handsome young graduate of the acting school had come back to help out the instructor. Cameron Mitchell invited Johanna out for a coffee; they fell in love and soon married. He was a poor boy, the son of a Pennsylvania Lutheran preacher, and had worked hard to make New York and the big time. At that moment he was working with theatre legends Arthur Lunt and Lynne Fontaine. Shortly after the marriage to Johanna he went off to war, where he served as a bombardier. After the fighting ended, he signed with MGM and the two moved to Hollywood. He enjoyed a long career as a character actor playing supporting roles, but he never quite found the leading man parts that would catapult him to stardom. His high points were the role of Happy in the Broadway and movie versions of Arthur Miller's *Death of a Salesman* and, of course, *High Chaparral*. Every summer he would come with Johanna to Saskatchewan, where he befriended a local hockey hero named Gordie Howe.

The couple had four children: Robert, Fred, Charles (Chip), and Camille. The marriage was rocky, and Cameron Mitchell eventually left his young family for another woman. "For me, my Dad was God and when he left, it crushed me," Fred once said. "I'd never put LuAn and my kids in that position." Cameron and Joanna finally divorced in 1961, but the relationship had died years before. Cameron would fade in and out of Fred's life. "I respect my dad," Fred would remember. "He came from nothing and he became a pretty good actor. He worked hard, but unfortunately his career took over." Camille, who was born while her father was making the film *Carousel*, told a journalist: "I hardly knew my father because my parents divorced when I was very young, but whenever I saw him die on television, I cried."

Fred had a typical mother-son relationship with Johanna, without any hint of the rancour that would follow. But his link to grandfather Mendel was truly special. Fred Mendel took Johanna's family under his wing after Cameron left them. Fred Mitchell went to school in Pacific Palisades, near Los Angeles, but spent his summers in Saskatoon with his grandparents and began working in the plant. It was a strange kind of life, divided between the spare Canadian prairies and the Hollywood glitterland. His father, during his periodic bouts of involvement with his children, would let Fred hang around on movie sets with the likes of Clark Gable and Jane Russell. In the mid-1950s he even found him a role in a short film about a bunch of Little League kids. The boy who played second base in the film was Tom Selleck, who went on to star in TV's *Magnum PI* and many movies. Fred went on to run a pork slaughterhouse.

His father found him another role, this time on *High Chaparral*. But it was the same summer that Fred Mendel wanted to take his grandchildren to Europe to celebrate his and Claire's fiftieth wedding anniversary. In the end there was really no choice — Fred Mitchell gave up the TV role to be with his grandparents. After high school he attended the University of Arizona, where he earned a degree in economics. He took some aptitude tests that indicated excellent business skills, and it was suggested he might consider a Harvard MBA.

"But grandfather didn't think much of MBAs," he said, so in August 1969 he moved to Saskatoon to become a management trainee at Intercontinental.

Two of Fred's siblings were drawn more to the other vocation of the Mitchell/Mendel family — the acting world. Both Chip and Camille attended the University of British Columbia, then studied acting in England. Chip would later act in a number of movies and several episodes of *King of Kensington*. Camille moved on to dramatic roles at, among other places, Ontario's Shaw and Stratford festivals, where a number of her performances drew critical acclaim. She was particularly skilled in light comedy, where she could display her quick wit and elfin charm. Both Mitchells had solid acting careers — in Camille's case, brilliant at times — but they also continued to receive some income through the family's ownership of Intercontinental.

The oldest son, Robert, was expected to carry on the family business in Saskatoon. But Robert was a tortured soul and could not handle the pressure of being the designated heir. He drifted in and out of the company and finally committed suicide as a young man. Fred, as the second-oldest, was spared the intense pressure at first. He worked hard but had no hunger for a big career at Intercontinental. "I loved my grandfather but I wasn't sure I loved the meat industry," he said.

Fred felt that other people in the organization resented him. They were constantly urging the young kid to take it easy, not to work so hard. At times, Fred listened to them. It took a while for him to see the light. "One day, I woke up and said if I'm going to lead this company, I'm going to have to make up my mind, work real hard, get real serious, and decide that's what I want to do. For a lot of years after that, mine was the first car in the parking lot in the morning and the last to leave."

His grandfather noticed, and Fred became the designated golden boy, the link between generations, the son Fred Mendel never had. His rise was meteoric — at twenty-six, he became vice-president of marketing. He had never worked outside the company, although he spent some time looking at the operations of U.S. meat packer Oscar Mayer and meeting with its top marketing and sales people. He even received some outside job offers, but "I had to be here; my grandfather was getting older."

Even then, Intercontinental was a highly paternalistic enterprise. The Mendels' love of art was reflected in their sponsorship of creative people, such as the acclaimed Saskatoon painter William Perehudoff. At one point Fred Mendel hired Perehudoff, who was still unknown, to paint murals in the company cafeteria, vibrant works of muscular, industrial realism showing men engaged in brawny slaughterhouse labour, slabs of beef dangling beside them.

The murals are still there, remarkable testimony to the work that continues in that rambling, crowded factory on Saskatoon's 11th Street West.

In 1976, Fred Mendel died at the age of eighty-seven. Though he was only twenty-nine, Fred Mitchell was the natural choice for president; his mother Johanna, then president, moved up to the role of chairwoman. Fred found a company in dire straits, with heavy debts and a recalcitrant management team. The boy president had to show who was in charge. "When I took over, I was forced to take out all our vice-presidents over a year-and-a-half because they didn't want to support me. And I figured if it was going to be them or me, it had better be them."

When he inherited the company's management, he became a partner of the Province of Saskatchewan, which had bought a 45 percent stake in Intercontinental as a window into the meat-packing industry. But after a few years Fred bought out the government. As a major employer who benefited greatly from government incentives, he was constantly beating back claims that his company received special treatment. Once his frustration boiled over. "I'm personally sick and tired of having my company run down," he told an agri-industry conference in 1983.

On a personal level, Fred's life had been the company for a number of years. While at university he had married a fellow student, and the couple stayed together for seven years. But according to LuAn, the former wife was a "big-city girl" from California and didn't like Saskatoon. After his divorce, Fred became one of the city's most eligible bachelors. In the early 1980s his personal life took a dramatic turn that would have serious repercussions for Intercontinental. He was watching television and saw a local show hosted by LuAn Gingara, a former Miss Saskatoon and a one-time contender for Miss Canada. He asked her out to lunch, and they got along very well. She was a schoolteacher's daughter of German and Ukrainian stock from Melfort, east of Saskatoon. After winning her beauty crown she had done some modelling in Toronto before settling back in Saskatchewan.

Soon the thirty-eight-year-old company president and the twenty-three-year-old beauty queen were seeing a lot of each other, and the family grew concerned. Johanna never took to this young woman with the big hair and the flashy wardrobe — or to the fact that she already had a child from a teenage relationship. According to LuAn, her boyfriend's mother would drop little hints about how to dress. At one point she said to the younger woman, "You know, LuAn, you're a nice person but you'll never be able to travel in our circles." Beneath the petty insults was the not-so-subtle insinuation that the young woman was an attractive, high-cheekboned golddigger who was out to sink her nails into a vulnerable and wealthy man fifteen years her elder. In the eyes of Johanna, Chip, and Camille, their loving son and brother had become a pawn in the hands of a manipulative woman who wanted to get her hands on their company and the wealth it represented.

LuAn was a formidable adversary. She was hardly sophisticated, but she was gutsy and possessed a plainspoken honesty, and she never allowed herself to be intimidated by the Mitchells' hauteur. And Fred clearly adored her. They were married in August 1986 in a wedding that was one of Saskatoon's social highlights. By now all the seeds of family discord had been planted: sister Camille did not show up at the event. Fred and LuAn proceeded to raise a family. Freddie was born in 1988, and Ryan and daughter Jinji-Jo soon followed.

The family's dread of LuAn seemed to only intensify when Fred's health took a sudden turn. For years, Fred had tended to cough and wheeze a lot. As his condition grew increasingly serious in the mid-1980s, he went to a doctor, and medical tests revealed that his pulmonary functions and lung capacity were operating at 25 percent of normal. The doctors diagnosed a rare form of mutant cystic fibrosis and estimated that he might have only a few years to live. In September 1986, Fred checked into the Mayo Clinic in Rochester, Minnesota, where he received confirmation of the earlier diagnosis — terminal cystic fibrosis. Fred sought medical treatment to prolong his life. In July 1986 he began an intensive course of treatment that included medications and vigorous physiotherapy and inhalation therapy. Throughout this time he continued working as Intercontinental's president and CEO.

As Fred struggled with his health, Johanna landed a bombshell in his lap. She was proposing a reorganization of the company in which all shares would be transferred to a family trust, with her as trustee. Through the trust, Johanna would in effect control all the company's shares. Fred owned 45,000 nonvoting shares, which he had bought back from the province in 1983. According to court documents filed by Fred, Johanna threatened to strip him of his management duties and of various financial compensations if he did not agree to the transfer. Fred signed the document — mainly, he said later, because he was determined to keep running the company.

In court documents filed in 1994, Fred said that during his medical treatment for cystic fibrosis he had suffered from acute stress, anxiety, and sleeplessness, which required him to take tranquillizers. As a result he was reduced to "a condition of vulnerability [which] made him susceptible to domination and influence exerted on him by others." Later, Fred would argue that his family's animosity toward LuAn was also a major factor in the power play. His mother and siblings wanted to drive a wedge between him and his wife. LuAn insisted that much of the resentment was rooted in family history: "Earlier, a younger woman took their father away. Now here was another younger woman and Fred had been a surrogate father to them."

LuAn says that the last time she saw Johanna was at dinner at a Los Angeles restaurant. Her mother-in-law rose to say she had to leave because Chip was throwing a party that night, to which LuAn and Fred were not invited. As she left, LuAn says, Johanna stopped to speak to her grandson, young Freddie. "Do you love your Mommy?" Johanna asked. When the child answered that he did, the older woman said simply: "That's too bad."

It was a painful time for Fred: he soldiered on, taking extensive treatment for his condition but never really getting better. Finally, in 1990, he took a leave of absence from the company and travelled to Palo Alto, California, where doctors at the Stanford University Medical Center had developed expertise in heart-lung transplants. Fred and LuAn waited in Palo Alto for a donor, occasionally going on drives in the area. On one such drive, a message came from the babysitter: they had found an ideal heart and lung in a cyclist who had just been killed in an accident. The transplant was carried out, and Fred's own healthy heart found its way into a fifty-one-year-old woman.

He came out of the hospital with a new view of life. "I'm certainly very spiritual now," he told the *Star Phoenix*. "It's very personal but I have a belief in God, a higher power, that I never had." He went on to say he had been depressed in the past by a lack of open communication in his life. Although he didn't mention his family, the implications were clear. "I used to carry my rock sack," he said. "It was full of big boulders. They went right back to my childhood. They were boulders of anger, boulders of blame, boulders of resentment, jealousy, guilt, hatred. There were negative boulders." The difference now was that every night he took out his rock sack and emptied it.

If Fred felt rejuvenated, his relationship with his family was anything but. At one point he asked his mother why things weren't working. The business was doing well, but the relationship wasn't. "If I could have gotten my family to talk to me, other things could have been different." One problem was that there was no forum for communication, no family meetings or family council. "Not only was there no forum, but a lot of subjects [simply] were not discussed," Fred said. "I tried, LuAn tried too, but we ran into walls and no interest or desire on their part."

Family relations were further complicated by the intermittent presence of Cameron Mitchell in their lives. LuAn admits that as a youngster, she was never really aware of Cameron. "Where I grew up, we got *Bonanza*. I didn't see *High Chaparral*." But Fred was proud of his father. When he and LuAn were dating, she got a call from him one night telling her to flip on the TV — *High Chaparral* was on and she could see his father in action.

In their later years, Johanna and Cameron had reached a kind of reconciliation, and the old actor was around more often. He was always looking for ways to revive his career. While Fred was ill, the family raised the notion that the Mitchells could sell the meat company and use the proceeds to make a movie starring Cameron and the rest of the acting Mitchells. Fred said no thanks, he wanted to hold on to the business.

The final split revolved around what Fred saw as a direct challenge to his role in the company. He believed it was triggered by a conversation with his mother in which he proposed more consultation: "All I know is I said to my mother, 'You know, Mother, I'd really like to see this family together. I don't feel we are close and if there's anything I can do ... If you have problems, I'd like to hear them and I'd like you to hear some of mine.' There was just a refusal to do that."

Fred contended that his mother — who controlled the company through the trust — and his siblings were obstructing his ability to manage. In particular, they were blocking a new business plan. Fred and his Intercontinental team could see more rationalization sweeping the meat sector. They planned to shift their beef operations out of Saskatoon to a Moose Jaw plant the company had acquired. Fred's plan was to fill the unused capacity in Saskatoon by closing down a Vancouver pork operation. Economies of scale would be achieved by consolidating all pork activity under a single roof. The company had had a successful 1994, but Fred was concerned that oversupply in the industry might wreak havoc in the next few years.

Managers who attended a December 1994 meeting at the company sensed something was up. One recalls that when the issue of consolidation was raised, Johanna "crossed her arms and said we'd talk about it in a month." It was clear to the managers that there was dissension in the family ranks, with Fred urging consolidation and Johanna resisting the idea.

Fred later alleged that the family began to cut him out of strategic planning. Some of Fred's legal advisers told him to hang in, but LuAn urged him to quit the company. When he left abruptly in April 1995, his exit was front-page news in Saskatchewan. "Over the past months, my management role has changed and that hasn't been acceptable to me," he told the *Star Phoenix*. "I'm not happy with the changes."

It was a bizarre time for the company's managers, who were torn two ways — they were still loyal to Fred, who had hired them, but he was now outside the company. Nobody would move on the business plan to close Vancouver and consolidate in Saskatoon. The company drifted as the pork market began to deteriorate as a result of oversupply and declining prices. Also, a rejuvenated Maple Leaf Foods, now under the control of Wallace McCain's family, was determined to pull more of the meat industry under its control.

Intercontinental's managers tried to resolve their torn emotions. "My policy was dedication to the company, and not to individuals, but it's hard to separate the two in a family company," says one manager, who felt pressure to pick sides in the dispute. "It was hell," another senior officer recalls. "It was difficult to rally any effort by the rest of the employees. There was a definite split among senior management in the direction of the company. Some managers wanted Fred back to lead the company. Others said his actions indicated he could not be a leader."

Chip, now installed as Intercontinental's president, was clearly out of his depth as a manager, and surrounded himself with outside legal and financial consultants. One key person was Gordon Campbell, a boyhood friend of Fred's and a financial turnaround expert who had advised the company for more than a decade. Although he was named chief operating officer, it was clear he was more of a big picture person than a details man. Meanwhile, the industry was going downhill, Intercontinental was losing money, and its major lender, the Bank of Montreal, was getting nervous.

The company was distracted by the carnival show among its family owners. At one point Fred showed up in the cafeteria, apparently wanting to keep in touch with what was going on. A senior manager started talking to him, awkwardly, and finally pointed out that he wasn't comfortable with Fred there. Fred decided he should probably leave. The two walked amicably to the door. So it became a front-page newspaper story that Fred had been forcibly escorted from the factory.

Inside and outside Intercontinental, Fred was clearly the people's choice. "The whole province was behind us," LuAn recalls. "In the restaurant having dinner, they'd say 'Fred, we're pulling for you and bless you, do what's right in your heart.' We were moved to tears several times. It wouldn't make a lot of sense to a lot of logical thinkers right now, who would say why don't you just take the money and run, this is ridiculous, game over and let go of it.

"It's like what Fred said to me one night: 'It's as if I had a baby, and I love that baby so much and that baby has cancer. And I don't care if I have to go across the world to find a cure for that child, well I'm going to do it and whatever it takes we're going to see to it that we're given every opportunity to cure that cancer.'"

Workers who were interviewed in the media said they wanted Fred back. There was a petition signed by more than 250 employees urging his return.

One manager, who worked at the company throughout this time, explains: "Fred was a caring man. He never acted like a president, never strutted around the plant, and he never pulled rank. Also, he had a lot of insight into the industry, he had a very good feel for it. When he walks through that plant, it's as if he were talking to friends."

But in early 1996 the war between the Mitchells escalated. A year after he left the company, Fred launched a suit against Intercontinental for constructive dismissal, arguing that the terms of his employment had changed to such an extent that they amounted to outright dismissal. Specifically, he said the other family members had changed the reporting relationships between senior managers and family members and had disregarded Fred's recommendations for restructuring. Also, the company had unilaterally cancelled Fred's corporate credit card and had determined that it would no longer pay Fred his bonus and performance incentives. The suit further alleged that the company had excluded him from "various sensitive and high-level discussions regarding restructuring the plant production and negotiations with the province of Saskatchewan." In all, he demanded payment of $2.5 million in lost income, as well as compensation for bonuses, benefits, interest, and legal costs. Later Camille would say the suit held little weight: "There was no one put above or beside Fred in the company."

The family quarrel was now out among the public. Intercontinental, with Chip Mitchell as president, countersued, demanding the repayment of sums alleged to have been borrowed from the company by Fred and LuAn. The suit claimed that Fred had abused his position for personal gain. The company alleged that Fred and LuAn had borrowed $441,160 to buy a house in Palm Springs, and that $385,262 was still unpaid. Also, that the couple had charged $137,000 on the company credit card and not repaid that sum. The company also listed $181,485 in personal expenses and $46,000 in dental expenses that had not been repaid.

According to the statement of claim, Intercontinental had suffered a $245,000 loss from the purchase, renovation, and sale of a house for Fred and LuAn on a Saskatchewan lake. The statement also said that the Mitchells had established a company, Save the Planet Holdings, for LuAn, and had directed Intercon to pay various expenses. In all, Intercontinental was asking for a judgment in the amount of $1 million.

The suit also raised the curtain on the family's struggle over the ownership of the company. It described Johanna's departure from the company in November 1993 to undergo open heart surgery, and again in 1994 to deal with the death of Cameron Mitchell. During that time, the claim said, Fred Mitchell neglected his obligations to the business. Further, it was alleged that he manipulated creditors and senior managers in an effort to gain control of the company.

Chip Mitchell told the *Star Phoenix* that "Fred's struggle to take control from my mother started perhaps five to six months after my mother had open heart surgery and a month after my father was buried (in 1994)." Chip added: "That's when he started his attacks on my mother. I'd always loved my brother until that point. But when you start doing things like that to a seventy-nine-year-old woman, it makes you wonder about a person." Camille said that Fred seemed to feel he was under some kind of deadline, and that he was determined to wrest the company away from his family members as soon as he could.

Fred replied that he was indeed trying to buy the company from his siblings and his mother, but they weren't acknowledging his efforts. Meanwhile, reports were circulating that Burns Foods Ltd., a major competitor — soon to be acquired itself by Maple Leaf Foods — was negotiating to buy Intercontinental, which rankled Fred even more. Fred couldn't understand why his own family wouldn't sell it to him. But any efforts by Johanna, Chip, and Camille to sell the company were undercut by the legal wrangling, which scared suitors away. Interviewed later, Fred said his relatives simply wanted to sell the company and use the money to make movies. "But when you've had your heart in the business, it's hard to sell to Burns or Maple Leaf and to the people you've been fighting for years."

In the midst of all this jostling, on April 30, 1996, the police charged Camille Mitchell with uttering death threats and with telephone harassment in connection with a call she made to Fred's home. The incident had allegedly occurred the previous October; the prosecutor explained that charges had not been laid earlier because of the odd circumstances. Camille pleaded not guilty, and her lawyer told the *Star Phoenix* that the calls were in fact attempts to make peace.

"I never made any threats," Camille said in an interview after Fred's death. "It was an attempt to call a brother I had always loved. I had called to say, 'We love you, why are we at odds like that?'" She added that the allegations of death threats were "part of the psychological leverage [being exerted] on this side of the family."

In the background, the two parties were moving toward a compromise. According to insiders, there was a growing sense that the company could collapse unless the battle was resolved. Instability and uncertainty were killing Intercontinental. Suppliers, customers, employees, and lenders were nervous. One weekend in November, senior managers received phone calls from a colleague suggesting that Fred Mitchell might be back in the plant that week. "I said to the caller, 'Cut it out. I've heard crazier stories but not many,'" one manager recalls.

But the following Tuesday, a group of top brass were called to a morning meeting in Chip's office. There was Fred, sitting in his chair as if he had never left.

Fred was coming back as vice-chairman, but the exact lines of authority were unclear. Chip was still president and nominally in charge. Asked if Chip was his boss, Fred said, "We're working that out." But he added that he planned to take full control of operations. In the background, Fred was being given time to buy out and refinance the Saskatoon operation. The family was under tight agreement not to rock the boat — to give the appearance that all was hunky-dory — while Fred raised the money. All lawsuits and charges were dropped.

Fred held a meeting of the company employees in the cafeteria, the vibrant Perehudoff murals providing a backdrop. "It was such a good feeling because everyone stood up and clapped," he remembered. The standing ovation was the first step to restoring morale. Then, as Fred had advocated, the Vancouver plant was closed with the loss of 237 jobs, and the hog operations were consolidated in Saskatoon. Finally, in July 1997, eight months after Fred's return, the other shoe fell: a deal was announced to split the business, with Fred taking the pork operations and Johanna, Chip, and Camille the beef business in Moose Jaw.

In refinancing the Saskatoon plant, Fred brought in a group of financial partners. Under the new structure the Mitchells owned a control stake of 41 percent. SPI, the producer-owned Saskatoon pork-marketing agency, had 16 percent and a Taiwanese partner took 15 percent. Merchant bank Roynat Inc., a subsidiary of the Bank of Nova Scotia, contributed $33 million and took a chunk of equity. An undisclosed silent investment partner owned the rest.

For Fred the timing was perfect. At the time of his return, industry conditions were starting to perk up. Some of the overcapacity was beginning to work its way out of pork packing. The company was beginning to enjoy stronger sales in Asia. Fred zealously pursued his strategy of moving the company away from straight meat-packing and into processing products with higher added value. He announced that the company would invest $14 million in the plant over the next three years, and would be embarking on an ambitious hiring program.

Soon after, Fred was able to report during an interview that Intercontinental's workforce had risen to more than 1,300 people, compared with 800 before his return, and that the company was making a profit again. He had been approached by Maple Leaf Foods and other suitors. "We've had several people interested in buying this company, but the reason we came back was not to sell it but to continue it," he said in his upstairs office, which in the 1940s had served as an apartment for his late grandparents. He indicated that he was contemplating taking the company public.

"This is my mission, our mission," he said, glancing across the table at

LuAn. "We put so much into coming back — we put everything we had on the line personally, and the motivation was that this has been my life. It's LuAn's in part as well, not as long as for me. When you have a dream and you're determined, nothing can stop you."

The plant improvements were proceeding, and the company was about to unveil a new pork-cutting room, easing pressure on its old, overcrowded cutting operation. The highlight would be a robotic cutting arm that would be able to slice apart a pork carcass so efficiently that LuAn would christen it "Jack the Ribber." A month later, Fred would rename the company Mitchell's Gourmet Foods Inc., because "it fits our markets and culture today." The former label, Intercontinental, suggests "the old killing and cutting image. We're a value-added processor now."

By this point, Fred hadn't spoken to his mother for two years, and the family was no closer to reconciliation. Each side blamed the other for not making an effort. In an interview, Chip Mitchell said that Johanna hadn't heard from Fred, and "I've tried to talk but he won't communicate." Johanna, in poor health from continuing heart problems, was dividing her time between Palm Springs, California and the family ranch, just up the road from the Intercontinental packing plant near Saskatoon. Chip and Camille both owned properties in Saskatoon, and Chip at one point was intending to sell his home in Belair, a wealthy enclave of Los Angeles, to move back to Saskatchewan.

Fred and LuAn were raising their three children, determined that the acrimony of the previous generation would not repeat itself. "We really are raising them differently," Fred said. "We talk to them very openly about jealousy, about trying to be happy for each other when good things happen and about trying to be a team member." The family was holding regular Sunday night family meetings during which they tried to discuss what was on everyone's mind. Fred and LuAn were reading Stephen Covey about the habits of highly effective families. "He has some very good suggestions," Fred said. "We believe in honesty and openness and not accusations. We have a completely different philosophy. Our children can sit down with us and say, 'You know, I hear what you have to say to another member of the family. I want to discuss it because it is important to us.'"

Fred was particularly proud when his ten-year-old son said he wanted to come out to the factory for part of the summer and work — "without any pushing and prodding." Young Freddie wanted to buy a Lego game and he needed some extra money. "I like the sense they want to be rewarded for initiative and hard work rather than [taking] an open pocketbook philosophy."

Except for the estrangement with Johanna and his siblings, everything seemed to be falling into place. But then Fred visited Stanford for his annual checkup, and died. LuAn was beside him when his body finally gave out. In her mind they both went to a beautiful place, a place alive with butterflies, which Fred loved. "I was with him in the place ... It helped me deal with it. I left the hospital and sat in the park. I told the children what their dad was saying was: Love the butterflies. When they see the butterflies, he's there too."

LuAn didn't hesitate about taking over the company. When she tried to explain the new challenges to her children, Freddie Jr. spoke up: "Let's do it and do it better than anyone else." She was also buoyed by the employees' response. At a wake for Fred at the plant, she stood for six hours shaking hands and exchanging hugs. Meeting with the board, she quickly assumed the post of chairwoman; Stuart Irvine, who had started on the shop floor thirty-three years before, moved up from vice-president, manufacturing, to president and chief operating officer. That was what Fred had instructed. Given his complicated medical history, he had left extensive instructions on what to do if he died.

In the aftermath of Fred's death, there were many questions. Could LuAn and her management team continue to run the company in the absence of Fred's firm strategic guidance? Would someone make her and her financial partners an offer they could not refuse? Could this mother of four — including her daughter from a previous relationship — shepherd the company through to the next generation? There was only one certainty for the Mitchell family: the wounds had not healed. LuAn had no doubt that the turmoil of the past few years had shortened her husband's life: "People know that Fred literally gave his life to save this company."

But this interpretation was still being disputed by Camille months after her brother's death. "He was exploited, he was an ill man," she said in an interview. "History was revised for him in a passionate way. We were best friends for thirty-odd years before everything went awry." The family, particularly her ailing mother, had wanted some kind of reconciliation, but "the family was ostracized. There was a financial closure, a legal closure but in our hearts we can only say prayers for the Fred that we knew, who we couldn't say goodbye to."

The fate of Intercontinental became clearer in the spring of 1999, when Kitchener-based Schneider Corp., itself a former family company, acquired a 32 percent share of Mitchell's Gourmet Foods. Mitchell's and Schneider, which is now a subsidiary of giant Smithfield Foods of Virginia, called it a strategic alliance: the initial investment would help fund a $50 million expansion of the Saskatoon pork plant. This was quite possibly the first move in a creeping takeover of Mitchell's by the U.S. meat company and its Canadian arm.

LuAn Mitchell, who was making plans to move her residence from Saskatoon to Banff, Alberta, said that her family would continue to be the major shareholder of Mitchell's, although she did not reveal the exact share. Still, the agreement gave Schneider the option of acquiring control by buying more treasury shares as it provided cash to Mitchell's for further expansion. LuAn said the company had looked at going public or taking on more debt to finance expansion, but decided the best option for expansion was seeking a large strategic ally. Fred, she said, had always approved of the way Schneider's had dealt with its employees — an obvious dig at Maple Leaf, which had been confrontational with its unions. She felt that its employee-friendly culture had survived the sale of the company by the Schneider family to Smithfield Foods.

Seven months after the sale to Schneider, Johanna Mitchell died in Palm Springs at the age of eighty-two. She was buried in that California city, in the family plot beside her husband Cameron, her son Robert, and her parents, Fred and Claire Mendel. "She was intimidating to some people," daughter Camille said a few days after Johanna's death, "but she was a loving, compassionate person." Camille pointed out that her mother had worked for thirty-five years in the family meat business and presided over some of its most successful times. Right to the end, Johanna was battling LuAn. The *Star Phoenix* reported that two weeks before her death, Johanna had filed a lawsuit alleging that she was entitled by an earlier family agreement to 10 percent of the proceeds from the sale to Schneider.

For Camille Mitchell, her sister-in-law's sale of a large stake of Mitchell's Gourmet Foods, only six months after Fred Mitchell's death, merely validated her mother's opinion of LuAn. From a strategic point of view, the deal did seem to make sense, but the question still lingered: Given all that Fred had gone through, all the years and tears and pain, what would he have thought of all this? "I've never done anything Fred would not approve of," says LuAn. "Fred would have been proud of this choice." But you can't help wondering whether Fred Mitchell would want to see his beloved meat-packing firm slipping slowly away from the family's hands.

FIVE

WENDY MCDONALD —
MOTHER AND CHILDREN

Wendy McDonald, majority owner and CEO of BC Bearing.

Photo by Suzanne Ahearne

A T SEVENTY-SEVEN, WENDY MCDONALD still comes to the office. On this
autumn morning she's navigating the staircase to the second-floor executive suites at the head office of BC Bearing Engineers Ltd., the company she
has ruled over for almost fifty years. Close behind are two toy poodles, Winky
and Dizzy, who will spend the day bouncing and barking around the office.
Ms. McDonald has perfectly coiffed silver hair and tortoiseshell glasses, and
is wearing an impeccable cream-coloured suit — but don't let the grandmoth-
erly image fool you: "I'm still the CEO and I have the right to go into anything
I want," says Ms. McDonald, who is every bit as vivacious as when she was
modelling as a young woman in the 1930s: "I'm still two-thirds owner, you
know. I get in there. When there's a problem, I do get involved."

Wendy McDonald admits that these days she leaves most of the day-to-day
business to her four children who work in the company. For BC Bearing of
Burnaby, B.C., a distributor of bearings and power generation equipment with
operations in six countries, she is officially chairperson and CEO, but unoffi-
cially a kind of roving ambassador and compulsive networker. On this morning she is just back from Calgary, where she attended a Mexico/Canada
business forum (BC Bearing has a branch in Mexico). She drops the names of
people she rubbed shoulders with — old pals like Alberta utilities tycoon Ron
Southern, and Tom d'Aquino, the head of the Business Council on National

Issues. While she handles a lot of the international schmoozing, oldest son
Robby MacPherson, fifty-five, runs the show as president, along with daughter Penny Omnès, fifty-one, vice-president for marketing and human resources,
son Bill Dix, forty-four, vice-president for international business, and Scott
MacPherson, forty-nine, president of BC Bearing's U.S. operations.

Robby, interviewed in the office adjoining Wendy's, says the roles are not
easy to separate — he and his mother work together so closely. "Her vision is
to expand globally. That's where she's coming from. She puts a lot of effort
into global expansion. Then she turns it over and tells me to do it: 'Here's what
I want done, these are the reasons why and go do it.' Sure we argue, but I'm
not a yes man. She has to have some very good ammunition when she asks me
to do something."

Although she is affluent and sucessful, Wendy McDonald's life has swung
the entire distance between tragedy and triumph. She has had three husbands,
all of whom died in accidents. She has faced down a mutiny by her second-in-
command manager while she was away on a business trip. And on top of that,
she has raised ten children largely on her own. She inherited BC Bearing from
her first husband in 1950 and developed it into a multinational business with
more than $130 million in annual sales.

Tragedy has continued to stalk Wendy McDonald, even at this advanced stage
in her life. Her adopted son, Kerry Dix, died a couple of years ago at age fifty-
one of a drug overdose, and one of Robby's two sons passed away three years
ago of leukemia. She has no particular insight into how she manages to carry on,
except to say that "every event makes you stronger." She believes she has a
purpose in life: to bring up her and her husbands' children and assemble a clan
that includes ten sons, daughters, stepsons, and stepdaughters (nine now with
Kerry's death), twenty-eight grandchildren, and nine great-grandchildren. Two
of the grandchildren have been involved in the business — Lance Ross, thirty-
five, the son of her oldest daughter Sandra, is marketing manager, and Chris
MacPherson, twenty-nine, Robby's surviving son, was second-in-command of
BC Bearing's Chile operation until recently, when he took a leave of absence.

Wendy McDonald is something of a legend on the West Coast — a rare woman
entrepreneur who took control of her company as a widow with small children
and has since built a reputation for perseverance and guts. Now she has one more
big act to orchestrate: she must engineer her own exit from the company she has
dominated for five decades. And that may be the toughest job of all. So far, so
good, she insists. In the past few years the family has forged a succession plan
that will, on her death or her exit from the company, split her two-thirds shareholding interest among the four children working in the company, with some

compensation for Sandra, who no longer works at BC Bearing. Robby, now president, will assume the title of CEO. But Wendy McDonald is the glue that has held it all together. The children and grandchildren pledge loyalty and affection to "Ma" — or TuTu, as she's known to the grandchildren. Will the group continue to demonstrate solidarity after she leaves? And can BC Bearing survive as an independent business into the next generation? "If they don't get along, they don't. I've done the best I can," she shrugs. Penny Omnès, Wendy's daughter, acknowledges that when her mother goes the family consensus may become unstuck. As an active member of the Canadian Association of Family Enterprise, she has seen the carnage that can result when family members feel they can only communicate by threats and lawsuits. "We'll have to come to grips with it. The courts are a losing proposition, and we want a win-win."

The fact that her succession is such a landmark event must seem utterly amazing at times for Wendy McDonald. Fresh out of high school in the late 1930s, she had no aspirations to be in the bearings business or any business at all. An attractive young woman, she had done a bit of modelling around her hometown of Vancouver. But she had a strong entrepreneurial background — both sides of her family had been in the shipping business. One night Wendy Stoker met a darkly handsome young man with a slim brush of a moustache. His name was Robert MacPherson, and he ran a Vancouver company called Northern Metals and Engineering Co., which made logging equipment. They started going out and got married in 1941.

Robert MacPherson was beginning to diversify his business. In the late 1930s he had become the regional distributor for a line of industrial bearings, instruments used to reduce friction in all kinds of moving equipment. On the resource-rich West Coast, the demand for bearings would grow strongly in the coming decades. Then the war broke out and Robert, who had a commercial pilot's licence, joined the air force as a pilot. In 1944 he was transferred to India with the Royal Air Force. He left Wendy — then twenty-one, with one small child and another on the way — in charge of the business and with power of attorney. She likes to joke that she didn't even know what power of attorney meant in those days.

Wendy found that she liked the business life. The bearings trade was booming, and the company was supplying two North Vancouver shipyards plus a Boeing plant that operated in the city during the war years. The bearings business became so strong that she incorporated a separate company called BC Bearing Engineers. Seeing the potential in Alberta, Wendy opened a branch office in Calgary, which originally supplied the agriculture sector but was well placed to profit from the oil boom when it began in the late 1940s.

Robert MacPherson came home in 1946, and for Wendy the game was over. He literally ordered his wife back into the kitchen. "Well, I wasn't happy at all. Of course, I wasn't," she admits. But she obeyed, and proceeded to have two more children over the next four years. By all accounts Robert MacPherson was a domineering and highly chauvinistic husband. He took to calling Wendy by a demeaning nickname, "Dumb Ma," and there was no suggestion that she would ever again play a role in the business. According to Penny Omnès, that dismissal explains her mother's overpowering drive to succeed: she yearned to prove to Robert and everyone else that she could run the company and do it very well. But all that would come later.

Over the next few years, Wendy MacPherson focused a lot of her attention on the family's property up the Sunshine Coast, at Halfmoon Bay on the Sechelt Peninsula. She had inherited some money and had a summer home, Red Roofs, built there in 1948. The property would become almost sacred ground for the family. It remains to this day a place where family members can go to slip out of their business roles. This is where the family tries to be just a family, not the owners and managers of an industrial company.

The Sunshine Coast has also been the site of family tragedy. In 1950, Robert MacPherson was flying from Vancouver to the cottage when he tried to land his Sea Bee single-engine plane at Point Roberts. The plane crashed, and he perished. Wendy did not hesitate — she felt she had to take over the company if her young family, now four children, was to ever have a livelihood. At that point she was twenty-eight and the business was grossing $250,000 a year.

It was not as easy as Wendy hoped. She once told *B.C. Business* magazine that "Bob was also the type of businessman who made little deals all over the place. It was really hard picking up the pieces. But all the suppliers took me under their wings, and I had a very good banker, a very good chartered accountant, and a very good lawyer ... but we had to eat for heaven's sake. You don't get fazed with that [hanging] over you."

Because Robert MacPherson had left two wills, there was some initial confusion about the transfer of ownership. One senior manager thought he could take advantage of the power vacuum and seize operational control of the company. "He thought it was time that I went out and played golf and looked after the children," remembers Wendy, but she made it clear that she had no intention of doing that. One of her first actions was a trip to Europe to visit some of BC Bearing's major bearings suppliers. When she came back, the mutinous manager had established his control. "While I was away, he tried to take over ... He rallied a few other branch managers behind him. When I got back I was fighting for my life." She fired him, but he struck out on his own and managed to lure away half of the company's thirty employees, including most of the salesmen with their vast store of contacts and customer information. Mrs. Mac, as she is known to employees, battled back, rebuilding her customer lists. "I was close to nervous breakdown that first year. My son Scott was only six weeks old and had been a preemie. He cried every night. And I was having to deal with people during the day and I then had to go home and cook the dinner and do the diapers. I finally got a good woman from England, and her husband came over and worked for us too."

The bearings business then, as now, was dominated by men. For her European trip she had notified her business contacts that "W.B. MacPherson" of BC Bearing would be visiting them. The companies would book lunch and dinner meetings at exclusive male clubs, then Wendy would watch with some amusement as they scrambled to undo their plans.

Meanwhile she had sorted out the MacPherson wills and begun to move on emotionally. Still a young woman, she got to know a charming young widower named Bill Dix, the vice-president of sales at Neon Products Ltd., a successful West Coast sign company. Talking to Wendy today, it's clear she still misses the gregarious Mr. Dix, who became her second husband. He was a talented artist, and Wendy took up painting as well. They entertained a lot and spent their spare time at the beloved summer place at Halfmoon Bay. He had two children from a previous marriage; then they had another of their own, whom they named Bill. In all, there were seven children, including five of her own with two husbands — all under the same roof.

On Valentine's Day in 1957, Bill Dix was at Red Roofs entertaining some of his colleagues from Neon Products. Wendy was with the wives back at their home in Vancouver's British Properties. At a nearby cottage, Bill's friend Sam Cromie, assistant publisher at the *Vancouver Sun*, had a group of his own people up for a retreat. Sometime during the evening, Dix and Cromie apparently wandered off from their groups to test-drive a new boat. It is still unknown what happened. The next morning the group noticed the two men were missing. Cromie's body washed ashore; Dix's was never found.

Somehow Wendy pulled herself together again, throwing her energy into the bearings business. As her personal life turned more tragic, her business life began to flourish. In the early 1960s, Canada's resource economy was taking off. In the Canadian bearings business the large manufacturers do not sell much directly to end users; instead, they work through well-established regional distributors such as BC Bearing. The local people know the needs of the clients; they can customize orders for them and help them retrofit used bearings. It is a very personal business, with local offices serving local businesses. Under this regime, BC Bearing expanded, setting up branch offices in places like Duncan on Vancouver Island, and Prince George in the Interior.

The children were starting to move into the company. There was never any question of working somewhere else. "I've always wanted to be in the bearings business," says Robby MacPherson. "I used to go to the office to sweep the floors, dust the bearings on the shelf. I went with my father. It was in my blood and I liked what I saw. You always learn something new every day in this business." Does he regret never having worked anywhere else? Not really, says Robby, although he is certainly familiar with the argument that heirs should find their own place in the world. "With what was going on in our industry in the sixties and seventies, we were clipping right along and didn't have time to think about things like that. You just had to get on and do things." If the company had been more established, there might have been time to explore other ventures. But not at fast-growing BC Bearing. In those expansion years, Wendy was fortunate to have access to a loyal and hard-working corps of employees, including her own children.

Robby MacPherson was sixteen when he started working in the shipping department in the summer; when he was eighteen he was sent to Edmonton and Calgary to work in sales for the summer. Only after he was established at the company did he go to get a sales and marketing diploma at Vancouver City College (now Langara College). After he graduated he returned to the company to help set up branches in Prince Rupert and Kitimat. For a while he was Northern Regional manager, which involved a lot of travelling in the B.C. Interior. Then he was manager for all of British Columbia, then vice-president of sales for Canadian operations. Finally, in 1988, he became president and CEO.

The other children followed a similar pattern — they entered the company right after high school and were quickly thrust into key roles in its expansion. The children were helping Wendy build the company; because their father, the founder, died so young, they are in essence first-generation enterepreneurs, too.

In the 1960s, Wendy met and married a mining promoter named Sidney McDonald, who brought three more children to the ménage, expanding Wendy's brood to ten children. The marriage was not successful, and the couple separated in 1966. Today, Wendy is loath to talk about her third husband or the circumstances of their separation. In 1969 he was killed in a mysterious episode. Some press reports indicate that he was beaten to death in a fight. Wendy won't discuss it, to avoid further pain for the McDonald children. Whatever the facts of his death, it left her once again husbandless and with more young children to raise.

Penny Omnès, Wendy's daughter, says her mother developed a routine during these years. She kept good help — cooks and housekeepers — around the house and devoted most of her own waking hours to the business. Life around the MacPherson/Dix/McDonald household was hectic, Penny says, but Wendy managed to wedge in some personal time. "On Thursdays she would take [time] off and take us shopping. We'd do dinner that night and every Sunday we'd do dinner. Every summer she'd take off and we'd go up to our summer place." At one point, Wendy had eight teenagers living in the house. Then they started to get married — three weddings alone in one chaotic year.

And the business kept growing. In the 1970s it could hardly have done otherwise, given the strength of the B.C. resource economy. BC Bearing opened branches in small cities close to the mines, lumber mills, and industrial sites that were its major customers. In 1979 the company made its first foray into the United States — with little success at first. The first failed attempt cost the company $30,000. "The hardest part was trying to get the [product] lines," she told *The Globe and Mail*'s Patricia Lush in 1994. "I got practically down on my knees to all our suppliers. They said, 'Just because you're a big company up here in Canada doesn't mean you can waltz into the United States.'" But she persisted, and the company established itself in the United States on its second try.

Her own children continued to be employed in the business. Her adopted family and her stepchildren, except for summer jobs as kids, did not get involved full-time. Even so, Wendy feels very maternal toward them. Kerry Dix, the real estate developer who died of a drug overdose — ruled accidental — "was a very smart boy, maybe too smart for his own good," she says. "I would think he was under business pressure. He wouldn't talk about business. I only saw him once a year — he lived in Hawaii and San Diego. He was on a different path."

She made a conscious effort to give each of her own children responsibility in a distinct area of the business so that they could develop without bumping into each other. "You've got to balance things with so many children in the business. We've grown so much, they can work in their own situations ... I always wondered where Penny would fit in — she left us for a little bit. But she's got a great personality, she knows the business, and we need the marketing aspect."

Penny Omnès, a vivacious, outgoing woman, has been in the company now for twenty-eight years. She got married out of high school but that union didn't last. She joined the family company with a high school education and picked up her business knowledge by just doing it. Eventually she went off to secretarial school, and when her mother needed an executive assistant, Penny offered her services. That was the start of a thoroughly fulfilling fifteen years, during which she travelled with her mother and learned a lot working beside her. They are still very close. At one point, Penny started getting nervous about what the future would bring if her mother wasn't there. So she acquired a college diploma in marketing. When her mother decided the company needed a marketing department, Penny was her choice to head it; then Penny recruited her nephew Lance Ross as her second-in-command.

When Penny's first marriage ended, her mother suggested that she get to know the French-born manager of the Delta Hotel at Whistler. Wendy was serving on a committee with Jacques Omnès and was impressed by the young man. Eventually, Jacques and Penny did meet — they had enrolled in the same cooking class — and they found that they quite liked each other. They started dating and eventually married. He has two children from an earlier marriage and she has two daughers, as well as two grandchildren. Currently, he's selling hotel franchises for a U.S.-based company.

Penny sees an important role for herself as the company's face to the outside world. She has become active in the worldwide association of power transmission distributors (in fall 1999, she became the group's president); her brother Robby and her mother have participated in bearings distributors' trade groups. This way, they have both sides of their business covered. Penny sees this as valuable networking, and it gives her a chance to travel. She is also involved in the Women Entrepreneurs Association of Canada, and with CAFE, Canada's leading family business group. She's a member of one of CAFE's personal advisory groups, or PAGs; these are groups of ten to fifteen family business people from various industries who get together regularly to swap ideas and war stories. She finds all of this valuable, partly because there are other women in the group with whom she can share experiences. "I feel that I'm a female and I'm being discriminated against by my brothers — sometimes I get that feeling," she says. "It's nice to see it's not just me who feels it. [I hear it from] the two other women in our group — it's still going on out there."

But wouldn't BC Bearing be less chauvinistic since it has been run by a woman? In fact, Penny believes the opposite is the case. The fact that Wendy is in charge makes the men overcompensate and become even more macho in dealing with a woman manager in their midst. "My mom used to say my father was terribly chauvinistic ... Two of my brothers are exactly the same."

According to Penny, the roles the siblings adopted as children in an often fatherless family have established certain patterns. "The role playing is still there. Robby had to be the father when we were kids. Mother expected him to just control the troops because he was the oldest son. It's continued on through life, and it's a pain in the backside. I'm fifty years of age now, thank you very much. You'd think I'd start to be treated with respect." Wendy is sensitive to these concerns. Like any mother, she wants everyone to be happy.

She worries that her son Robby is a lot like his father — closed-mouthed, inward-looking, quietly controlling.

Penny does see some improvement in conditions for women at the company, but also perceives a permanent glass ceiling — men will always be represented more heavily at the highest ranks. "Women are pushed out of the higher end — it's still the mindset that we're inferior. We've always had to do [more] — I do three times what my brothers do. But that's the way life is, and my mom's done the same. Look at the load she has. It's just the way of the world."

Still, there is an upside to being part of a close family business. When the family gets togther, the atmosphere is very relaxed, close, and loving. In fact, the relationships are similar to those in any family — it's just that these sisters and brothers are already spending so much of their time together. "You do care for your family," Penny says. "It's just that sometimes you could kill them. But that's life."

Bill Dix, her half-brother, says he has had one advantage in the sprawling family — he's a half-brother to both the MacPhersons and the Dixes, who are Wendy's adopted children. "I see the family issues on both sides." He too joined the company right after high school and worked his way up, finally finding his place in international operations. But he acknowledges that Robby is the clear day-to-day manager of the company. "Every business has to have a leader, and that's Robby."

Robby MacPherson insists that BC Bearing is a different company because it is run by a woman. His arm sweeps around him, gesturing at the native art, paintings, and mementos from Wendy's endless travels. "Just look around here, you've got the women's touch, the art and everything else. She just does it a little differently." He does concede, however, that in contrast with popular stereotypes of women in management, his mother is not a consensus decision-maker. She asks questions, but she makes decisions on her own. He also says she is more inclined to make up her mind of the basis of a hunch, or intuition, than he is.

In recent years, BC Bearing has had to confront new business realities. In the late 1980s and early 1990s the economy of British Columbia began to nose-dive. Mining companies, in particular, complained of the high cost of doing business in the province and what they perceived was an antibusiness attititude fostered by B.C.'s NDP government. Wendy McDonald felt that to succeed, BC Bearing would have to establish itself as an international company. She opened branches in Mexico and Singapore. Meanwhile, South America was opening up as a rich source of minerals. In particular, Chile had entered a period of political stability following the end of military rule. As exploration slowed in Canada, Canadian mining companies became much more active in that part of the world. BC Bearing would have to follow its old customers, in addition to finding new ones.

She first visited Chile in 1988 on a trade mission with Michael Wilson, then trade minister in the Conservative government of Brian Mulroney. She emerged as a vocal supporter of free trade, and was a member of the government's international trade advisory committee. In 1993 the company entered the Chilean market with a joint venture partner. In 1997, after the signing of the Canada–Chile free trade agreement, BC Bearing bought out its local partner and began expanding on its own in that mineral-rich country.

Chile accounts for about 12 percent of the company's total sales. Wendy holds a lot of hope for its Chilean operations, as the mining industry expands in that part of the world. But she admits that the company has had problems in Chile — basically startup glitches stemming from the company's fast expansion over the past two years. Bill Dix says there have also been cultural barriers — BC Bearing has had to learn how business is done in that Spanish-speaking country. For a while, Robby's son Chris was attached to the Chilean subsidiary.

Even with this expansion, Wendy found some time to devote to a succession plan. She admits that she delayed the process too long: she had wanted to start planning as early as the 1960s, but events always seemed to push succession to the side. By the 1990s, the situation was getting serious — the children were moving into their forties and fifties, and she wouldn't be around forever. The children already owned one-third of the company's shares. When Rob MacPherson died, he had left them to his four offspring.

BC Bearing's board of directors has played a large role in executing Wendy's succession plans. She depends heavily on this group of family members, long-time friends, and community figures. (Among the eight, she and Robby are the two family directors.) One of the critical events, instrumental in getting all the children onside, was a retreat held in late 1997, at which the four children got together to iron things out. Accompanying them was director Gordon Steele, an entrepreneur himself and a cousin of the family. Wendy herself did not attend. "You've got to figure out where you've got to go — it wasn't easy," daughter Penny says of that tense weekend.

Under the final arrangement, Wendy's shares are to be divided equally among the four kids. (Their sister Sandra will also get shares, but the other four will then buy her out.) However, voting control will be in the hands of a trust, Wendy McDonald Holdings. The trustees — who will ultimately determine the voting direction of the company — are three directors. Two of these, cousin Gordon Steele and Ottawa lawyer Brian Stocks, are outsiders. The third,

Robby MacPherson, is an insider. Significantly, Robby is slated to become CEO when his mother leaves the company.

On an October morning, outside Robby McPherson's second-floor office the Fraser River is carrying masses of logs on their way downstream. Robby is clearly pleased with how things have turned out. As the family member who is also a member of the voting trust, he feels he is first among equals. As for his mother's future role, "she stays in the company as long as she damn well wants. It's her company. She can do anything she wants. She leaves me alone to run the company, so I don't care if she's CEO. The suppliers want someone on top."

But when his mother goes, won't things become unglued? Robby points out that there is a shareholders' agreement among the children to settle any unsolvable disputes. The assumption is that if one owner doesn't like how things are going, the others will buy him or her out. Asked what else has to be resolved, Robby is adamant: "We're done." Will they still get along? "Got to. The other option isn't good."

His sister Penny insists that Robby should not be considered the dominant sibling. "I don't think it will be his company, not in my mind. That's why mother has built it like she has, that everyone is basically in different areas. We've had our own family meetings and it's no secret if Robby retires, I will take his position." Wendy, too, is adamant that the company does not belong to Robby just because he will be one of the three trustees. She insists that the two directors involved in the trust are fair people "and they would know how to deal with things."

Robby admits that the company could change as events unfold. Currently he is comfortable with the executive team's mix of family managers, old loyalists, and outside recruits. He also concedes that the company could conceivably be sold at some point, but it's important now that family members are in control. He believes that family companies are different from other kinds of businesses. "We do look at our employees in a different way than public companies do. We go farther than the standard company in terms of employees and their problems." Could BC Bearing have an outside CEO? "Ma has built the company in a certain way. If the right person is in here and understands the family structure and where it is coming from, and the family wants that spirit to exist, I suppose it is possible." Penny is also fairly open to the idea of an outsider as CEO at some point. It's a matter of capability, pure and simple, she says. It reflects her view that the business should be the business and the family should remain the family, and that the two are different spheres.

Her own daughters are not interested in the company. One is a full-time mother and the other works in the vibrant West Coast film industry. "They both worked here but don't like the family dynamics. When I die my shares will likely be sold. That hurts — I've invested a lot in the company and I'm proud of what I've done. My brothers will probably buy my stake and it will stay in the family."

Conversations with family members in late 1998 suggested that, while the succession plan was in place, siblings were having trouble coming to grips with the implications. One of the main problems was communication: family members were not talking to each other about what their new roles would mean. When they tried to communicate, they did so through their mother, which put a heavy load on a woman in her mid-seventies, even one as formidable as Wendy McDonald. But a year later, Robby, Penny, Scott, and Bill had made some progress. The four had held two family meetings in September 1999 and resolved to schedule regular monthly meetings. Many of the fears and tensions seemed to be lifting as the three brothers and their sister began to plan for life after Mom. And they were talking more among themselves.

Penny says the family is determined to move toward a more active board, and that two long-serving directors have retired. And when would Wendy finally retire as CEO and let Robby take over? Penny says that her mother won't change her role until she is comfortable that the four children are working well together.

So where will BC Bearing be in ten years? Robby is confident the company will still be in operation and under family ownership, although a lot bigger, both domestically and internationally. BC Bearing would like to expand dramatically through internal growth and acquisitions. It is developing alliances, including a working relationship with Canadian Bearing of Mississauga, the dominant bearing distributor in Ontario. But the company has hit a bump. In 1998, the family had been aiming at sales of $175 million in the year 2000. But 1998–99 turned out to be a dismal period for BC Bearing, which got hammered by the slumping B.C. economy, the downturn in some commodity prices, and the problems in its Chilean unit. Penny Omnès concedes the company would now be happy with sales of $150 million in 2000.

Behind the scenes, BC Bearing is trying to set the foundations for higher growth. It is improving its computer capability, with a goal of becoming Web-enabled for customers and suppliers. As customers simplify their supply chains, the strategy is shifting away from individual orders toward integrated supply contracts with big customers. "We will supply a full bucket of products. Instead of a [client] company having one hundred suppliers, they have ten," explains

Penny. BC Bearing hopes to be one of those ten. Penny also expects increased competition from rivals moving into Canada from the United States.

It's still a long way ahead in the future, but at some point the McDonalds/MacPhersons/Dixes will have to decide what to do about the third generation. Lance Ross has worked in the business for fifteen years, starting out as a shipping clerk and moving up to the marketing department under Penny Omnès. A university dropout, he has laboured to upgrade his skills through a constant array of courses, and he is very active in the local sales and marketing club. He feels all this activity makes him more useful, and "if something surprising happens, I still will be valuable in the marketplace."

The other third-generation family member who's been active in the company is Robby's son Chris, who worked in Chile for a time before taking a leave of absence from BC Bearing. One reason for Chris's leave was to enable him to spend some time training with a supplier company. The family decided that the young man had been thrown too quickly into a difficult assignment in Chile, and should be given more time to develop his skills. Chris is expected to rejoin the firm and take up a post in Mexico. Meanwhile, Penny's daughter, Penelope Braidwood, thirty-one, had reassessed her career and left the film business to join BC Bearing in late 1999.

Lance scoffs at the idea that it's him against Chris for BC Bearing's future leadership. "This company is large and there is a lot of room to grow. There are a lot of years and a lot of things can happen. I hope each of us has a skill set to complement each other. I chuckle when I hear it's him versus me." Meanwhile, Wendy isn't all that sure she's finished with her succession planning for even the next generation, let alone the third. With just the tiniest glint of mischief in her eyes, she admits: "I may still change it — we'll see how things go. Who knows?"

SIX

THE BENTALLS —
UNCLES AND NEPHEWS

Bob Bentall of Vancouver's Bentall Corp., with his wife, Lynda.

B OB BENTALL ABSOLUTELY REJECTS the idea of the family business. Oh, he believes in families starting businesses, but he disputes the iron law that founders should strive, above all, to ensure that a second generation or a third generation carries it on. He is flatly opposed to dynasty building. "When the founder, or whoever ran the business, finds his time is over, it's wrong to pass it over to the kids," he says passionately. "One-half of one percent of the population has the ability to be a real leader. The chances for an heir to be able to run his father's business is remote."

Strange words indeed from a man who, along with his brother, inherited a major construction company from his father, and who once ran one of the West Coast's most successful and ubiquitous family businesses. The company founded by Charles Bentall built a large chunk of downtown Vancouver. The four towers of the Bentall Centre office complex are one of the city's most visible landmarks. Yet Bob Bentall clearly has the courage of his convictions. He blocked his own nephew David's ascendency to the presidency of the Bentall Corp., the family's property development company, questioning the younger man's competence. Largely for that reason, he split painfully from his brother Clark, David's father. The two factions carved the company in two, with Bob taking the property development side and Clark's family the construction company. He sold Bentall Corp.'s control block to outsiders and championed a chief executive officer from outside the family. And he basically blocked his own children from reaping vast rewards from what their grandfather, uncle, and father created.

Still chairman of Bentall Corp., now a publicly traded company, Bob Bentall, seventy-seven, pours most of his energy and enthusiasm and his money into his private charity, which operates a performing arts centre for talented Vancouver inner-city children. Interviewed in a boardroom overlooking the neighbourhood where the centre is located, he is adamant that this is where his passion lies now. In fact, the centre admirably reflects his views on family and business. He is trying to unlock the talents of inner-city youth who lack the resources and family support to succeed. In the same vein, he feels that wealthy and advantaged family business members shouldn't be handed the good life on a platter. They should find what they are really good at and pursue it on their own.

About a mile away, in downtown Vancouver, a few blocks from the Bentall Centre, Bob Bentall's nephew David is also finding a life away from the family business. David is a bit at loose ends. He was pushed out of Bentall Corp. a decade ago because of his Uncle Bob's opposition to his becoming president. Now, through a forced auction process, he has reluctantly sold his controlling interest in Dominion Construction, the company that was the cornerstone of the Bentall empire and that he headed for ten years.

For the first time in his life he is not part of a Bentall family enterprise. Like his Uncle Bob, he is involved with helping disadvantaged kids — in his case as part of a Christian inner-city organization. As he spoke to me he was borrowing the organization's office for a while as he plotted his future career. He has managed to find a new challenge: he is one of the leading organizers spearheading the campaign by Vancouver and Whistler to bid for the 2010 Winter Olympics.

David Bentall, forty-four, is a tall man with thinning hair and an open, gentle, and vulnerable manner. His feelings run very close to the surface. He has decidedly mixed emotions about being severed from the business that has been the Bentall life force for eighty years. The auction of Dominion Construction, won by his sister and brother-in-law, was a shock because he had intended to purchase the company himself. True, he had never seen himself as a construction guy — he enjoyed property development, the part of the business kept by Uncle Bob in the big company breakup a decade ago. At the same time, he says, "I would be lying if I said I wasn't disappointed. I would have enjoyed the opportunity to continue to represent my family."

Barney Bentall is also getting on with his life. In fact, he has spent more than thirty years trying to distance himself from the Bentall property empire. A nephew of Bob Bentall and a first cousin of David, Barney, now forty-four, has succeeded marvellously in shaping his own identity outside the family business — he is a popular Canadian rock'n'roll musician. But while he was establishing himself on the bar scene in his twenties, there were times when joining the company seemed an easier alternative to a life playing two-bit clubs in western Canada. When he was twenty he was playing in a bar on Vancouver's Hornby Street in the shadow of the Bentall Centre. He was fired from the gig and found himself sitting down with "some sleazy guy, trying to talk him out of $200 for me and the band. Part of me was saying, 'I don't have to take this,' but another part was saying, 'This is your life, and it's what you make of it.' I knew I needed to make my own way in the world."

That is the closest Barney has come to an epiphany. He deliberately chose the tough, demanding life of a musician over the certainties of a career in a family business. He has watched his cousins grappling with the challenge of finding their separate identities in a world in which the word Bentall means a corporation. "For better or worse, I chose to go out in the world. You have to establish yourself on your own merits." He adds: "When you're playing at some dive in Saskatoon, it really doesn't matter if you're a Bentall."

David, Bob, and Barney Bentall have all been shaped by their relationship to the company, which was founded by Charles Bentall in the early decades of the twentieth century. Their life stories are about how a family business moulds lives, forces choices, causes heartache, and defines people forever. The responses vary widely from person to person: Bob embraced and then rejected the family business concept; David was hurt by it and is now liberated from it; and Barney has spent his life steering clear of it.

Bob and David Bentall do not talk much to each other these days. Mention one's name to the other and a certain frostiness creeps into the conversation. Yet these two men were once close; both are admirable citizens with plenty of sincerity and social commitment. They exemplify the bad things that can happen to good families when a successful business gets in the way. Speaking of his brother Clark and his family, Bob says, "These were not bad people — there were just complex things [we had to deal with]. People went on with their lives." As with the McCains, the Bentall story highlights the strong risk of family breakup once the issue of succession raises its head. This conflict can easily be heightened by a clash of visions about how the business should function. For Bob Bentall's wife Lynda — herself a central player in the breakup — the division was almost inevitable: "In a situation like this, you throw money and power issues into the middle of already difficult relationships."

Barney Bentall has watched the family split unfold from a safe distance. He's the son of Howard Bentall, Bob and Clark's Baptist minister brother. Barney is in a rare position — he is a family insider, yet his career path took him far outside the company. He considers himself lucky to have escaped from the nest. He never had any regrets. "I saw with close proximity what [the business] could do. It's more natural where the company is now." He agrees with his Uncle Bob that you can't keep handing the company off to the following generation. "It's not a workable concept. It exacts a toll on people. Bentall Corp. is doing very well now with professional managers, and it's overseen by a group of well-qualified directors. It is thriving. The family ownership percentage is a smaller piece of a much bigger pie."

Passing on the business is a profoundly damaging exercise, agrees Bob Bentall: "You damage the business and you damage the family." If you want a business to thrive and grow, he says, you have to get the best people to run it. Invariably, these people are not family members. So the owner has to decide how to tap other sources of talent, perhaps by selling to outsiders or handing the business over to employees to run without interference. By keeping family members in the business, you are almost guaranteeing mediocrity, he argues. For example, if the company needs to be downsized, can management trim family members as easily as other, more talented people? Not likely. As for the plight of the heirs, "It's best for children to do what they have a passion for. Then they know when they go into this chosen activity that success is because of themselves."

Looking back, Bob Bentall now regrets that he didn't get out of the company as a young man so that he could head to Alberta to get into business on his own. Not that he didn't enjoy the development game — "I loved the business." He just wishes he had seen all the options. He might have changed his engineering specialty — to mining, say, from civil engineering — or taken on a different field such as law or accounting. But there was never any question that he would continue in the business. After all, he was a Bentall.

Few families are so much a part of Vancouver's fabric as the Bentalls. They built chunks of the city, including Bentall Centre and the Sun Tower, and Dominion Construction put up GM Place, the city's hockey and basketball showplace. The company can be traced back to Charles Bentall, a British immigrant who came to Vancouver in 1911 and joined a fledgling company called Dominion Construction. Eight years after Dominion hired him, Charles Bentall bought the entire company. He came from a poor farming background in England, and his spirit was constantly buoyed by his strong Baptist faith. He had a well-developed sense of broader social goals. After his son Bob decided to join the company, Charles emphasized to him the responsibilities of corporate stewardship. His precepts were these: "Whatever you earn, you give back; you take care of staff; you live within your means; all this money is not yours." These words would guide the son in later years when he was wrestling with the future of the company.

David warmly remembers his grandfather, who died when he was about twenty. Charles was, the grandson recalls, "an unshakeable, immovable rock." He emphasized moderation and thrift. He would tell his grandchildren that if they saved $90, he would always put up the final $10 to buy a $100 Canada Savings Bond. Charles's life was remarkable for its lack of ostentatiousness. He lived in a beautiful downtown residence but for years only occupied part of the house. He was his church's Sunday School superintendent for more than thirty years. "He would give you a hug and hold his face close against yours," David recalls. "There was a warmth there, but he was also a man's man." He wouldn't tolerate what he considered inappropriate behaviour. "If there was anything that was an untruth, if anyone was caught stealing, there would be a severe response. He was clear about what was right and what was wrong."

Barney Bentall was also attached to his grandfather, even though he grew up in Calgary. "I would sit for hours and listen to his stories," he recalls. Barney deeply appreciated the old man's personal account of starting something from zero. Family members saw this connection between grandfather and grandson and assumed that Barney would be pulled into the business. But that was not the real link between two men. Barney, like his grandfather, saw himself as an entrepreneur. As a kid in high school he started his own small construction company, whose major product was barbwire fences. As a young man he built his own house and furniture. In fact, Barney felt that building and engineering were more in his genes than rock music. But the modern construction business wasn't about building, he discovered. It had become highly specialized — a far cry from when Charles Bentall, a self-taught immigrant with a grade-school education, could design whole buildings. Barney couldn't see himself in the modern development game — the roles were too confining. Music, which came less naturally to him, allowed him to be more creative and to be involved in more facets of the creative process.

To Barney, his grandfather was "a very strong man" who was able to emigrate from England, penniless and unknown, and build a major company. Such a powerful mystique creates a challenge for the generations that follow: "Everyone who comes after him in the business wonders, 'What am I made of? Was all this just handed to me?'" It's somewhat easier for the second generation, says Barney. These people can grasp the significance of the company, the struggle to create it, and the fear of losing it. The troubles come when the third generation tries to find its place in the world. Barney spent a good part of his early life trying to stay out of this third-generation trap.

As Vancouver grew into a major financial and corporate centre, Dominion Construction flourished; it spun off a sister company, Bentall Corp., which emerged as one of Canada's premier commercial property developers. Two of Charles Bentall's sons, Clark and his younger brother Bob, came into the company. Barney's father Howard, a minister, took a radically different role, although he would inherit shares in the company and play a part in charting its future. Howard, who preached in Calgary, had to be one of the most affluent Baptist ministers in Canada. He developed his own charitable foundation, which gives money to various causes.

In 1955 Charles Bentall had a severe heart attack that forced him out of the president's role. Clark, the older son, took over. It was not an easy time for Bob, who resented the primacy of his older brother. In later years he admitted that he and Clark fought some fierce battles. "The more Clark would say no to my expressions of how the business should be run, the more I would fight to get my way," Bob once said in a speech to the Vancouver chapter of the Canadian Association of Family Enterprise. Yet the brothers were able to find ways to work together. Clark proved to be the consummate marketer. David says his father tried to understand what the customer wanted and what kinds of services, dimensions, and materials were needed for a project. Bob was the inside man, a cerebral type much taken to management, strategy, and financing.

The company was growing and could easily accommodate both men and their styles. Clark visited New York in the 1960s and was much taken with the Rockefeller Center. He took this vision of a spectacular multitower office complex back to Vancouver and turned it into the Bentall Centre. There was no overt talk that David would go into the family business, but there was a lot of intangible reinforcement. In fact, explicit discussions of succession were avoided until it was far too late. His father used to send his school report cards to his uncles, perhaps to impress them and get them to support David's claim for leadership. As a boy he caught one other strong hint: "One day in grade five, Dad said, 'Turn off the TV and do your homework because you can't be president unless you do your homework.' Dad always assumed I would head up the company."

He went off to the University of British Columbia, but not for an engineering degree like his father, uncle, and the company's other senior officers: David took a business degree instead. He got married in his last year of university. While he was on his honeymoon in Hawaii, Uncle Bob called him asking if he would like to come work with Bentall Corp. over the summer. David is still sensitive to the irony that it was Bob who extended the invitation. At that point David saw himself and his uncle working as a team building up the property development business.

Meanwhile, Barney was growing up in Calgary, living a fairly normal middle-class life far removed from any reminders that he was part of a power-ful business family. For him, the Bentall legacy hit home during the wonderful summers he and his family spent on the coast, mainly at the family compound on Keats Island in Howe Sound. His uncles and grandfather had cottages and boats on the island. His father Howard kept a powerboat there on which he would transport his family for extended tours of the coast. And there were the physical monuments in Vancouver — the downtown skyscrapers that carried the Bentall name.

During the summers, Charles Bentall was very much the patriarch trying to keep his family together. He would assemble the extended clan for barbecues once a week. Barney admired this effort: "This was a man trying to keep his family strong." But when Charles Bentall died there was no one to really hold it together. For Barney there were distractions — his own growing family and his life as a musician. He began to question why he needed to meet with his far-flung cousins, since he really had nothing in common with them. "What is the reason to get along except for the company?" he would ask. Still, today he feels some sadness that the cousins do not see one another anymore. Attendance at the summer place and at family gatherings had once been mandatory. When the core began to collapse, the pendulum swung abruptly the other way. Nowadays he would like the family to find some middle ground where members could meet because they really want to.

But if he was physically removed from the company, Barney still felt forces pulling him into Bentall Corp.'s vortex. Howard felt that Barney and his three sisters should find their own way in life, but he worried about the instability of the music business. There was pressure for the young man to attend univer-sity, clearly as part of a career path that would lead to Bentall Corp. And Barney did go for two years, taking arts and commerce courses before decid-ing that it was not really advancing his music career. He quit and devoted himself to music. There was a "ten-year freeze" during which he and his dad did not really find a common ground. But as Barney developed as a musician, and his reputation spread, his family began to accept his decision. When *Maclean's* ran a profile on the bright new rock star, Howard Bentall agreed that his career was probably a good thing. At one point in their reconciliation, Howard told his son that he had felt some of the same pressures to join the company. "He knew how I felt," Barney says. "It brought me to tears."

Meanwhile, David was doing well in the family business but yearning for a broader experience. He was prone to questioning his elders' authority and often dissatisfied with how the company conducted business. So in 1983–84, against his own father's wishes, he took a job with Cadillac Fairview Ltd., a major developer based in Toronto. He now remembers it as "the happiest two years of my life." He had gone to Toronto with the idea that he would stay for a couple of years, get some varied experience, then settle back into a long and satisfying career with Bentall Corp. "I think that if I could do it over, I wouldn't come back unless I was invited back. I reapproached the company after two years and they managed a way to reintroduce me to the business."

He came back to a company whose unified facade was starting to crack. Clark and Bob had run the company amicably for years, papering over any philosophical differences. For example, Bob had argued for a stronger board than Clark could countenance. Then a series of events blew things apart. Bob had become increasingly concerned about the viability of the family business concept and was arguing more and more for leadership by professional management. Clearly, that could leave David out of the loop. Meanwhile, Clark's aspirations for David, and David's own hopes and dreams inside the company, were beginning to grow. Bob had joined the newly formed Canadian Association of Family Enterprise, which brought together family companies to share their stories and their solutions. But the sad experiences he heard from many CAFE members, rather than inspiring him, only highlighted for him how family businesses could degenerate into snake pits.

As often happens in these family business sagas, a powerful outsider with some strong views entered the scene. Bob invited Lynda Wager, a psychologist and consultant, to address a meeting of CAFE's Vancouver chapter. He was so impressed with her message that he invited her to work with him at Bentall Corp., where he had succeeded Clark as president. In her view, the family business was an outmoded, even primitive form of business and social organization. The model might have worked in agricultural times, but it did not in modern industrial societies. She endorsed a kind of tough love approach — give the children education, a way in the world, but show no favouritism and extend no special treatment. Simply tell them it is extremely unlikely that they will inherit the company — and even less likely that they will manage it.

David had worked hard to master the business, but sensed he was being frozen out by his Uncle Bob. A meeting was called in 1986 to discuss the future of the company, and David was advised that he did not have to be there. "I think any objective observer would find it strange if there was a meeting called to consider the future of the business, and the only member of the next generation who was working in the business — myself — was advised it was not necessary to be there."

Led by Charles, the Bentalls had developed the institution of the annual family council. It was a social occasion, but it also had a serious side. In a 1985 speech to the local CAFE group, Bob described how these gatherings worked: "As the president, I give a state of the union message and both Clark and I see ourselves as being as vulnerable to penetrating questions as the executives of any public company. In a very real sense, it's our annual general meeting." Family forums are a concept much loved by consultants and experts in family business circles. Such councils bring all the clan members and their spouses together for a frank exchange of views. It is a chance for the senior family members in the company to explain what is going on and how the business is performing, in a context where there is also a lot of socializing and levity.

Lynda Wager felt that the Bentall family councils had deteriorated into brag sessions at which members flaunted their material wealth, their lifestyles, and their children's accomplishments. In 1986, Bob invited Lynda to the family council in the hope that she could unleash some of the honest feelings that people had about the company. Her hard-edged comments triggered outpourings of emotion among the thirty-five to forty Bentall kin in attendance. People cried and screamed at each other, Lynda recalls. The Bentalls never again held these family forums. "Bob was shocked," says Lynda. "Until then, no one had talked about the jealousy and anger."

Barney was at that meeting but is reluctant to discuss the details. It is safe to say that it was "a bit dramatic." He attributes the split that followed largely to the succession issue. "It's sad, but once you get past the pain and the fractured relationships, it may be all for the better." He is relieved that for all the bad feelings, the conflict never entered the courts.

The Bentalls grappled to find a solution to the rupture between Bob on one side, and Clark and David on the other. "Bob came up with a plan for the future of the company and it did not include [Clark's] son," Lynda recalls. So it was decided that the only real solution was to split the organization in two. Bob wanted to keep and run the development arm, and he was supported by Howard and by the Worster family, the descendants of a former trusted manager, who held a minority interest. Clark and David were handed the old Dominion Construction Co., the business that Charles Bentall bought back in 1918. The two brothers went their own ways, rarely speaking to each other, and in recent years Clark Bentall's health has deteriorated. The conflict, Bob says, "was a pivotal event but it should not define the Bentall family and the company." The problem was that "we needed to be professionally managed and he [Clark] was against that. He felt it should be run by the family." David's response is that professional management doesn't necessarily exclude the family, if someone in the family has been trained to fill that role.

Bob's relationship with Lynda Wager in time became more than professional. He was divorced from his first wife, and married the consultant. He also continued to practise what he preached by moving Bentall Corp. away from a family business model. In 1992 the Bentall family sold 23 percent of the company to New Jersey–based Prudential Insurance Co. of America and a B.C. government pension fund. In 1994, Bob stepped aside as CEO in favour of a bright young nonfamily outsider, Mark Shuparski. Then in 1996 the family sold 57 percent of the development operation to the Caisse de dépôt et placement du Québec, the mammoth Quebec pension fund. The $70 million deal packed a powerful symbolic punch — control had passed from the Bentalls, the West Coast entrepreneurial clan, to an institutional investor, from eastern Canada, no less.

Bentall Corp. was poised to enter the twenty-first century as one of Canada's largest owners and developers of commercial office space. Under Shuparski it was laying the groundwork for a fifth tower of the Bentall Centre, but the Vancouver market was no longer its main focus for expansion. It had moved aggressively into Seattle and was planning to spend hundreds of millions of dollars on a California foray. As of mid-1999 about 63 percent of the company's assets were in the United States, with 56 percent in Seattle and 7 percent in California. According to Shuparski, the company was planning to increase its California holdings by 20 to 25 percent over the next two to three years. Company officials stated that even so, Bentall Corp. would retain its strong Vancouver presence.

Driven by his and Lynda's uncompromising views, Bob Bentall removed his own children from the company largesse. Originally, he had frozen the value of his estate, kept the voting shares for himself, and issued nonvoting shares to his three kids, Bob Jr., Laura, and Ruth. "And they got education, houses, and cars," he adds. But one day, one of his daughters came to him and said the shares meant nothing to her — that they were more of a burden than anything else. So he bought the shares back from all three children and channelled them into a foundation. His children would no longer participate in the growth of Bentall Corp. Today he senses that his children harbour some resentment over the deal they accepted, "but I believe in my heart, after I'm gone the kids will say, 'Dad did the right thing.' In time, they'll come to grips with it."

Lynda says that otherwise, the Bentall children would have come to develop a dependency ethic. They would be constantly waiting for the money to bail them out. "There is serious damage done to children by creating a safety net,"

she says. "They've grown so much since then, they are growing as people."
Passing on the family company, she concludes, represents "an ego drive that
takes on damaging proportions." Bob continues with that thread. "When you
pass on money, a father is really buying friendship and adulation from the
kids." He says his son Bob works with a family camp ministry on Keats Island.
Daughter Laura has been a secretary at a church in Modesto, California, and
Ruth is living in Vancouver.

After going public and selling great chunks of the company to outside
investors, Bob, Howard, and the Worster family still hold about 20 percent of
Bentall Corp. Bob and Lynda have transferred their own shares to their foundation for deprived Vancouver kids. It provides everything from counselling
to clothing and tutoring, but a very large component is Ailanthus, the performing arts centre that the couple built on Commercial Drive in Vancouver.
Unprepossessing from the street, the centre is bright and airy, with a gymna-
sium, workrooms, and computers. From the centre's boardroom there is a view
of neat houses and yards — not your typical mean streets. But Bob and Lynda
insist that drug deals are regularly conducted in the parking lot.

The Bentalls are not your typical bleeding heart social activists. They are
scornful of the welfare state, which they say is creating a dependency culture in
the downtowns of cities. There are lots of programs for youth, they argue, but
nothing that truly challenges them, that strives to turn exceptional young people
into potential leaders. They have created a tough-minded and unabashedly élitist
organization the purpose of which is to provide opportunities for only the
brightest and most talented children. The couple is clearly interventionist —
they closely monitor marks in school and provide tutoring. The idea is to strip
young people away from this easy "socialist culture" and challenge them. It's
exactly the same tonic that they prescribe for children of entrepreneurs. "My
own kids had a great safety net and it took away their motivation," Bob says.

The foundation's structure reflects the Bentalls' contempt for classic charitable organizations. Their operation functions on a twenty-eight-year plan —
at the end of that period, the couple will have liquidated the foundation and
spent all the money. (The centre cost about $5 million to build; operating costs
are about $3.5 million a year. The Bentalls were also building a new, $1 million
residence to house some childen on site.) There is no succession plan, nor are
there any entrenched vested interests. The land and building will be given away
at the end of the foundation's life. Ailanthus depends on no public funding or
fund-raising, and expects nothing back financially from its bright young
protégés. Says Bob: "All we ask of those kids is nothing more than if a child
crosses their path some day, they will do something to help that child."

Bob remains a proselytizer on how family businesses should work. He believes strongly in activist boards, not just yes-men and yes-women serving the interests of the family. He argues that when Clark and he were running Bentall Corp., the company didn't really have a board, just a meeting each year to file the annual report. When the two brothers split, Bob put a real board in place.

He also dismisses the common view that family companies treat employees with more compassion — that they draw their workers into a more caring culture that reflects the close and warm relationships of the family owners. Bob says that's hogwash. Because of the lack of accountability in family companies, employees often feel they have an obligation to butter up their bosses. Lynda supports his view: "The moment the family is out of the company, you hear employees say, 'Now I'll tell you the real story.' When they're honest, employees see the company as incredibly paternalistic." Also, employees face tremendous pressures in their relationships with family members. For example, they get nervous when dealing with an underperforming family member. Can they use discipline? Can they fire? Ultimately, the company suffers from this ambiguity.

David Bentall, meanwhile, is learning to cope with life outside Dominion Construction. The construction company acquired in the family split was not a small business — annual sales amounted to about $275 million. David shared the ownership with his two sisters, Helen and Mary. In 1993, after three-and-a-half years with Dominion, David was handed the presidency; two years later he became CEO. He brought a more aggressive marketing approach to the company, which he believes helped it prosper.

But in early 1998 he and his brother-in-law Phil George, Mary's husband, agreed it would be much better if the company was owned entirely by one of the three family parties, and David decided to make a takeover bid. The three groups could not agree on a price, which triggered an auction process to settle the ownership and the price. Helen decided to sell, and in the sawoff between David and his other sister, Phil and Mary George ended up submitting the higher bid. "My brother-in-law felt the business was worth more than I did," shrugs David, who still seems dazed by the turn of events. At first, David intended to stay on as president while retaining a small shareholding in Dominion. But he decided that the Georges should be able to bring in their own president. After more than twenty years, David was not involved in a Bentall family company.

Now liberated from his status as an heir, David says he has learned some hard lessons. At least one of them lies close to his Uncle Bob's view: Don't lose perspective about the sanctity of the family company. "A family business is only a legal construct," he says. "Don't get your shirt in a knot over it." Also, children who are potential heirs owe it to themselves and to those in the family to work outside the family business for a fairly long stint. "For me two years were not enough. Five as a minimum makes sense — five to ten years wouldn't be too long. You get a sense of what's yours and what comes from your family. There's no substitute for that." (Barney would argue that a few years working for another company in the same industry doesn't really add up to finding your own way in life.)

David, an avid athlete, turns to a sports metaphor to clinch his idea: "If the coach's kid is on the team, the coach can't help but be particularly interested in his own son. Kids should play on teams that are coached by someone else. There has to be a chance to have a sense of your own self outside of that."

David believes that almost all family business leaders want their offspring to do well in the business, and almost all family members active in the business want to succeed. Yet the existing owners have the power to decide when the next generation will have the chance to lead: "The power falls to those who have it until they decide to relinquish it. It will always be that way." Some next-generation family members try to grasp power before it is surrendered. But succession is *always* timed by the preceding generation. Sons and daughters have to recognize this reality, and if they don't like it they should move on to something else.

Also, family members should be careful about what kind of informal roles they play in the company. When David was in the business, he was advised by a trusted third party that he should be "a defecation disturber." "I believed in being an agent of change, to help improve the business. I believe one of the prerequisites of leadership is a healthy disregard for the status quo. I took this man's advice and openly sought change in the business. Looking back, the company did need change, but the son of the chairman should not be leading that change." He suggests that young people in family business either support the leadership or, once again, move on to another employer.

He takes to heart Lord Acton's axiom that power corrupts and absolute power corrupts absolutely. "I have tried to hold power lightly," he says. "[At Dominion Construction] I sought to have an executive committee and a board, not a rubber-stamp board." Like his Uncle Bob, he supports the idea of a powerful and independent board that can mediate on divisive issues: "When family communications broke down, my father and uncle didn't have a court of friends or advisers to fall back on."

As for his own children, he doesn't know what's in store. He has a daughter in university, and a son who shows some interest in architecture. For the moment, he has the Olympic bid to keep him busy. In addition, he is planning to write at least one book — no, not about the Bentalls, that great curse and pride of his life, but rather about male friendship. He and two other Vancouver men are part of a ten-year covenant of friendship. He'll write about what that has meant to him.

David has developed yet another fascinating sideline, one that's packed with irony. He travelled east to Toronto in the spring of 1999 to be part of a panel of speakers for the Business Families Foundation, sponsored by Philippe and Nan-B de Gaspé Beaubien. The other panelists were Sonja Bata, a director of the Bata Shoe Organization, and Fred Eaton, former president of the now defunct family department store chain. The de Gaspé Beaubiens were so impressed that they invited David to become one of the foundation's facilitators — a prospect that both excites and amuses him. "I will be an adviser to family businesses based on the scars on my back," he jokes.

He has another reason to smile. His ailing father recently celebrated his eighty-fourth birthday. Clark's brother Bob came to the party, and so did Barney's father Howard. There was no discussion of succession. Bob and David had a chance to chat about the house where David lives with his father and family — a house built by Bentall Corp. with Bob as the project manager. Maybe time does heal, after all.

Once friends, then adversaries, and now trying to find a middle ground, Bob and David Bentall are coming to grips with life without Bentall Corp., although Bob remains chairman. Surprisingly, their attitudes are moving closer together. Says David: "I have been hurt often in the family business. I'm stepping off the field and will not play the family business game anymore. Now that I have left the business, it is clearer to me that for a long time, I was compromising who I am by trying to conform to the mould of our ongoing business."

Barney Bentall is simply relieved that he never got involved that deeply and that his music has proved to be so personally rewarding. Rejecting Bentall Corp. meant getting on with a real life: "I don't know what possessed me then, but I knew very clearly — I had strong feelings that the family business was not the path I should take."

SEVEN

THE DE GASPÉ BEAUBIENS —
POWER COUPLE

Philippe and Nan-b de Gaspé Beaubien in their office on the thirty-third floor of Place Ville Marie.

THE YOUNG HARVARD BUSINESS school graduate came home to work as a salesman in his family's business. The return was a disaster. His father had built the electrical supply business through his hard work and iron will, and he wasn't about to share authority with a twenty-six-year-old kid. Father and son quarrelled constantly, until one seemingly trivial event broke the back of their business relationship. A customer came to the family offices asking for a lamp. The buyer might normally have been directed to the second-floor showroom, but the son — for reasons he cannot recall — agreed to fetch one from the upstairs storeroom. He was walking back down with the lamp when he confronted his father on the stairs. "What are you doing?" the father demanded. When the son explained, the father exploded: "The showroom is upstairs. It's not downstairs. You take that lamp back up to the showroom and bring the customer up — right now."

Philippe de Gaspé Beaubien II placed the lamp in the middle of the stairs and brushed past his father. "He looked at me as I walked out, never to return again, and it broke his heart and it broke my heart," says the son, now seventy-one and looking back on events forty-five years ago. "I loved him dearly and I would still go home every Sunday to see him as I used to do." But the two men never worked together again. Within five years, Philippe says, his voice breaking up with guilt, the electrical supply business had fallen into bankruptcy. Yet today he can empathize with his father. His view had been, "I built this company and I set the rules." It was all perfectly human and understandable.

Philippe de Gaspé Beaubien can detect a pattern here. His family has been doing business in Quebec for more than 350 years. That is *thirteen* generations. Yet it is hardly a record of unsullied accomplishment. Never has the Beaubien family succeeded in passing a family company in its entirety from one generation to the next. His bitter departure from his own father's business — because of an argument over a lamp — is a sadly typical chapter in the annals of the Beaubien family. Today Philippe sits on the other edge of the generational chasm. He is watching as his own three children — all in their thirties — take control of Telemedia Inc., the Montreal-based broadcasting and publishing company that he has built over the past thirty years, and he is praying that family history won't repeat itself.

That 350-year record of succession futility has served as a kind of negative inspiration for the courtly Philippe and his elegant wife Nan-b. Memories of past failures have driven them to pursue every possible means for ensuring that their own succession works. It has also propelled them into high-profile roles as the power couple of family-business counselling in Canada. They are absolutely obsessed about the subject of how to manage and maintain a family enterprise. Stung by their own family's track record, the de Gaspé Beaubiens are making enormous efforts to follow best practices in their own company, seeking rational and progressive ways to pass the business on to their children, Philippe III, thirty-nine, Nanon, thirty-eight, and François, thirty-seven. "We have decided to try to see if we can break the mould," says Philippe, sitting in his office on the thirty-third floor of Montreal's Place Ville Marie complex, with its clear view of Mount Royal. "We decided we would like to see if we can do it in our own family — and only time will tell us if it will work."

More than that, the de Gaspé Beaubiens have devoted a chunk of their personal fortune to building the Montreal-based Business Families Foundation (formerly the Institute for Family Enterprise), which is dedicated to educating families in business on how to manage their enterprises, particularly the issue of succession. They attract clans from around the world to sessions at which case studies are picked apart and experts from Harvard Business School and other emerging hotbeds of family business studies share their wisdom. Family retainers and consultants are instructed on how to advise owners of family businesses. Their motivation is purely altruistic, the couple says. "We're devoting most of our time to giving back to the community and helping those families," says Philippe.

The de Gaspé Beaubiens offer the Cadillac of family business courses.

However, Philippe insists that the term should be "families in business, not family businesses." The phrase *family business*, he explains, has taken on negative connotations. When fast-growing companies in the United States were recently surveyed, he says, they would not admit to being family businesses, even though family members were prominent in their ownership and management. For them, "family business" was equivalent to nepotism, incompetence, and Mom-and-Pop (i.e., small-bit) operations — nothing they would want to be associated with.

The company that spawned the foundation, Telemedia, is certainly no insignificant business. It is the publisher of some of Canada's major consumer magazines, such as *Canadian Living*, *TV Guide*, and *Homemakers*. The company's role in magazine publishing propelled the family's youngest child, François, Telemedia's head of publishing, into prominence as the Canadian magazine industry's leading spokesman against American split-run magazines. Some critics argued that the principal result of an anti–split run policy in Ottawa would have been to shelter from competition the two dominant domestic magazine publishers, Telemedia and Maclean Hunter. The telegenic François lost his battle: under a compromise agreement reached in May 1999, American magazines have been allowed some market penetration in Canada. Recognizing the new reality, Telemedia was seeking a minority U.S. partner for its magazine division.

As a broadcaster, Telemedia has been heavily involved in the consolidation of Canada's radio industry. Over an eight-month period in 1998–99, it emerged as a national radio broadcaster, adding forty-seven stations across Canada to its existing stable of twenty-seven clustered in Quebec and Ontario. The new stations, in British Columbia, Alberta, the Maritimes, and Northern Ontario, join a complement that already includes Montreal's CITE-FM and Toronto's all-sports THE FAN.

A public company until recently, Telemedia was taken private by the de Gaspé Beaubien family in the fall of 1997. The stock had not done well since the company launched its initial public offering of nonvoting shares in 1986. The buyback mollified some unhappy institutional shareholders, who got a chance to cash out their underperforming investments. Philippe says the children felt that a simplified ownership would make it easier for them to make decisions about the business, and the buyback does not preclude them going public again when they see fit.

The de Gaspé Beaubiens are an impressive couple. Philippe is tall and patrician, given to wearing pinstriped shirts with plain white collars. Nan-b at sixty-three looks fifteen years younger, with her unlined face, blond hair, and tasteful suits and blouses. The couple are famous for their singlemindedness, determination, and ability to extricate whatever they want from any situation. The force of their personalities is such that they are not universally loved, but they are never underestimated. Some observers say they are so strong-minded, so domineering, they surely couldn't give up the reins of the family business all that eagerly. They appear to be a francophone version of Tom and Sonja Bata — a very strong business and marital partnership and a hard act for any kids to follow. And yet they have made their exit moves — they no longer have any ownership or management links with Telemedia, although Nan-b still sits on the board of Gasbeau, the family holding company. They haven't physically moved very far away — the parents' foundation occupies space in Telemedia's head offices in Montreal, although Philippe insists that the glass walls between the two offices are more like steel barriers. He does not meddle, he maintains, although he does talk to his children informally a lot. And obviously, he still cares about the business and the role of his children in it.

The children have informed him that there is not going to be one single business leader in their generation; rather, they are going to share authority in the family holding company by setting up an "office of the chief executive officer," consisting of all three of them. Their father shakes his head — "I think it is crazy" — and worries that such ambiguity at the top never works. His training is from the Harvard Business School, which in his time espoused a theory of leadership based on a military structure. There was no place for splitting leadership in the organizational chart. And yet, he muses, surveys of family businesses show that many owners fully expect that in the next generation, their firms will be run by teams of family members, not just a single entrepreneur. Teamwork is in the spirit of the age, he admits — look what is happening in today's workplace. He worries about this three-headed structure. Even so, he says he is very supportive and is trying to stay out of their way.

He is also wary of the history his children are swimming against — a history both glorious and futile. Philippe can trace his Canadian family directly back to the 1630s and 1640s, when his ancestors emigrated from France — from Britanny and Amiens — and established themselves as coureurs de bois and fur traders. This trading habit took them to the far ends of the North American continent. His forebears helped found the cities of Chicago and Detroit and ranged as far to the southwest as the current state of New Mexico. Warming to the story, Philippe talks about Charles Beaubien, who journeyed from Quebec to St. Louis, where he worked for a French trading company, and then took the Santa Fé Trail all the way to what is now New Mexico. He was captured by natives and pestered by the Spanish and yet became a wealthy trader in that part of the world. In time, Charles became a huge landowner with holdings of two million acres. But he lost a lot of that land to expropriation by the expansive U.S. government. "Our family lost a lot of land to American governments," Philippe wryly observes.

Scratch a piece of Québécois commercial history and you will find a Beaubien. They were seigneurs, importers and exporters, financiers, and brewers. Frontenac Brewery, which became part of the Carling O'Keefe group, was once a Beaubien family holding. The history encompasses commercial and investment banking, including the establishment of Lévesque Beaubien, still one of Quebec's financial services powers. They bought and sold real estate, founded hospitals, and provided land for the largest Montreal cemetery. All this enterprise was admirable, but little of it was transferred from one generation to the next. "They thought about succession, but I don't know what it was that made them fail," Philippe muses of his ancestors. "They lived life to the fullest and they let the second generation take over without planning it. The idea was: I'll do my bit and let them take over." Nan-b agrees: "I don't think they ever had the training or they ever thought about the issues and how are you going to solve this, or settle this, or talk about that. They were not people who were good communicators."

Philippe's father was a brewmaster, but the family's Frontenac Brewery was sold out from under him. As the middle child, he had little input in a family that still practised primogeniture — the oldest son inherited all the spoils. So Philippe I founded and built an electrical supply and distribution company. He expected Philippe II to follow in his footsteps, but as the standard bearer of the next generation, the young man was independent-minded. Following an undergraduate degree at the University of Montreal, he applied to the Harvard Business School and its MBA program. "I was listening to my inner soul, I wanted to excel," he says. At the same time, Philippe II, whose mother died when he was twelve, felt family pressure to stay home.

Philippe I was a very strong man who demanded total fealty. It was very much in the spirit of Quebec at that time: the church was all-powerful, and university professors demanded that "you listen to me" and allowed no resistance. "It was a very authoritarian culture, and my father was very authoritarian," Philippe recalls. As a significant fundraiser and organizer for the Liberal Party, he was also a very important man in Quebec. The father adamantly opposed the Harvard adventure, so the younger Philippe was forced to borrow for his tuition and lodging. When he was accepted at Harvard, his father scoffed and suggested he would fail miserably. "That comment was a terrible blow to put on me for I'd never studied in English in my life," Philippe recalls. But the period at Harvard was broadening, and he graduated in the top 10 percent of his MBA class.

While at Harvard he met Nan-bowles (Nan-b) O'Connell, a young beauty with porcelain skin and impeccable Boston lineage, who was a psychology major at Smith College. At that time, marrying an American woman was taboo in the closed community that was Quebec. Also, if they settled in Quebec, Nan-b would have to give up a scholarship she had won to study psychology in Switzerland. Philippe promised the young woman's father that if they got married, he would make sure she gained all the education she wanted — and she did, eventually acquiring a PhD in psychology from McGill. So the two married and moved back to Quebec. "I didn't speak French, had only a vague idea of where Canada was, and had no intention of sacrificing my career to a marriage," she told reporter David Olive in a 1986 interview for *Report on Business* magazine. The two would become a team, and in time Nan-b — while pursuing a career in counselling and therapy — would be recruited by her husband to become Telemedia's head of human resources.

Philippe returned to Montreal from Harvard to immerse himself once more in the family business. He was the oldest of the children, and he was expected to serve. Nan-b was worried about the future, for the two Philippes had trouble getting along. The younger man, armed with a Harvard MBA, did not appreciate the smothering presence of the domineering father. "I was close to my father-in-law," says Nan-b. "I could see both sides. They were into a pattern and they had trouble breaking it." Then came the big blow-up over the lamp on the stairs, and Philippe was gone from the family company, without a job or immediate prospects. Father and son later reconciled personally, but they never patched up their business quarrel.

Philippe drifted into management consulting, which kept him away from his new wife and a young family that was beginning to take shape. It was a good job, and it exposed him to a variety of industries. He was, for example, a consultant to Dominion Corset of Quebec City, which at that time called itself the largest brassiere maker in the British Empire. Today he can't believe that a Canadian company would have held such an exalted position in the garment industry, which has largely departed North America for the Third World.

He was then recruited by McKim Advertising, and joined their Montreal office as a marketing specialist. He still dreamed of having his own business, but he made the most of his new role. At one point he heard that McKim's client, General Foods, was sending a group of people to Montreal from its New York offices. So he had his stepmother cook some fine Québécois tortière, which he served to the assembled New Yorkers. The message was that Quebec had a distinctive cuisine and General Foods would have to tailor its ad messages to that special market.

Later, when General Foods needed a local distributor to handle its new Hostess potato chips in Quebec, Philippe stepped forward and established his own company to bid on the contract. He won the job and quit McKim to become a potato chip distributor. He built the company from 5 to 150 trucks and to 16,000 trade accounts. As the company grew outside Quebec, he had to move to Toronto with his young family. But he sensed a resentment in General Foods against a former advertising colleague who was grabbing a big piece of the action. It was getting harder to do business in this atmosphere, and he eventually sold the distribution company back to General Foods. He went back to working for a Quebec manufacturer.

Then in the mid-1960s, a once-in-a-lifetime opportunity knocked. The organizers of Expo 67, the world's fair scheduled for Canada's centennial year, needed an operations director to manage the fair. They approached Philippe, and he accepted the post, even though he had only three-and-a-half years to prepare an event that generally took more than five. The Russians had pulled out of holding the event, leaving Canada to fill the breach. The organizer who hired him explained: "Philippe, I am looking for a crazy French Canadian. Why? My team is basically English and I need a French Canadian and he has to be crazy because if he takes this job, he has no chance. This is an impossible job." Still in his thirties, Philippe couldn't resist the challenge.

Expo 67 was a nerve-wracking, exciting, and often frustrating 183 days, but it clinched Philippe's reputation as someone who could get things done. After the fair ended he entertained a number of job offers and finally joined a tiny company called Quebec Telemedia, which owned an AM and FM radio franchise in Sherbrooke. The company was controlled by Southam Inc., Power Corp., and a Hamilton, Ontario, entrepreneur named Paul Nathanson. Philippe came on board with the understanding that he would be able to acquire a 15 percent stake. But his demands for ownership were continually put off by the owners.

As Philippe agitated for some ownership, Nathanson and Southam sold their interests to Power Corp., the Montreal-based conglomerate, which by the early 1970s had ended up in the hands of Paul Desmarais, the immensely shrewd empire builder from Sudbury, Ontario. Desmarais's key lieutenants urged Philippe not to leave the company, because they needed him. Desmarais continued to add broadcast properties to Telemedia, but he was having trouble with regulators over his media cross-ownership which included both newspapers and radio stations. To take the heat off, he agreed to sell Telemedia to Philippe for a reported $10 million. Although the price seemed steep at the time, the de Gaspé

Beaubiens were able to acquire the company for little cash down and 6 percent financing. Philippe was always comfortable carrying a fair bit of debt — something that has not always won him fans among the investment community.

He was able to build the company, first by turning its ailing stations around and then by expanding into new markets and products. He gained a reputation for buying sickly properties and restoring them to blooming good health. He acquired the Canadian version of *TV Guide* from American media magnate Walter Annenberg. He bought *Canadian Living* from John Labatt Ltd., revived it, and converted it into one of Canada's most successful consumer magazines. He even took a fling on the back-to-the-land periodical *Harrowsmith* and its sister magazine *Equinox*, although both were eventually sold. And he led Telemedia into investments in Cancom, the Canadian satellite company, and Rogers Cantel, the embryonic cell phone provider. In 1986, Telemedia went public with a share issue that raised $20 million. The company did reasonably well, but it never met the growth expectations of analysts or the levels of profit that institutional investors expected. Of course, the de Gaspé Beaubiens continued to control the company through their stranglehold on the voting shares. Essentially, the nonvoting shareholders were along for the ride.

In the early years, Philippe and Nan-b were clearly preoccupied with building something for themselves. The idea of a family business that would be handed down was remote. Their thinking began to change in the mid-1970s when Philippe, a leading member of the Young Presidents Organization, had to travel to an international YPO convention in Hawaii. Traditionally, the couple had never travelled together by plane — they felt it would be unfair to rob their children of both parents should there be a plane crash. This time, because the trip was so long, they considered breaking the rule. But first they sought a little advice. Their lawyer advised them that if the plane went down, their children would have to sell the business because there would be nothing left to pay the estate taxes. "That's when I realized I had to cope with the continuity of the family and I realized it was a family business," Philippe says. "So I took insurance out on my life in the name of the children and we went on the trip. That was the turning point. That's what made me realize I was not an entrepreneur — I was a family business owner."

In time, the de Gaspé Beaubiens began to divest themselves of some of their noncore assets in Telemedia. In 1988, Telemedia sold off its 13 percent of cell phone provider Rogers Cantel, which brought a nice sum of about $170 million. Until then, Telemedia had not made a lot of money for its owners. "If Philippe made two cents, he'd borrow five cents to put into the business," says

Nan-b. After the Cantel sale, "It was the first time in our life that we had 'cash-cash.'" The question was what to do with it. Thus, the windfall coincided with some introspection on the part of Philippe and Nan-b regarding how best to return some of their wealth to their community.

The answer came about in a bizarre way. The couple decided to take a boat cruise of Antarctica offered through the YPO. The trip was a disaster from one perspective — Philippe was seasick for twelve of the sixteen days. But at one point, people began putting up notices on bulletin boards, offering discussion groups on various topics — estate planning, life insurance, yoga, the usual things. The de Gaspé Beaubiens saw the notices and decided to post their own page offering an evening's discussion of family business issues. Philippe and Nan-b had been thinking of their own succession and the family's long history of failed generational transfers. When they showed up in the ship's dining room for their discussion night, the place was packed. "We were floored to see that practically the whole ship was there," Philippe recalls. "They were all in family businesses." The session lasted three to four hours because people didn't want to stop talking. Philippe and Nan-b had hit a nerve.

So the de Gaspé Beaubiens began a whirlwind exploration of the state of the art of family business. They plunged into the topic with no lack of ambition, resources, and connections. They started talking to academics about the scholarly discipline of families and business. It was pretty thin stuff so far, but some interesting work had been done, particularly at the Harvard Business School and by a few well-established professor/consultants, such as John Ward of Loyola University in Chicago. Some academics contended that they could not truly teach family business as a separate discipline, questioning how it was different from any other business. Nan-b was disgusted: "What do you mean? We can live it but you can't teach it?"

Another challenge was the entrepreneurial community's innate scepticism of universities and colleges. Any project would have to operate outside academe, while drawing on the expertise that many professors were capable of offering. The de Gaspé Beaubiens also talked to professionals in the field. Lawyers, accountants, and consultants were doing good work, but they were narrowly specialized. There were experts in estate planning, and taxation, and governance, but nobody was bringing all this together in a package. Also, the experts had not really lived the experience — they could not provide the credibility, or the searing recollections, of real businesspeople. "Consultants don't have the answers — people who provide estate planning haven't lived it. It has to be the families themselves," says Philippe. The de Gaspé Beaubiens' challenge would be to merge all these perspectives into a single program. Canada already had a family business organization, the Canadian Association of Family Enterprise (CAFE), but its strengths were networking and peer counselling, not education. To deepen their understanding, the couple roamed the world, talking to members from about a thousand family businesses to find out what they wanted and what had worked for them. The couple had found a void that they could fill on their own.

The de Gaspé Beaubiens created the Business Families Foundation as a kind of haven where families from around the world could come to talk and learn about their challenges. The immediate response was gratifying. One family from Latin America sent thirty of its members. The foundation immersed the families in a wash of information and guidance from top experts, including battle-scarred family business warriors who had lived the experience. The price was high — as much as $2,500 a person for a four-day immersion retreat. To refine the case study method, the institute produced videos of "typical" family crises featuring fictional characters, such as siblings "Ginny, Tim, and Bert" who were conspiring against one another for control of the company. The foundation also launched a lecture series in which high-profile families could tell their own stories with candor, under the assurance that their words would not slip into the media.

Some of Canada's larger family enterprises signed up for the program. The Sobeys, the supermarket family from Stellarton, Nova Scotia, have made use of the services. Rémi Marcoux, the founder and chairman of the large printing company GTC Transcontinental, has become an active member. Marcoux, whose offices are right beside Telemedia's in Place Ville Marie, has three children in their twenties and early thirties: two daughters, Natalie and Isabelle, work in the company, while son Pierre is a journalist in Washington, D.C. Isabelle, a lawyer, urged her father to attend some of the de Gaspé Beaubiens' events, but he was sceptical that it would do any good. "I like the business very much and I'm far away from retirement," says Marcoux, fifty-nine. But his family kept nagging him, and he finally relented. "I could see Philippe had developed lots of experience — it's very well put together. He has been a great help to me in planning my succession."

The one area the de Gaspé Beaubiens have found difficult to penetrate is the world of small business, yet this is where their work is most needed. Most small business people don't have the time or energy to consider such issues as proper governance, codes of conduct, and the broad challenge of passing the business on. Also, they cannot afford the high cost of the de Gaspé Beaubiens' seminars. So in early 1998 the institute made a deal with CAFE whereby the national association became the distribution channel for the institute's education programs for small businesses. "They [CAFE] are very good at bringing people together in networks," says Philippe. "We can do the educational [aspect]; we will train the trainers, the families and professionals. It suits our strategy because it approaches small businesses, which is the strength of our economy." It is too early to tell how well the marriage will work. The de Gaspé Beaubiens are not used to sharing authority, and there is the culture gap: the world of well-cut Italian suits meets the more diverse CAFE culture of golf shirts and chinos, big hair and heavy jewellery.

The de Gaspé Beaubiens believe that family business challenges are pretty much the same everywhere, whatever the business's size and wherever in the world it is based. They believe it is possible to build models so that families can anticipate problems before they happen. Nan-b cautions that there are powerful societal values working against family businesses. To succeed, families have to work as teams, not as isolated individuals. Yet today's values, both in business and in society, place tremendous emphasis on the individual leader — the single owner, entrepreneur, or star CEO. "Nobody wants to share power today," Nan-b says. "So everything we are doing is really countercultural." Philippe despairs about the worship of the lone hero, and about the business media's glorification of "the single authority in the business that we identify all policy and growth with. In family business, they have to accommodate themselves to more of a team. He doesn't lord it over the others even though he is the leader."

For high-powered, wealthy people, the de Gaspé Beaubiens preach a message of modest living and unostentatious lifestyles. They are disciples of the popular book *The Millionaire Next Door*, which espouses the importance of living frugally in order to build wealth. The successful business family, says Nan-b, should follow the 10 percent rules: it should live 10 percent below its peer group, save 10 percent of its income, and give 10 percent away.

In Philippe's view, Canada and other Western nations cannot afford to pass up the tremendous benefits that families in business can offer. He argues that they are usually closer to their customers, closer to their employees, and more flexible than their publicly traded counterparts. "They are more profitable comparatively than other companies because they put their hands in and they work at it 100 percent. They are creators of imagination, of creativity, of employment. They are very good for the communities in which they work because they really give back to the people they know and with whom they are involved."

Nan-b, whose perspective is more that of a counsellor, has seen the human scars that can be inflicted when family businesses become battlefields. She worries that many groups of brothers, sisters, and cousins don't see all the options. For example, families should be learning how to sell the company without breaking up the family, and in a way that won't ruin the business or imperil the jobs of the employees. If the foundation can help companies make that transition, it will be doing a good job, she says. But all too often, companies simply descend into mediocrity as incompetent or greedy family members drive it into the ground. The de Gaspé Beaubiens recognize that family businesses badly need outside managers who can bring new ideas and motivation to the table. Yet the best and the brightest managers often shun family enterprises, realizing that certain jobs, usually the top jobs, are not available. So how do you "sell" the family company to outside professionals?

Philippe suggests a winning recruiting pitch: "I'd like to convince you to join my family business because we are in great need of the best professional management people, and often that professional skill may not exist among the members of the family." He says it is important to note that the family makes a distinction between ownership and management. "The big issue that is plaguing a lot of families in business is the confusion between the two — that people cannot see the responsibility and dignity of the ownership function in a family business, which is very different from managing. It is a great responsibility to be a great owner and to work with that. So I would say that the majority of families in business are going to have a tremendous need for managing, and that is not necessarily a given privilege of the members of the family ... If they can find that kind of people, this is a more interesting environment, a more secure environment, and there is more future benefit if that family is cognizant of the importance of that role."

He observes that in the largest widely held public corporations there is an "unknown ownership structure" that comes to the foreground at annual meetings when slates of directors are elected. And in public companies there is usually less job security for professional managers, he says. The average tenure of a CEO in a public company is less than five years. He doesn't have the exact numbers but is confident that the average tenure for a CEO in a family company is much longer. (Some studies say the average CEO in a private family company stays for six times as long as in a public company.)

In grooming their own children, the de Gaspé Beaubiens started early, assembling the kids for regular weekly meetings when they were nine, ten, and eleven. "We'd ask their opinions and basically keep them abreast of what was happening in the company," Nan-b says. People who know the couple say they were almost fanatical that their children absorb the right expertise, the right training, the right insights. There are never any half-measures with this highly controlling couple. All three children attended the Harvard Business School to get their MBAs. But Philippe and Nan-b were determined not to indulge the children when it came to natural entitlement. Philippe describes what their thinking was: "We love our children so much, we will give them all the education we can, all the love and caring we can, but we will not give them shares, we will not give them money, and we will require that they go and work somewhere else." Then he adds: "And we changed our minds on all three."

It's a refreshing admission of fallibility by this perfectionist. One reason for the compromise, he says, was a glitch in the career of Philippe III, whom his father refers to as "de Gaspé." All three children have worked outside Telemedia in consumer goods companies. The understanding was that they would spend at least five years somewhere else before even considering a berth at Telemedia. But a number of years ago *The Globe and Mail* ran a positive profile of the family, which featured an attractive picture of the children, identifying them as "the successors." Philippe III had been in line for a brand manager's job at General Foods, but after that article appeared he was told the company wanted to promote people who aspired to spend their careers at the company. The young man insisted that was his intention — that he had made a solemn commitment to General Foods, and that no spot had been promised him at Telemedia. But he also sensed that his career at General Foods had plateaued, so he asked his father for a job, arguing, "Dad, do you think it's fair just because I carry your name that I'm not allowed to go into the family business?" That seemed to be a just statement, the older man says. Philippe III joined Telemedia ahead of the scheduled time.

The children not only joined the company but also moved smartly up the ranks under their parents' ownership. On the question of nepotism, Philippe is brazenly disingenuous. He insists he never promoted the children and that his children never reported to him. He admits he did hire Nan-b away from a hospital to come and work with him in human resources. But she reported to the president of the company, not to Philippe, the chairman. Still, it was difficult, he says, because she would tell him things that were happening in the company and he would get angry. "It's not easy for couples to work together. Don't do it until you have ten years of married life, because you'd better put your [married] life in order before adding the business."

As Philippe entered his mid-sixties, he was determined to establish a succession plan. He wrote to each of the children, telling them of his plans to relinquish the ownership role. He gave them options: the business could be sold and they could share in the proceeds; or he could put all the assets in a bag and

they could choose the parts they wanted; or they could take it all for themselves to own as a group. He arranged a meeting with Nan-b, the children, and
a facilitator. The facilitator said his one request was that nothing be decided
on that day. But the children ignored this call for patience: they placed their
hands on each other's in the middle of the table and declared together, "We're
in." This Three Musketeers–type gesture was an immensely touching moment
for their father, who even now has to wipe away tears as he talks about it. (The
children have politely refused to be interviewed on the issue of the family business, saying it is still too early in the process to undertake such conversations.)

   This solidarity was just what the parents had hoped for: they had always tried
to allay any jealousy among the three children by emphasizing that each brings
special gifts to the organization. Their father likes to describe the trio as a ship:
"You, de Gaspé, you're the rudder, you're solid, you know where you are going.
Nanon, you're the hull of the boat, you keep the family together." As for
François, he is the the sail, energetic and engaging. "A sail by itself will flap in
the wind," their father says. "A rudder can do nothing, and the hull of a boat
just floats. But put the three together and you get things done."

   In the de Gaspé Beaubiens' world there are three spheres of activity, and
each has its own leader. There is the family, headed by Nan-b; the business, in
which leadership will be shared by the three children; and the ownership, of
which Nanon has been elected the "steward" or leader. Philippe emphasizes
the critical role of ownership in the family constellation; to him it means more
than personal control and power. "It's the responsibility that comes from the
stewardship — it's rented, it's not given to you. The question is what do you
do with that? What are the responsibilities to your community, to your employees, to directors, to managers?"

   To denote the different relationships, the family uses separate tables for its
discussions: a round table is used by the active owners to thrash things out; a
square table is for situations where the parents are invited to join the discussions; and there is a diamond-shaped table for everyone affected to gather
around, including the in-laws. Both Nanon and Philippe III are married —
Nanon to Don Mattrick, a Vancouver software entrepreneur. Philippe's wife,
Annette, is a manager with a major chartered bank.

   Interviewed in 1999, Philippe II said he had been hearing rumours that the children would eventually sell the company — that they were just waiting for an
advantageous price — but maintained the situation is just the opposite. The three
young de Gaspé Beaubiens had lived with the company all their lives, and now
they wanted to put their stamp on it. "They want to grow it — they just don't
want to sell it. What are we on this world to do — just to take advantage? They

feel they have a responsibility and a stewardship to those who depend on them." Philippe was deeply touched when he told the children he was giving the company to them, and his son Philippe insisted, "'Excuse me. You're not giving it to us, you're loaning it to us.' I think he meant, 'This is a legacy, this is our way to leave a legacy. We'll be damned if we're going to just take what you have left us.'"

Nan-b, reflecting her usual concern about family harmony, is more sanguine about the issue of selling the company; she says the children should feel free to do that too. "I feel very strongly about that. If the next generation isn't totally committed to carrying this out and all the work that it takes, then for heaven's sake don't do it because you'll end up destroying the family and the business."

Philippe and Nan-b have placed one ironclad condition on their gift of the company to their children: the successors have to establish a proper governance structure. That means preparing a number of key documents — a constitution, an owners' code of conduct, a conflict resolution process, and a shareholders' agreement that outlines what happens to the ownership structure if one of the three wants to leave the company. These principles are to be presented to the parents for their assessment and comment. This is one area where Nan-b and Philippe feel they can offer useful counsel. The process is harder than was first expected. The children were confident they could whip together the code of conduct over a weekend. In fact, it took two years. In 1998, Philippe and Nan-b invited their children to join them on a trip for Philippe's seventieth birthday. The children surprised him with a gift of the code of conduct, nicely bound in a book.

Now that the children have taken over, the parents are strongly aware that they have to keep their distance. Philippe, perhaps remembering his own father, is worried that he said the wrong thing during a recent conference call with the children, that he seemed too intrusive and overbearing. "I've got to be very careful. We're the founders and have to learn to listen more, and ask questions. That's a big step. Are we doing it right?" The one thing in the family's favour, he says, is that the process wasn't delayed until he and Nan-b were in hospital beds — or in coffins. "Most people who start, build, and are identified with a business find it very hard to distance themselves from the decision-making or even the ownership of the business during their lifetime."

He concedes that there are some difficult moments when he is in his office alone and there is a meeting of the board in another office around the corner. He has clearly been ruffled by the children's enthusiasm for changing things — they have decided to shake up the board and get some new blood as directors. Also, discussions are taking place about changes in management, and in direction. The father feels loyalty to his old colleagues and appointees, but he accepts that his children will want their own people in place.

In some ways he is comforted by how aggressively they have taken charge. He has seen too many transitions where the younger generation has owned the shares but "they don't own the issues." The children in these companies assume that Dad and Mom will continue to look after things. When the parents are no longer in the room, Philippe says, the children can't fall back on them anymore. "I'm not on the board, I'm not in management — I'm gone," he says, pointing out that there's more than enough at the foundation to keep him busy.

Nan-b, still in her family counsellor's mode, insists that she doesn't worry a lot about the outcome of her children's decisions. "The only thing that I really would be upset to see is a tremendous fight among them. I don't think that is going to happen. Whatever they decide, as long as they will remain friends and close, the rest I couldn't care less."

EIGHT

THE WOLFES —
COUSINS

The late Ray Wolfe, founder of the Oshawa Group Ltd.

I T WAS CLEAR THAT AN ERA HAD ENDED at Oshawa Group Ltd. when the photos of the founding fathers came down shortly before Christmas of 1998. For years the lobby of the food wholesaler's west-end Toronto head-quarters had been graced by portraits of the company's now deceased builders — Max and Maurice Wolfe, the brothers who created the company in the early twentieth century, and Maurice's son Ray Wolfe, the smart, shy man who built the small wholesale business into a grocery retail and merchandising giant. If it was the end of one era, it was also the beginning of a new one. The Sobey clan, a close-knit family based in the small town of Stellarton, Nova Scotia, was now in command of the Oshawa Group, having completed a $1.5 billion takeover.

The removal of the pictures, by some departing Wolfe family members, shocked and saddened long-time Oshawa Group employees. They were used to seeing the reassuring images of Max, Maurice, and Ray Wolfe at the entrance to their offices. The photos were tangible links to a better time. The Wolfes had presided like a benevolent royal family over Oshawa Group and its predecessor company Ontario Produce for eight decades; family members had penetrated every corner of management. At one time as many as nine Wolfes worked in the company, which was the leading franchisor of IGA super-markets in Canada. But times do change.

The removal of the Wolfe mementoes was a tangible reminder of who had won and who had lost in the dynastic battles that have shaken Canada's supermarket industry. For some employees there was the bitter irony that the tables might well have been turned, if not for the shifting fortunes of family business. A decade earlier it had been rumoured that the much bigger Oshawa Group was a likely candidate to take over the Sobey family's supermarket group. Within a few years the reverse had happened. It was a signal of how far and how fast Oshawa Group had fallen.

The Oshawa Group takeover is essentially a story of third-generation failure, and of the inability of Toronto's Wolfe family to deal with the issues of succession and leadership. When the company consisted of two brothers, decision-making was simple and direct. Once some children were added, it got more complicated. As more and more cousins became involved, diverging priorities were brought to the table. Some worked in the business but held no voting shares; others were voting shareholders but had no management roles. Some held key leadership roles; others aspired to them. Some wanted to invest in the company's future; others wanted to cash in now. In such situations, decision-making becomes complicated — in fact, often paralyzed — as interests sharply diverge and brothers are pitted against brothers, cousins against cousins. "In the end, the only thing they all had in common was that their last name was Wolfe," said a director of Oshawa Group during the final days of the company's independent life.

As long as Ray Wolfe was alive, it was possible to keep these conflicts under control. But the death of the entrepreneur in 1990 sapped the will and direction of the company and left it rudderless. He had delivered growing revenues, profits, and shareholder returns. His demise triggered ten years of leadership crisis. The end of Oshawa Group as a Wolfe family business can also be seen as arising from Ray's failure to provide an enduring succession. Ray's son Jonathan Wolfe always expected to some day run Oshawa Group. He was designated from an early age as the successor-in-waiting. And he seemed to do all the right things — he went to a well-regarded American school, and he spent several years in Paris working for one of the world's most elegant department stores, Galeries Lafayette. He returned to join the company and worked his way up through a number of jobs. He became the special mentoring project of Allister Graham, the wise and loyal family outsider who was Ray Wolfe's right-hand man. When Ray Wolfe died, Jonathan took the big step, taking over as president and chief operating officer.

But in September 1997, Jonathan Wolfe's dream fell apart: the family rejected him as the next CEO and embarked on a search for a new successor. That set up a bewildering series of events that led to the Sobey family's dramatic purchase of Oshawa Group in late 1998. Jonathan's own family essentially turned against him, telling him he would not run the company and that an outsider was better qualified. Yet while the business could find a new leader, the family could not: there was no one to bind together the diverse interests, as Ray Wolfe once did. The Wolfes' lack of family cohesion led to the end of its association with Oshawa Group.

In the small towns of Ontario, from Fenelon Falls to Tweed to Brighton, Ray Wolfe is still spoken of in a kind of hushed reverence. If he were alive today, Ray, a shy man, might be a bit abashed that grown men speak of him as a kind of grocery god. But he made men rich, and he made them important people in their own communities. They owned the big IGA supermarkets, often the only major stores in town, and that provided them with an automatic entry into the community's élite. Ray was the moving force behind IGA, the franchise system that brought full-line supermarkets to the communities beyond Toronto and later to other parts of Canada. An urban Jew with family roots in downtown Toronto's shops and markets, he mingled easily with the stolid rural stock who became his franchisees in east-central Ontario, the Maritimes, and the West. He backed them when they needed money, he was patient when they weren't able to deliver big returns. And they worked hard for Ray Wolfe. He was to them a solidly reassuring figure with a quiet savvy.

The Wolfe family came to Toronto in the early twentieth century from Lithuania. Two boys, Max and Maurice, immigrated with their mother. In 1911 a teenaged Max Wolfe spent $65 on a horse, a wagon, and a barrel of apples and started supplying produce to small grocers and street vendors in Toronto. The venture proved profitable, and three years later he persuaded his brother Maurice, a furniture retailer, to join the business, which they called Ontario Produce Company. Building on Max's wagon, the brothers quickly expanded, moving into the importing, exporting, and trading of fresh fruit and vegetables. Their clientele expanded to include wholesalers, hospitals, hotels, ships, railways, and other institutions.

The Wolfe brothers lived long and industrious lives — Maurice died in 1978 at eighty-nine, and Max in 1987 at ninety-four. For many years Max was the company's link to its past. In his nineties he was still coming into the office in the mornings, then strolling over to the produce markets where the big trucks were rolling in bringing California lettuce, Florida oranges, and a host of other products. At one time the centre of the produce business was around St. Lawrence Market in Toronto's downtown; in later years Max shifted his attention to the rambling Ontario Food Terminal complex on the Queensway in the city's west end.

Maurice and Max were traders, street-smart and instinctive; Maurice's son Ray was brainy and sophisticated, with a deeper strategic purpose that would build a major Canadian company. A graduate of the University of Toronto, he was the best educated of Maurice's four sons, all of whom worked in the company. Besides Ray, there were Leonard, Jack, and Harvey. Ray worked briefly at a Montreal produce house and in 1941 joined the family company to become general manager of Ontario Produce in Ontario. It was clear from the start that he was the second-generation Wolfe who was most likely to carry on the business. He served in the Royal Canadian Air Force during the Second World War, then came back to the company to become its general manager.

In the late 1940s, the grocery industry was changing rapidly. As Ontario Produce's business developed, its main customers became the big grocery chains. But the chains were now beginning to bypass wholesalers and fill their produce requirements directly from the supplier. "New sources of business had to be found if Ontario Produce was to survive," says a brief company history published in the early 1990s. Ray concluded that if the chains were no longer going to be large customers, the only option for Ontario Produce was to enlist more independent grocers as wholesale customers. But independents were finding it harder to compete with the big chains and were having survival problems of their own. Ray's mission was to make the independents more competitive while allowing Ontario Produce to broaden its base of business.

He took the first step by acquiring Oshawa Wholesale Ltd., a small Ontario distributor of groceries, tobacco, confectioneries, and health and beauty aids to independent grocers. The company took the name Oshawa Group. That broadened the family's product range and its network of independent merchant customers. Ray also looked to the United States for ideas. He came upon the Independent Grocers Alliance (IGA), a Chicago-based franchise group that gathered independent grocers under a single banner and marketing approach. It was a franchise program: a central franchisor owned the brand and supplied the stores, but individual storekeepers owned the local business. This model combined the group buying and brand name clout of a big chain with the entrepreneurial opportunities of the independent store owner in his own community.

In 1951, Ray persuaded the American IGA organization to grant Oshawa Group its first Canadian master franchise; he then offered the IGA program to his company's 750 independent store customers. At first, only forty-nine stores with a combined annual retail volume of less than $5 million took up the chance to buy, advertise, merchandise, and sell under a single banner. It wasn't a lot, but it was enough to launch IGA in Canada, and it laid the foundation for Oshawa Group to become a merchandising force. Ray Wolfe's bright new IGA supermarkets helped revolutionize grocery retailing in Canada.

The new franchisees came to appreciate Ray, whose credo seemed to be, "If you work hard for IGA, IGA will work hard for you." He selected his franchisees carefully, based as much on character as on financial clout or track record. "His strength and his secret was his belief in people, his ability to pick the right people as dealers," says Stan Pilot, sixty-seven, who joined the IGA group in its first year of business in Canada and is still a franchisee in the system. "If he believed in you, he backed you to the hilt."

In 1951, Pilot was twenty-one and working in downtown Toronto, when he read an ad in the paper offering a supermarket on Dixon Road in Toronto's west end. He and his brother-in-law applied and ended up with an IGA franchise. He remembers the operation being run along traditional lines — someone would call Pilot's IGA store in the late afternoon asking if it needed a produce order; Oshawa Group buyers would go down to the market the next morning to fill the order and deliver it the same day. In the late 1950s, Pilot and his brother-in-law decided to part company, and they sold the business. Pilot found himself out of IGA and looking around for something to do.

One day he ran into Ray Wolfe, who asked, "When are you coming back in?" Pilot explained that he didn't have a lot of his own money, but that wasn't an obstacle for Ray. "Can you come up with $500?" he asked. Pilot said he could. So the young man ended up with another IGA store, this time in suburban West Hill, east of Toronto. The volume numbers were not good, and Pilot was worried. "If it doesn't work out, I'll pull you out of there," Ray promised. Indeed, after four years it wasn't working out, and another chain had set up shop in the neighbourhood. "I was broke," remembers Pilot. "I woke up one night in a cold sweat. The next day, I told Ray I'd like to come and see him. I told him, 'Ray, it just isn't working. After four years, I'm going behind, not ahead.'"

Ray did not hesitate to offer Pilot the choice of two new stores. The young man picked one in the booming northwestern Toronto suburb of Bramalea. This one worked out spectacularly. After a period of scurrying between the two stores, he was able to sell the West Hill operation. With the volumes from Bramalea he was able to pay back all the money he owed — "huge numbers," he says now. The patience and confidence showed by Ray impressed Pilot and led to his lifetime association with the IGA group. He sold the Bramalea store in 1996 but remains a partner with his son-in-law in an IGA in Brighton, Ontario. His son owns an IGA in Fenelon Falls near Peterborough, Ontario.

Dealers like Stan Pilot held Ray in a kind of wonder. He was soft-spoken but had a warmth that drew people in. He also knew it was the little things that mattered. One day Pilot happened to be at Oshawa Group headquarters with a grocery order. He was looking for the computer room when he ran into Ray Wolfe. "I'll take you down there," the older man said, over Pilot's protestations that the company president must be too busy. "He made you feel there was no one more important than you," Pilot recalls. "I'd come in and sit down and have coffee with him. The man awed me in every way, I thought I was way below him."

As the postwar Canadian economy flourished — particularly in central Ontario — the company kept growing as more and more independent grocers joined the IGA group. In 1959, Oshawa Group went public by issuing nonvoting shares; this allowed the Wolfe family to raise huge amounts of equity capital while retaining control of the company. Oshawa Group was among the first family companies to find a way to tap public markets without giving up the full clout of voting control. Canada's model of voting and nonvoting shares has vastly benefited its family businesses.

As Ray built the company, he was able to centralize his control even within the Wolfe family. Shares were held by a number of Wolfes, all of them belonging to the families of Maurice and Max. In the early 1970s, Ray demanded that the voting shares be held only by Wolfes who were actually employed at Oshawa Group. The others would have to trade in their voting for nonvoting shares. This reorganization created two classes of Wolfes — those who worked at Oshawa Group and held voting shares, and those outside the company, who held the nonvoting A shares. This changed the family dynamics, creating an in-group and an out-group. Under the new arrangement, Ray controlled one-fifth of the voting shares, as did each of his brothers, Leonard, Jack, and Harvey. The final, fifth share was held by Max's only son Harold. All five of these voting shareholders were working in the company at that time. According to the shareholders' agreement, Ray, as the leader of his generation, held the right to vote the proxies for all the voting shares, subject to an annual review. Clearly, power was centralized in his hands as long as he lived and the company continued to perform.

Fueled by its public share issues, Oshawa Group embarked on an ambitious expansion through the 1960s and 1970s. The IGA concept grew, partly through the Wolfes' opening of company-owned stores as well as franchises. These corporate stores were testing grounds for new concepts, and were often handed over later to franchisees, who were known as associates. In 1961 the Wolfes founded Food City, the first discount supermarket chain in Canada. They also spread out geographically, buying regional suppliers such as Bolands Ltd. in Atlantic Canada; a Quebec distributor that become known as Hudon and Deaudelin Ltd; and Codville Distributors in Manitoba, Saskatchewan, and northwestern

Ontario. The company also picked up a number of small chains and wholesalers. Meanwhile, Ontario Produce was expanding, adding to its operations at the Food Terminal and establishing a packing plant on the Holland Marsh, Ontario's produce heartland just north of Toronto. And Oshawa Group moved into the food service business, making a couple of acquisitions in the 1960s.

In 1972, Ray suffered a serious heart attack that took him right out of the company. His brother Harvey was installed as president and CEO, and from all accounts it was not a happy transition. Under Harvey the company undertook an ill-fated diversification. One of his initiatives was an expansion into ultra-large retail complexes based on France's hypermarchés. These superstores offered both groceries and general merchandise under the same roof. Unfortunately, Harvey was twenty years ahead of his time, and the concept fizzled. He also moved Oshawa Group into peripheral areas such as construction; he even bought a company plane. Financial performance and share prices were floundering.

Ray recovered his health, came back to the company, and sent Harvey to the sidelines. Harvey left Oshawa Group's management and moved into real estate investing. But as the owner of one-fifth of the family's voting shares, he remained a director — a position that entitled him to attend board meetings. It made for odd meetings, directors say, providing a crackle of tension and dissatisfaction even when the company was doing well. It also suggested what was to come — the first crack in the Wolfes' united front. One company source later told *The Globe and Mail*, "Harvey sucked on his rancour for a long time. He was very, very bitter. His brother had put him through the meat grinder."

In those years it was clear that the company belonged to Ray, whose business style was both gentle and controlling. He was not a great delegator and liked to keep his hands in a lot of small decisions. He avoided snap decisions and preferred to sleep on things. This meant he could be a procrastinator when it came to tough calls. He hated to sell assets he had acquired even when they were clearly bleeding the company. "Selling them would be an admission of failure," an insider points out. One example was a mushroom farm in Pickering, Ontario, whose presence in Oshawa Group's portfolio became a kind of ongoing boardroom joke. Despite the farm's stubborn refusal to earn decent profits, Ray held on to it year after year. Yet at the same time he was very shrewd — he never overpaid, either for people or for assets. He could also be exceedingly secretive — a private owner in a public company — and this frustrated independent members of the board.

While he was building Oshawa Group, Ray was also building a family. In 1940 he married Rose Senderowitz, the daughter of a Toronto baker who had emigrated from Romania. Rose graduated in sociology from the University of Toronto the same year she married Ray. She followed him to Vancouver while he was in the RCAF, then returned to Toronto to work at an organization that placed orphans with foster homes. This set off a lifetime of volunteerism that made Rose a prominent citizen in her own right. In 1959, Rose visited Israel, an event that inspired her to fashion herself a role as a fundraiser for Jewish causes. In 1975 she began serving on the University of Toronto's governing council, an appointment that led to her election as chancellor of the university in the 1990s, after Ray died.

There were two children, both born in the early 1950s, both serious young people who got good educations. Jonathan, shy and cerebral, studied in the United States at Swarthmore College and worked in Europe before coming home to Oshawa Group. Elizabeth pursued a law career, and served as general counsel for Oshawa Group before quitting to spend time with her young family.

According to employees, Ray watched the sad saga of Montreal's Steinberg family with great interest. Sam Steinberg was a brilliant entrepreneur who built the dominant Quebec supermarket chain, which was a powerful rival to the Wolfes' Oshawa Group. But Sam failed to pick a clear successor in the second generation, perhaps because he had wanted a son and ended up with four daughters. When he died, daughter Mitzi moved aggressively into a dominant position, leaving her sisters suspicious and resentful. Steinberg's descended into an abyss of family disputes and litigation; in 1989 it was sold to the Caisse de dépôt et placement du Québec pension fund and entrepreneur Michel Gaucher. As he watched this debacle unfold, Ray became determined to quickly anoint and groom Jonathan to succeed him.

To outsiders, the selection of Jonathan made sense. He was, after all, the only son of the dominant Wolfe branch, and he had grown up in the business. He had been mentored both by Ray and Allister Graham. By the mid-1980s he was running one of Oshawa Group's most important divisions, Oshawa Foods, which supplied Ontario's IGA stores. A 1986 article in *Report on Business* magazine describes how Jon tried to avoid being drawn into the family business, but ultimately couldn't resist his father's entreaties. He finally joined the company in 1976. "Ray Wolfe was delighted with his son's decision," the article's authors observed, "for while there are nine Wolfe family members at work throughout the $3 billion retailing concern, Wolfe Sr. thought for a while that his own children might not play a role in the company."

The article described father and son as a winning team who had helped

Oshawa Group become a formidable power in grocery retailing and distribution at a time when other industry titans, notably Dominion Stores, were slipping. "This outward reaching is the calculated result of planning by the three generations of Wolfes who run Oshawa. Max Wolfe, the nonegenarian who founded the firm with Ray's father Maurice, is Oshawa's honorary chairman and still tours two of the company's warehouses daily; Ray, who suffered a heart attack in 1972 but plunged back into the business after his recovery, runs herd over the whole company; and Jonathan, thirty-three, is president and general manager of the Oshawa Foods division, the largest money-maker in the group, accounting for 35 percent of total sales."

Despite this rosy view of the succession, many inside and outside the company were sceptical of Jonathan's potential. "Jon was given the Ontario region, but he didn't do a good job, he was not really a master merchant," said one nonfamily insider. The most common adjective used to describe Jonathan was "intellectual," and in the food retail industry that was not considered a high compliment. "The grocery business is a dirty-nails kind of business," another former manager comments. Jonathan didn't have dirty nails, and he was uncomfortable with those who did. And he was not good with people — a major liability when you are dealing with franchisees in small towns and local communities. Jonathan may have been intelligent and sophisticated, but he suffered for another very simple reason: he was not his father. He was cast from another mould — he spoke several languages but not the language of his own grocery people. The sons and daughters of entrepreneurs are often considered uncharismatic, even when, as in Ray's case, the charisma is of a shy and subtle nature.

While Ray was alive, Jonathan's supposed personality flaws were not a problem. But in January 1990 the entrepreneur's damaged heart finally gave out, and he died suddenly. His death threw Oshawa Group into momentary confusion. Jonathan clearly lusted for the job of CEO, but the rest of the family was not convinced he was ready — or that he would ever be ready. Ray's brother Harvey and his cousin Harold, two key power brokers, had little love for the distant Jonathan. The family installed Allister Graham, the longtime lieutenant of Ray — a man who began his career as a clerk in the meat department — as chairman and CEO. He would also serve as mentor and caretaker until Jonathan was ready to assume leadership. In the meantime, Jonathan, at thirty-seven, would move up to president and chief operating officer.

It was a different company from the one Ray had built in the 1960s and 1970s. Oshawa Group was no longer just about groceries — the company had diversified into pharmacies, most dramatically with the 1988 purchase of the 109 drugstores of the Boots chain, which was renamed Pharma Plus.

It had moved more aggressively into food services, and it was even taking a shot at discount department stores with its Towers chain. But Oshawa Group was a peripheral player in both pharmacies and department stores and would eventually get out of both activities. The company, once an innovator, was beginning to look sluggish. The organization had been built on strong regional divisions, and that made it difficult to drive change from the top. In many ways Oshawa Group was still essentially a wholesaler based on regional divisions, not a retail chain. That close-to-the-ground profile had been the chain's great strength in its early years; now it seemed to be a liability. In addition, strong competitors were emerging, led by the resurgent Loblaws chain under owner Galen Weston's rejuvenated management team, which included marketing whiz Dave Nichol and his President's Choice line of store-brand gourmet products.

For the first couple of years after Ray died, the franchisees saw no change in the operations of the retail chain. But it soon became clear that this was not the old Oshawa Group. "The contact wasn't there and the communications were bad," says Stan Pilot. One problem was that the corporation was getting a lot bigger, which meant that the person-to-person relationships of the old days were disintegrating. The company sold its key warehouse operations in Ontario, and franchisees began to complain about shoddy deliveries and inconsistent responses to their queries. The franchisees felt that the quality of merchandise was suffering, and their grumbling intensified. Especially in Ontario, the supermarket franchisees felt abandoned by head office.

It was no coincidence that the family wasn't getting along either; indeed, there was a leadership crisis at the top of Oshawa Group. Jonathan's management was generally unpopular. Ray had intended that his son continue to receive coaching from Al Graham, but according to employees, the younger man often resisted counsel. He preferred to go his own way, and increasingly isolated himself within the company. One former manager says that while he did sell some of the company's peripheral assets, he also allowed the core business — grocery merchandising — to weaken. And he seemed to resent Graham's leadership, perhaps because he felt that the CEO's job should be his. Every proposal had to be stickhandled through the two men, for Jonathan would almost certainly oppose any decision made by Graham. "They did not trust each other," says one manager. "Jon thought he should be CEO and instead Al had the job. I had to walk a beam between the two and get them both to agree to things. That was because when one agreed, the other disagreed, and decision-making slowed down."

The dissension between Jonathan Wolfe and Allister Graham underlines the potential weakness of transitional management in a family business. In theory, the arrangement made a lot of sense: Graham, a respected senior manager, would guide the company for several years until Jonathan was clearly ready to take the final step. Then there would be a seamless transfer of power, with Jonathan taking over as CEO. But for transition leadership to work, both caretaker and CEO-in-waiting have to accept the idea. In fact, the rift between the two hamstrung the company at a time when it needed a strong hand on strategy. Graham, left alone, could certainly have made the decisions that desperately needed to be made at Oshawa Group. But he was a caretaker, forced to share power with Jonathan as president. And Jonathan, who was no dummy, while he had the vision to do what was necessary, was burdened by the ambiguity of his role and his own simmering resentments.

To Jonathan's credit, he did understand that things needed to change, and he tried to develop a strategy. The goal was to turn Oshawa Group from a decentralized wholesale company into a more centralized supermarket chain with its finger on the consumer's pulse. The hope was for head office to become more directive, and this didn't sit well with regional managers, at least at first. It would mean the overhaul of a model that had served the company well for at least forty years. Oshawa Group employed the high-profile McKinsey consulting group for more than two years to come up with a strategy. Even the consultants were frustrated by the saw-off at the top of the company. Observers say that while Jonathan was a visionary, he could also be erratic and changeable. He fell in love with consultants easily, but he failed to move on many of their recommendations. In addition, the company's shares were not performing: in the great bull market of the 1990s, its stock basically stood still. For some of the Wolfes — particularly the older ones — their continuing affiliation with the company was becoming less important than their financial planning.

In the 1970s and 1980s, the strong leadership of Ray Wolfe and Al Graham had papered over many flaws in the company. For example, Oshawa Group was suffering from the classic family business weakness: there were just too many Wolfes in the company, and they were not all stellar performers. Most of them had never worked anywhere else in their lives. Ray, Jack, and Leonard all held key positions at one time; so did Jack's children Rick and Rhonda, and Leonard's son Myron. Both of Ray's children had been involved in the company, and Jonathan continued to be. Max's son Harold was a vice-president in charge of real estate. Ab Flatt, the husband of Harold's sister Phyllis, was a senior executive in the drugstore operations. Their two sons Stephen and Joel also became managers, although not until relatively late in the game.

A company director argues that this was a prescription for mediocrity:

"Several members of the family would not have held equivalent positions in a competitive situation." He adds that the presence of so many Wolfes had a negative impact on those employees who were not members of the family. Talented employees began to realize that no matter how well they performed, there were some jobs they could never aspire to. It's not that all the Wolfes were incompetent — in fact, some of them were quite talented and would have succeeded admirably in any business. One sad aspect of this story is that outsiders tended to lump all the kin together as a mediocre lot, and disregarded the substantial talents of some family members.

How does a company deal with such flagrant nepotism? "You try to surround the ones who are weaker with outstanding people," one manager says. "It was an unspoken truth in the company." It is often argued that when family members who are barely competent are allowed to hold down key jobs, it tends to breed incompetence throughout an organization. If you tolerate poor performance from family members, you soon begin to tolerate it from other managers and employees. At a time when rival companies such as the born-again Loblaws were strengthening their management ranks, Oshawa Group was saddled with a pack of Wolfes, not all of whom deserved their titles and salaries.

Yet it is hard to be too harsh on family members who want to join a family business — it is in their blood. Max and Maurice and the small produce cart were part of the Wolfes' heritage. As young people they swept floors and pushed carts around the warehouses. They were out at the Food Terminal on Saturday mornings while they were still in grade school. But when family members got inside the company, they often found little mentoring, training, or career development. Managers who were not Wolfes might expect some guidance, but not so the family members, who were expected to pick up the trade by genes, instinct, and osmosis.

Even so, Oshawa Group's managers and directors felt that there were some highly competent Wolfes right under their noses. A number of former managers believe that the next CEO should not have been Jonathan, but rather his sister Elizabeth. In their view, she had both the technical grasp and the people skills. But when Elizabeth had children, she chose to move out of the company. Another strong candidate might have been Rhonda Wolfe, Jack Wolfe's daughter and Ray's niece. In one observer's eyes she was the best "merchant" of all the Wolfes in the company. That's a strong compliment in the retail business, in which being a merchant — that is, a buyer of merchandise that will move off the shelves — suggests an instinctive grasp of the trade. Unfortunately, Oshawa Group was a male preserve in terms of top management. Rhonda, in fact, became a casualty of one of the company's strategic lurches. As a buyer for Towers, she was left without a job when Oshawa Group sold that department store chain to Hudson's Bay Co. in 1990.

Attempts were made to deal with the concerns and demands of the family shareholders. In 1994 the Boston consulting organization Conflict Management Group was hired to mediate a new shareholders' agreement that was more in line with the 1990s than with the 1970s. That process was dominated by Harold Wolfe, an undynamic manager but a man who truly loved the company and was concerned about the quality of its governance. He believed strongly that the company should embrace the findings of the Dey Committee report, which had been prepared for the Toronto Stock Exchange. Its recommendations amounted to a blueprint for corporate governance in a public company.

Under the guidance of CMG, the family embarked on a year of meetings in a Toronto airport hotel, which eventually produced a new, fifty-eight-page family shareholders' agreement. One close observer of Oshawa Group's history suggests that the Wolfes needed such a long agreement because the family members no longer trusted one another. The agreement contained all those things which such shareholder pacts contain, including provisions for the sale of voting shares among family members. Under the new agreeement, Harold surrendered his right, as one of the original voting shareholders, to precipitate a sale of the company on his own.

There were also provisions to create a family council to act as a forum for discussing family and business issues. This was a highly positive development for a clan that had problems communicating, and in which bitterness and envy ran deep. But not all family members took the forum seriously, and Jonathan in particular seemed to resent it. It gave Harold new authority as the head of the family council — authority that could be seen as undermining Jonathan's inherited right to leadership. However, the agreement also confirmed that Jonathan would become CEO as long as he showed the requisite skills and performance.

The family had also fallen in line with Harold's concern that Oshawa Group be run as a true public company rather than as an instrument of the Wolfes. The board, which had been dominated by Wolfes, would now have a strong coterie of independent directors. This would inject new blood and forceful personalities, who would naturally clash with some family members.

Despite the new shareholder agreement, the family was no more united than before. Oshawa Group's performance continued to lag — its sales and earnings were flat, and it seemed unable to make the difficult changes that were needed to revive its fortunes. Family members were growing increasingly unhappy about the choice of Jonathan as future CEO. Jonathan's uncle Harvey, still a smouldering presence on the board, had little confidence in his nephew.

Harold and Jonathan mistrusted each other. Rick and Myron Wolfe, both of whom had controlled large chunks of voting shares, were suspicious of the change process and concerned about their future roles. At one point Jonathan had given one of his cousins a negative performance review, which would have meant no annual bonus. The decision had to be overruled by Al Graham, who was still the CEO. In September 1997, Harold, Myron, and Rick finally made their move: they decided that the choice of a future CEO should be opened up to outsiders. The board instructed Allister Graham to undertake an executive search, and the headhunting firm of Egon Zehnder was hired to look for a new CEO to replace Graham when he took his retirement.

Some employees speculate that from this moment on, Jonathan was quietly working toward the sale of the company. According to this theory, the long-time heir was taking the view that "If I can't have the CEO's job, no one can." Jonathan will not be interviewed on this matter. In any case, other managers saw no evidence that he was thinking this way — in fact, Jonathan offered himself as a candidate for the CEO's post. Yet his attitude clearly had changed: he began to exclude people from his inner circle and was starting to operate more in the mode of a temporary president.

To outsiders, nothing seemed different: the search for a new CEO was kept tightly under wraps. Indeed, if the Wolfes have one strength as a family, it is their ability to close ranks, to keep their lips sealed, and to avoid battling each other in the press. But inside the family ranks there was considerable uncertainty in the early months of 1998. Family council meetings were held and the tension at them verged on unbearable. At one point some members put it to Jonathan to show he had a vision for the company: *Show us this vision*, they challenged, *and you can still become CEO*. Jonathan did not take up the challenge and was eliminated from the race. Late one night, when no one was at the office, he cleaned out his desk and was gone — no ceremony, no speech. He was clearly bitter, as were Rose, his mother, and Elizabeth, his sister. At the annual meeting on June 18, 1998, Al Graham told the world the news: he was retiring, Jonathan had resigned, and the search was on for a new CEO.

Oshawa Group was already negotiating with someone highly qualified to lead the company. John Lacey had been a grocery retailer in his native South Africa before immigrating to Canada to join Loblaws and emerging as one of this country's most sought-after professional managers. He had built a remarkable reputation as a corporate fixer at companies such as Scott's Hospitality and W.I.C. Western International Communications, both family businesses that he polished up to be sold. He had a knack for increasing the value of companies, allowing shareholders to reap handsome returns when the firms went on the block. Lacey met his prospective employers at a series of meetings at the fusty Old Mill restaurant and conference centre in a leafy ravine in Toronto's west end. At one point he told a group of Wolfes that he might like to work for a family business but only if the family was committed to the business. The Wolfes' reply was that they were committed.

Mr. Lacey joined the company in September 1998 and immediately set to work fashioning its new strategic path. Some people have the theory that his mandate was essentially to buff up Oshawa Group and then sell it. After all, that was the message of his track record. But others who worked closely with him insist that he wanted to run and build this company. In any case his appointment did signal a dramatic shift for Oshawa Group — a professional manager had been hired from outside with the mandate to make sweeping changes. Even as the Wolfes supported his hiring, he made some of them nervous, for their entitlements were no longer safe. Lacey began to study Oshawa Group's divisions and evaluate their potential. It was clear that he intended to add value to the business and to operate it for all the shareholders, not just the Wolfes. Lacey was supported by an increasingly activist board, led by such luminaries as Stanley Hart, the president of Salomon, Smith Barney in Canada; Larry Stevenson, the CEO of Chapters, the bookstore company; Charles Winograd, the deputy chairman of RBC Dominion Securities; and Peter Morrice, the former president of Canada Trust.

Behind the scenes, the mindset of some Wolfe family members was shifting. They were no longer strongly committed to owning a wholesale and retail food business. The family had been approached by potential buyers in the past, but nothing had come of it. Still, those approaches had got them thinking. They had already lost out on millions of dollars of shareholder value because the stock had been a market underperformer. Also, family members sensed that the company had changed — it was no longer small and personal, and family influence was diminishing. Some felt threatened by Lacey's determination to shake things up, although others were heartened by this new energy. Harvey Wolfe had no great interest in holding on to his shares; Harold was sixty years old and wanted to pull back a bit from the company. But at the same time, he wanted any sale to follow an orderly and acceptable process — one that was run by the board, not the family.

The critical factor was that there was no Ray Wolfe around — no clear family leader who could bring the various interests together. As John Lacey tried to work his magic, some members were clearly interested in holding on. Others had decided they wanted to sell the thing and move on. The desire to pass on a family legacy was no longer at work. The world had changed — the board was taking more initiative, family leadership was sorely lacking, and the company was facing wrenching change. What's more, a number of key share-holders had no direct descendants, or at least none who wanted to play a lead-ing role in the company. "Why do families keep businesses?" one family member asks. "For reasons of legacy." Those reasons no longer applied.

Inside the company, Lacey fingered Oshawa Group's beleaguered Atlantic wholesale division as a candidate for sale. It was #3 in its market, behind Sobey's and Loblaws, with little likelihood of moving up. He first approached Doug Stewart, the CEO of the Sobey family's Empire Corp., a seasoned grocery executive who once headed Oshawa Group's Ontario division. Stewart relayed the news that the Sobeys, who owned the top chain in the Maritimes, weren't interested. Lacey then called up Richard Currie, the CEO of Loblaws, who immediately indicated an interest in buying the Atlantic arm. This prospect alarmed the Sobeys, who now reconsidered their competitive position, and took a closer look at Oshawa Group as a whole.

The Sobeys, like the Wolfes, were moving into the third-generation leadership of their family business. But whereas Jonathan Wolfe's rise had been rocky, Paul Sobey, forty-one and the product of a Harvard education, seemed to win easy acceptance as his family's standard bearer. Paul was following in the footsteps of the second-generation leaders — his father David and uncle Donald — who for their part had succeeded their own father, the company founder Frank Sobey. Perhaps it was the Sobeys' relative isolation in rural Nova Scotia that made them immune to the usual public discord — or perhaps they simply kept the dissen-sion more carefully hidden. There were as many as ten Sobeys in the company, and there was no indication of festering quarrels. The Sobeys were also putting some thought and effort into being a family business — they were clients of the Business Families Foundation. They had a family council at which members would meet and iron out matters. For some time the Sobeys had been looking to expand more aggressively in central Canada. The restiveness of the Wolfe family and the restructuring of Oshawa Group gave them such an opening.

October 1998 was a decisive month. Lacey was negotiating the sale of the Atlantic division to rival Loblaws. Harold Wolfe, a key player, was preparing to leave on a bicycle trip in Israel on behalf of Hebrew University. While there, he was in a bike accident and suffered serious injuries, cracking ribs and break-ing a collarbone. He lay in an Israeli hospital and could not be moved. In the view of some observers, the rest of the family exploited his absence to speed up the sale process. Harold, with his obsession for process, had emphasized that the board would have to manage any sale of the company, not the family. His wishes would ultimately be ignored.

On October 24, newspaper reports out of Toronto disclosed that the Sobey family's holding company, Empire Co., had sent a letter to the Wolfe family bidding to buy the entire company, taking out both Class A and Class B shareholders. The Sobeys were prepared to pay $70 for each of the voting shares and $35 for each of the A shares. The Sobeys, no doubt shrewdly exploiting the divisions in the Wolfe family, had set a quick deadline of October 30 for the family to accept. All of this was apparently news to Lacey, who was phoned by a reporter with the leaked letter the night before the story ran. He found it very curious. Lacey had previously arranged a three-day senior management meeting, which happened to coincide with the Monday following the release of the Sobey offer. He went to the meeting and said he would do anything possible to assist the family; then he cut off the session after just one day. Clearly, there were other things on everyone's mind.

There followed a week of frantic and often bitter negotiations, complicated by the fact that Harold was flat on his back in Israel. Without Harold's input, family members hired New York investment bankers to assist in the sale of the company. The board, meanwhile, was extremely unhappy that the family had not disclosed to it the letter from the Sobeys. This was yet another skirmish in an escalating battle between the activist directors and a family that still acted as if the company was a private entity. The family said it had no choice in the matter: the Sobey letter had stated that if the deal was made public, the offer would be null and void. Besides, the family's impulse had always been to keep things quiet. As the week progressed, the board appointed an independent committee to review the fairness of the offer; it also tried to find a white knight that would increase the value for all shareholders. The directors' meeting on October 28 was particularly rancorous: the directors enacted a poison pill to try to buy time and to help boost the bid for the Class A shares.

The Wall Street investment bankers did their job for the family — they were able to persuade the Sobeys to hike the $70-a-share bid to $116 and then to $135. Thanks to the board's efforts, the Sobeys also threw in another dollar a share for the A shares — not great but a decided improvement. On November 2 the family accepted the offer. Harold, frustrated and frozen out of the decision-making in an Israeli hospital, was the last to relay his acceptance. The Wolfes were no longer the owners of the company that Maurice and Max had founded and that Ray had built. As a group, the Wolfe families were richer by about $250 million. It was a nice sum, but in terms of the megadollars being tossed around in the takeovers of the 1990s, it was hardly enormous.

The end of the Wolfe family's rule was fast and furious. John Lacey co-operated with the Sobeys on the handover, but it was clear that he would have no role in the new public company that would be formed by combining the operations of Oshawa Group and the Sobey stores. He left in December with a handsome cheque for three months' work, and resurfaced shortly afterward as chairman of another, more seriously troubled company — the Loewen Group, a chain of funeral homes based in Burnaby, British Columbia.

The product of the Sobeys–Oshawa merger, a debt-burdened company with $10 billion in annual sales, would trade publicly under the name Sobeys. Doug Stewart, the former Oshawa Group executive, would run the new supermarket giant, the largest such company in Canada. Rick and Myron left the scene quickly; Harold retired. His nephews, Stephen and Joel Flatt, stayed around until the end of January 1999 to help with the transition. Jonathan, as he pursued his new business ventures, had little contact with his cousins, aunts, and uncles. With the company gone, there was even less to unite a family that had clearly lost its will to speak with a single voice.

NINE

THE WILSONS — EIGHT GENERATIONS

The late Peter Wilson, right, and Dave Wilson, seventh-generation owners of Wilson Fuel.

L ESLIE WILSON CAME HOME to Truro, Nova Scotia, a couple of years ago, leaving a high-profile job she liked in Calgary. But the family business was beckoning. Now thirty-one, she's working for her father Dave as a marketing and advertising specialist for Kerr Controls, a heating equipment distribution company and one of a cluster of companies owned by Dave and his brother Peter. "I felt like it was time to come home and get a feel for it," Leslie says.

The timing also had something to do with the fact that her father was seventy and her uncle fifty-nine, although neither showed signs of slowing down. Leslie and her six brothers and cousins — all in their twenties and thirties — have also reached the stage of life where they are interested in carrying on the family tradition. It helps that the Wilsons have a pretty impressive track record in passing on businesses to their children. Leslie is part of the eighth generation to work in the family holdings, which at present range from heating oil to gas stations to ski hills. The children of this generation, some of whom have been working away, feel it is time to take a look at what their parents have built and to decide if there's a role for them in Nova Scotia.

Leslie, a former journalist who worked as communications director for the National Sports Centre in Calgary, has joined the family company at a pivotal moment. The Wilsons' core business is heating oil. They own Wilson Fuel, a company that sells oil to consumers in Halifax and Truro, and they manufacture and distribute furnaces to burn the stuff. Combined with the family's chain of gas stations, petroleum is at the core of what they do. The business has hummed along nicely over the past twenty-five years, providing a comfortable lifestyle and good education for the kids. But Nova Scotia is about to be swamped with natural gas piped in from Sable Island. That fuel is enjoying a wave of enthusiasm and support, particularly from the provincial government. The Wilsons, with their base in oil, wonder how they are going to fit into the new energy market. "I couldn't have picked a more interesting time to come home," says Leslie, in an understated tone that recalls the old Chinese curse, "May you live in interesting times."

Don't count the Wilsons out: adaptability seems to run in this family's genes. Whenever confronted with precipitous change, the Wilsons have always calmly moved their business in a new direction. In the late 1700s they were merchants and chandlers, bringing supplies and fuel to the remote communities of Nova Scotia. They later switched from selling wood to selling coal, and then oil. A generation ago the family got out of the construction business to concentrate entirely on fuel. In the seventh generation Dave and Peter built a string of fifty-five gas bars, which now form part of a group of companies with annual revenues of $90 million and a full-time workforce of 350 people. The brothers admitted they had their plates full: they faced a hefty business challenge at the same time as they were bracing for a new generation to take over the companies.

The Wilsons don't come to mind immediately when you think about Atlantic dynasties — the McCains grab bigger headlines, the Sobeys engineer larger takeovers, and the Irvings wield much more wealth. All are part of an unusually strong core of family businesses that have developed in this part of Canada. Think of the chocolate-making Ganongs of St. Stephen, New Brunswick, and the diversified Jodreys of the Annapolis Valley. Many of these enterprises are generations old. Moosehead Breweries of Saint John is as old as the country — it was founded in 1867 by an ancestor of the current owner, Derek Oland. Oland observes that private family companies stick out in Atlantic Canada because of the relatively small number of publicly traded companies. And even the public companies, such as Sobeys, may have family shareholders in control. It's just the family way.

But for pure staying power, nobody beats the Wilsons of Truro and Halifax. In the first seven generations — since ancestor William Wilson moved to Nova Scotia from New Hampshire in 1788 — there have been no big blowups, no public spats. "We say we're not going to pull that stuff," says Dave Wilson. "We keep out of each other's hair." This formula has made the family one of the longest-running clans in Canadian business, right up there with the Molsons, whose ancestor started brewing beer in Canada about the time

William Wilson was running provisions. The Wilsons are proof that family business need not be all about court battles and mudslinging. Now in the late 1990s, the brothers were trying to make sure that the same model of problem solving and sweet reason was carried into the next generation.

Robert Blunden, a business professor at Dalhousie University in Halifax, says the Wilsons seem to be doing a number of things right. Like other enduring dynasties, they have been able to transfer their values of hard work and loyalty to succeeding generations. "You have to start at a young age, before the child is fifteen," says Blunden, a co-founder of the Halifax chapter of the Canadian Association of Family Enterprise. The Wilsons have also recruited talented nonfamily managers and delegated real authority to them, he adds. The brothers generally got involved in the big issues, but left the operations to senior managers.

As Dave Wilson likes to say, the brothers were successful in warding off feuds because they didn't get in each other's way. And that's because the operations are fairly far-flung. In Truro, Dave owns and runs Kerr Controls Ltd., a $35-million business which distributes heating, air conditioning, and refrigeration equipment in Canada and the United States. He also manages another family firm, Parrsboro Metal Fabricators Ltd., a manufacturer of furnaces and heating equipment that supplies Kerr and makes half its sales in the United States.

In Halifax, Peter served as president and (with Dave) co-owner of Wilson Fuel Co. Ltd., a regional heating oil supplier and distributor of gasoline to the chain of Wilson gas stations, fifteen of which are owned by the company and the rest by private dealers. In 1998, Wilson Fuel had revenues of $38-million. Then there are the ski hills — Crabbe Mountain in New Brunswick and Wentworth in Nova Scotia. Dave owns the hills through Kerr Controls, but everybody in the family benefits. "We all ski together," he says. Sports are a big source of bonding for this family. They're all outdoors people. They have cottages on a lake outside Truro, and the males of the eighth generation play basketball together. Leslie was a long jump champion in college and an award-winning athlete in the province. The sports side may all be inherited from the brothers' father, George, who was a pretty good Senior A hockey player for the Truro Bearcats in the 1930s.

It helped that Peter had another life that kept him pretty busy. He was not around much in the early years, when Dave was building his own business. As a young man he studied mechanical engineering at university. He then pursued postgraduate studies in Britain, where he met his wife Rose. He even worked for a time for Shell Canada. But the tug of the Maritimes is strong, and Peter decided he could pursue his professional life closer to home. After he came home in the 1960s, he joined the faculty of the Technical University of Nova Scotia, where he stayed for twenty-nine years and headed the industrial engineering department until his retirement a few years ago. All the time he was working at TUNS (now part of Dalhousie), he stayed fairly active in the family business — an arrangement negotiated with the school. The university link allowed the Wilsons to spot talented young graduates who could be recruited by the Wilson companies, which probably hire more engineers for businesses their size than any other Dave knows in Canada.

The brothers had read a lot about all the quarrelling and division in other family companies in recent years. The sordid example of the feuding McCains in neighbouring New Brunswick has been on their minds. So a couple of years ago they started thinking seriously about a succession plan. They were prodded as well by the fact that a number of their children who had worked away were pondering coming home. So Peter, Rose, and Dave — who is divorced — travelled to Toronto in May 1998 to the biennial conference of CAFE, just to see how other families were doing it. As he listened to even more horror stories, Peter kept insisting that the Wilsons' priorities were clear: "The family comes first and the business comes after that. If we ever thought that it would make our [children] go after each other's throats, we'd sell the business first." Still, Dave points out, pride is also a factor in their planning: "We want to continue that legacy and stewardship. You want to see it preserved."

The first step, they felt, was to involve the children in the succession process. After all, whatever happened had to be acceptable to them, so why not let them craft a succession plan and present it to the parents? The five kids who live in Nova Scotia embarked on regular monthly meetings to share ideas and find a model for succession they can embrace. These five include Leslie and her brother Steven, thirty-four a recent MBA graduate of the University of Western Ontario, who joined the company in July 1998 and has been working on Wilson Fuel's response to the natural gas issue. Three of Peter's children were also involved — Ian, thirty, was director of store operations for the Wilsons' gas stops; James, twenty-seven, was installing software at Wilson Fuel; and David, thirty-one, was working full-time for a Halifax venture capital firm while spending a lot of spare time thinking about the family companies. These five made sure the two cousins outside Nova Scotia were kept informed: Dave's other son, Gregor, twenty-eight, was training to be an outdoor guide in Kamloops, while Peter's youngest, Christopher, twenty-one, has been studying at McGill University. Everyone was working on their timetables so that they could welcome Gregor and Christopher into the talks, whenever they can get home for a while.

According to David, Peter's son, the children all realized that they were going to be partners at some point, and wondered how they could work together. The monthly meetings were a first step toward figuring that out. There were no strict deadlines, although at some point they would present something tangible to the parents. He expected that in time the meetings will become a permanent institution — a kind of cousins' council. "Our parents are getting to the age when they should be able, if they want, to step away from the business. It was our responsibility, given that they had wanted to pass on the businesses, that we should provide them with the means of doing that."

During the first year of discussions the children mostly met by themselves, without the help of outside experts. But as they got into the larger issues — Who gets what? Who works where? — they realized they would need a facilitator to help them through the process. So they engaged David Chapman, a counsellor with a psychology background. The children don't seem concerned that Chapman lives thousands of miles away in Minnesota; he is experienced in helping family firms and has achieved a good rapport with the cousins during his get-acquainted sessions.

The succession will be tricky because of the number of people who will be involved in ownership and management — as many as seven, up from two in the previous generation. John Ward, the prominent professor in family business at Loyola of Chicago University, is one of a number of experts who have noted the value of "pruning the family tree" — that is, limiting the ownership and management to a few persons, or even just one person, to minimize the possibility of sibling rivalry and later management conflicts. The Wilsons are moving in the opposite direction, but they also have a strong desire to make sure everyone gets his or her due. Clearly, what is often most efficient for the business does not always jibe with the ideal of family democracy.

One of the big challenges has been to make the important distinction between the wealth of the family business and the administration of that business. A lot of business clans get it confused. They think the two aspects are inextricably tied up — that if you own a company and the wealth it generates, you have to manage it too. Not so, the experts say. Peter Wilson felt that if the children can capture the distinction between wealth and management, they may be able to minimize any dissension. Outside managers are often better suited to run a company; the family can focus on nurturing ownership and value. Peter was encouraged by the cousins' meetings: "Still, there might be problems when rubber hits the road, when they have to come up with solutions."

His son David, the venture capitalist, says it is hard for children to address such issues with emotional detachment. "I look objectively at hundreds of companies but it's interesting to see how hard it is to look with the same objective eyes at a business that has the same last name as yours. It makes it more difficult, so having an outsider involved is really important." When he invests in a company as a venture capitalist, one of the things he demands is a board of directors with independent members. That's what he would like to see for the Wilson companies, which have rarely enlisted outside directors. "It's hard to get a family business to think they need an outside view," he concedes. This outside voice will become even more critical when the parents aren't there to provide guidance, and when sorting out governance issues gets more complicated because there are seven owners instead of two. As for management roles, he points out that the Wilson children shouldn't be automatically excluded, and that family members can train and prepare themselves for leadership roles. "But it doesn't necessarily have to happen. There are other good people."

Peter Wilson explained that outside directors have been recruited in the past, but they never worked out particularly well. But as issues become more complex, and as the pressures on the company mount, "we need some form of adjudication on management issues. For example, who's the president, whether it should be a professional or an insider; and how family members are contributing. And the children seem quite keen on that." After exchanging their own points of view, the children plan to canvas the key managers to get their input on how the company works and how the succession might evolve. Then they will try to develop a real plan.

There are a number of complications. The children have to sort out a succession strategy for four different businesses, each with a different ownership structure. Wilson Fuel has been owned 50–50 by the two brothers. Dave owns Kerr Controls, and through it the ski hills. But Parrsboro is held by a family trust, with the children as beneficiaries. "We're concerned about finding a way to co-ordinate each of these for the common good," says Steven, Dave's son. "Right now it's easy for the two of them [Dave and Peter] to resolve things. But when you add more bodies, it's more difficult." He points out that some family members are involved in one company but not in the others. Each person wants to see his or her company do well, so there will have to be a system of checks and balances. The children will go so far as to look at the transfer prices by which products move from one company to another — for example, from Parrsboro to its distributor, Kerr Controls.

One thing in the kids' favour is that together they can muster a fair bit of expertise. James is studying to be a certified management accountant; Ian has an environmental degree; and Leslie takes a journalistic and marketing perspective. Steven had worked in a number of areas in the family businesses before heading off for his MBA. The assumption was that he would work somewhere else for a couple of years, but with the succession and natural gas issues looming, his father asked him to come back sooner. David has plenty of non-Wilson experience to bring to the table. He recently returned to Nova Scotia after working as a venture capitalist and engineer for six years in the San Francisco area. Before that, he earned a bachelor's degree from Dartmouth and a postgraduate degree in engineering from Stanford University. He came home because he wanted to get involved in the Wilson businesses, but an opportunity arose to work for the Atlantic Canada Fund, a $30 million fund for small high-tech companies backed by two levels of government and seven chartered banks. It seemed a great opportunity: come home, work as a venture capitalist, and have some input into the family companies.

He sees one big challenge for the Wilson companies, and for any family business. As a venture capitalist, he always makes sure that the managers of his investee companies receive proper financial incentives. "In entrepreneurial companies, you do that through stock options so that employees have the same goal as [the owners] do — that is, maximizing shareholder wealth. I see what a powerful incentive share ownership can be." So how does that translate for a closely held family business? Managers may be compensated quite adequately, but it is the incentive structure that ensures they are moving in the same direction as the ownership. So how do you do that?

He realizes that many family businesses are mature businesses — in the case at hand, the Wilsons are an eighth-generation mature business. Can the Wilson companies still be entrepreneurial and striving for change at this stage? He believes they have to be. "Your markets, even though they're mature, change dramatically. And if you're not entrepreneurial in that market you're not going to be successful. You've got to be continually looking for new opportunities and new businesses, which is not unlike what I do with young technology companies." David doesn't have an answer regarding how to incorporate an incentive structure into a family business so that managers see it as an entrepreneurial opportunity. It is possible to give people compensation that mirrors performance and acts somewhat like public shares, but it's not the same. "Equity is such a powerful motivator. But if equity is completely taken out of the equation in a family business because it is only going to be handed down to family, then you're really losing a valuable tool to make sure an organization is entirely entrepreneurial. So you've really got to address that head on."

David says that outside his full-time job, the Wilson companies are taking up more than half his free time. "Family businesses tend to be all-consuming," he says. He wonders whether his emotional attachment to this cluster of companies is all that healthy. "When I'm a shareholder in a company through my venture funds, I'm entirely objective or I try to be. But family business is much more complicated."

Life was a lot simpler in the nineteenth and early twentieth centuries. The Wilsons, like most dynasties, believed in passing on the company through the male heirs. Women just didn't get involved to the extent that Leslie possibly will. The brothers say that sibling spats were avoided simply because each generation contained one son who emerged as the natural leader, and the others seemed to accept his status. Frank Wilson, their grandfather, was clearly the leader of the fifth generation, and his brother Bert, who also worked in the company, didn't question that. Because Peter was away so much and had his teaching life, he and Dave didn't really rub against each other. It's not at all clear whether a single leader will emerge in the eighth generation. The children say they may adopt a more collegial model, which will be the pattern in many family companies in the twenty-first century.

It's been 210 years since William Wilson left Londonderry, New Hampshire, and settled in Nova Scotia as a supplier of provisions to what was then a British colony. He had a sailing vessel and used to ply the coastline. His son got into construction and moved the family to Truro. The Wilsons were masons who specialized in stone buildings. When a munitions ship exploded in Halifax harbour in 1918, levelling large parts of Halifax and Dartmouth, it was the brothers' grandfather Frank who directed the reconstruction of Dartmouth. The businesses have evolved since then, but there have been some constant themes — fuel, construction, and provisions. In the 1930s, George Wilson moved the family out of construction to focus on selling wood, coal, and ice. Around the Second World War he expanded into furnace oil, which remains the family's core operation.

His son Dave went off to private school and later to university. But he was not a success at higher education and was advised to take a year off to reassess his future. He came home and never went back to school: in the postwar era there were just too many opportunities to explore. It was Dave who pushed the company into the manufacturing and distribution of heating equipment, including furnaces. Dave found he was taking increasing responsibility for the business — and for the upbringing of his brother Peter, who was ten years younger. Their mother died when Peter was in high school, and their father's health was deteriorating. Dave became a kind of second father for Peter, even serving as his brother's scoutmaster. He also encouraged his younger brother's academic career. He well recognized the advantages that Peter could bring to the Wilson enterprises: "He helped us in technology with computers, and from the academic world he brought a different insight. He was analytical." And of course, he spotted bright young people to hire, a valuable service in the Maritimes, whose brightest graduates often leave to pursue careers elsewhere.

George Wilson died in 1975. By that time there was not a lot of value left in his oil distribution business. The OPEC oil crisis was in full swing, and petroleum prices were soaring. Governments in the Maritimes, as in most regions, were trying to discourage the use of heating oil. Also, there had been little succession planning. The two sons split the shares in the business. Their two sisters got no shares but received financial compensation. (None of the sisters' eight children are involved in the companies.) "He [George] felt his job was done with this transfer of shares, and then nature took its course," Peter observed.

Some things, however, did not die with their father, such as old rivalries. George Wilson had been a business acquaintance of a hard-driving entrepreneur named K.C. Irving, who was building a sprawling empire with interests in energy, forestry, the media, and just about anything else he could corral. The two men were able to speak to each other on a "George" and "Kenneth" basis. Irving would occasionally drop by the Wilson Fuel offices in Truro and offer to buy the company from George. There was always a bit of verbal sparring between the two older men, who seemed to warily like each other. At one point Irving told George: "If you sell out to us, you don't have to worry. We'll look after David." The Wilsons just rolled their eyes — they weren't about to sell to the Irvings.

For the Irvings and their Saint John–based business empire, the Wilsons must seem like bugs on their windshields. But the two clans have maintained a respectful rivalry over the years. One might call the Wilsons the "anti-Irvings." They just seem to be on the different side of almost every issue. The Wilsons squared off against the Irvings in the late 1980s, when the Wilsons were trying to break into the provincially regulated gasoline business in Nova Scotia. One of Peter Wilson's former students, now a manager with Wilson Fuel, figured there was a market opportunity in selling gas a little cheaper from the pumps. At that time, there were no independents in the province. In a series of hearings held across the province, the Irvings, who own a big gas station network, strongly opposed the Wilson entry.

The Wilsons argued that they would inject competition into a market controlled by Irving Oil and the other integrated giants. The brothers were successful in winning public opinion to their side. Eventually the province deregulated the industry, and the Wilsons became gas station operators, now holding a small percentage of the provincial market. They tend to be low-cost suppliers, often in locations where Irving and the majors don't operate. Peter says his Wilson gas stops probably save Nova Scotians $50 million to $70 million a year by offering a competitive alternative. The Wilsons can't come near competing with the Irvings in terms of the capital they can bring to the market, "but we keep our cost base low and fight them on price."

In the 1990s, natural gas was about to start flowing in Nova Scotia, and the Wilsons decided they had to get involved somehow. They applied to become the local distributor for natural gas in the small communities in three counties in the northern part of the province. Dave and Peter were prepared to set up a joint venture with a New York gas company. But the province decided there should be one superdistributor of gas for the entire province, and that cut off any chance of local participation. And there would be two finalists for that honour — Sempra Energy, a huge California-based utility, and Maritimes NRG, a consortium of Westcoast Energy of Vancouver and — guess who? — Irving Oil. "This time, we're right up against the Irvings full bore again," says Dave. In late 1999, Nova Scotia's utility board recommended the Sempra bid, handing a rare defeat to the Irvings.

The province's decision to shut out local participation left the Wilsons "a little in limbo," Dave says. His son Steven had returned from MBA school to lead the family's strategic response to the arrival of natural gas. But now, says Dave with some concern, "maybe Steven will have to go to greener fields. There may not be an opportunity for his skills here at home." Steven agrees that the natural gas issue has cast a shadow over the succession issue and his own future. "Our family business is tied up with the oil heating industry in Canada," he says.

The Wilsons are concerned that the provincial government seems to be favouring natural gas over oil. This raises the possibility of subsidies for the distribution of gas. Former Liberal premier Russell McLellan publicly indicated at one point that he would seek subsidization of gas distribution to meet his goal of bringing gas to all of Nova Scotia within seven years. In its lobbying, the heating oil industry had argued that the price of oil on world markets has made its fuel competitive in terms of pure economics — that is, as long as the economics remain pure. It just hopes that consumers will be allowed to choose based on that equation. Meanwhile, the Wilsons continue to search for a role in this new energy equation. Steven Wilson speculates that there may be consolidation among the heating oil suppliers and that the family could add to its presence along that line. And, of course, the Wilsons do make gas furnaces, and they could expand that business.

If the Wilsons lose their strong oil furnace market in Eastern Canada, they will step up activity in Ontario and the United States. Steven is confident that "we can find our niche. But if we have to fight government and the natural gas companies, that's difficult."

As the new century drew near, the Wilsons were obviously nervous. Could they find a way to participate in the gas business? Will their oil business come under increasing pressure? Will they have to sell some of their businesses? The ski hills, hurt by poor snow conditions in 1998–99, are obvious candidates for a sell-off. The family has taken a leading role in the heating oil association, lobbying to get its message across. David Wilson, the thirty-one-year-old venture capitalist, takes a more detached perspective. For family businesses to survive, he says, they must adapt. He believes that in every generation there has to be a major shift in the business — "you have to have a fundamental change in order to be viable."

He says that his father's generation changed the business by diversifying into gas stops and heating equipment, and that there will be change in his generation as well. "In fact, if you look at history, it's almost a ten-year cycle of business opportunities. We sell gasoline now. Well, how are fuel cells going to impact that business? Our parents went through that, and we're going to have to do it. There's opportunity in it too." In the past the family has tended to be reactive, adapting to survive rather than moving according to a strategic vision. While they made the right responses, that approach may not be possible in this generation.

John Ward, the small business guru, agrees with David. In *Keeping the Family Business Healthy*, he writes: "This is quite possibly the most important lesson that successful family businesses teach: the need to combine strategic revolutions with changes in leaders, be they sons, daughters, or outside managers. These new leaders, arriving every twenty to twenty-five years or so, naturally bring their own ideas to the business."

David says the children see this as more than a succession — it's an opportunity for some kind of strategic renewal in the face of the natural gas challenge. "It's not just a handoff to us, it's not that easy. It makes us anxious but it motivates us to get a structure in place that's going to work."

During the summer of 1999, the Wilson family seemed to be coping well with these challenges. The cousins were meeting regularly and Peter and Dave continued to prepare for their own exits, although Peter told the family he felt he could work another ten years. Peter had a mild heart attack in the spring when he suffered a fall, but he was given a clean bill of health. He enjoyed an active summer, at one point sailing his boat up the coast to Sherbrooke and back in heavy fog. Then, in late August, while attending the theatre in Wolfville, Nova Scotia, he became acutely sick. He and Rose left during the intermission and he died of a massive heart attack in the car. His death at fifty-nine was widely mourned in Nova Scotia. The Halifax edition of the satirical magazine *Frank*, in an unusual tribute to a public figure, described him as "one of the nicest, most interesting, most eclectic and most respected Nova Scotians of his generation."

Peter's passing jolted the family, giving even more urgency to the issue of succession. Leslie was now clearly committed to taking over Kerr Controls from her father; Steven was more involved in Parrsboro, as well as in other projects. At Wilson Fuel, the employees were anxious for some sign of direction, and Peter and Rose's second-oldest son, Ian, moved into the president's job. "We just had to accelerate the process," Dave Wilson explained. Peter and Dave had always assumed, he said, that "I'd be the first out the door. Then, boy, he's just not here anymore."

There were changes at the ski hills too. An effort to sell Crabbe Mountain to a New Brunswick businessman fell through and Dave continued to operate it. However, the cousins had leased Ski Wentworth from Dave, and were considering long-term plans to develop it into an all-season resort, testing out the validity of the business model. Dave's younger son, Gregor, was back from British Columbia and working at Wentworth.

David, Peter's oldest son, says the cousins are now much more focused on making the transition happen. Over the next couple of years, they will work on the ownership transfers, resolving whatever issues remain. They now have a more concrete timetable, rather than just a conceptual idea of where they are going. His father's death, he says, was a message: "Get your act together. You can't leave these details hanging."

TEN

THE MOLSONS —
THE FIRST FAMILY

Eric Molson with the brewmaster of Molson's Air Canada Centre brew pub in Toronto.

THE NAME ON THE HULKING OLD BREWERY on Notre Dame Street East in Montreal says "Molson" in large letters. The labels on the beer bottles rolling off the production line say "Molson" too. Across the street, in the company's head office building, the walls of the fourth-floor hall are lined with portraits of ancient Molsons. The man who founded the company 215 years ago was named John Molson. And a group of his descendents still controls 60 percent of the Class B voting shares of the parent company, Molson Inc. Yet Eric Molson, the chairman of Canada's oldest brewer, insists this is not a family company. "We are a large public company where the significant shareholder happens to be the same family that started the business a long time ago," says Eric, sitting behind his dark wooden desk in his dark, wood-panelled office.

He argues strenuously that the Molson family participates in the brewing company merely as shareholders. Certainly they are large owners of shares, but they are not much different from the thousands of public shareholders who also participate in the ownership of the company. Oh yes, three Molsons do sit on the fourteen-member board — Eric, his brother Stephen, who runs the Molson Foundation, and his forty-five-year-old cousin Ian, who is likely to succeed Eric as chairman. At annual meetings, Eric regularly votes his family group's proxy in favour of management. But, he argues, a board dominated by independent directors charts the governance of the company, and chooses the

CEO, who is not a Molson and who may never again be a Molson. The company went public in 1945, and a Molson has not been president since Percy Talbot Molson committed suicide in 1966. The family's role is to be supportive of management; no Molson today sits in a senior management position. In fact, the only Molson involved operationally in the company is the youngest of Eric's three sons, who has just joined the marketing department.

If this were a family company, Eric says, the overriding goal of the family in the company would be to advance its own interests. The company would be a vehicle for the family — it would exist for the family's purposes. But for the Molsons, "we see ourselves as representing all the stakeholders, not just other shareholders but employees, clients, society, even societies. We have a lot more to worry about than just ourselves." On another occasion Eric has said, "The Molsons are not wealthy, but we are guardians of wealth."

Eric Molson apparently believes in this distinction. So Molson's may not be the oldest family company in Canada, but it is certainly the country's oldest family-controlled company. It considers itself the second-oldest Canadian-based company of any kind — only four years younger than *The Gazette*, the surviving English-language daily newspaper in Montreal. Hudson's Bay Co. may be a much older company — it was founded in 1670 — but, Eric argues, it was a British company until the 1800s, well after John Molson brewed his first bottle of beer in a Montreal brewery in 1783. The Eatons, whose frittering away of the family legacy has been much lamented, are mere pikers in the dynasty sweepstakes — they can trace their retail roots only to the 1850s. With the demise of T. Eaton Co. Ltd., and Sears's purchase of the Eaton's brand, Molson Inc. is the most prominent surviving family company whose reach stretches right across the country, and whose family name remains a strong national brand. The Molson family must now contend with the same pressures that killed Eaton's — it must find ways to maintain dynamism and change in a company where the modern-day heirs may not live up to the legacy of the ancestral founders and builders. The Eatons failed miserably to adjust; the Molsons have done well in the past but have stumbled in recent years. The next few years will be a test of the resiliency of Canada's oldest family brand.

Among old Canadian money, the Molson blood is the bluest of the blue. Yet the head of the family's sixth generation, Eric Herbert Molson, sixty-two, is the plainest-spoken, least blue-blooded guy you'll ever meet. Strip away the fancy schools, the Princeton degree, the fine houses, and the art and artifacts in the corner office and you find a man who simply likes the beer business. On a Friday morning in May, he's wearing a rumpled white shirt, a bland print tie, and a pair of grey suit pants. His office is a mess because he's been moving boxes of documents back from Toronto. Molson's, he announces proudly, is shifting its executive offices back to the city that spawned it. He has no idea how to dispose of all the boxes of papers and artifacts. Surely some archives would be interested. "What do you do with this?" he asks, showing the visitor a small, degree-like document celebrating his chancellorship of Concordia University.

There are rumours that Eric Molson is a painfully shy man, someone who backs away from any public notice. It is said that he once made a videotape of a speech to staff members, rather than have to address the group directly. And that he is indecisive and ineffectual. But if Eric is bashful or backward, he is not showing it today. He is effusive, even emotional, especially about the family's twin passions, beer and the Montreal Canadiens, whom he calls "a precious and delicate hockey team." It is hard to think of a team of dentally challenged hockey players as delicate, like some flower, but if anyone can, it's Eric.

The Molsons exemplify a kind of relationship that's rare in Canada — they are a pure ownership family, but they are not a managing family. Unlike the Eaton brothers, who hung on to management roles until the company sank into financial crisis, the Molsons long ago ceded operational control to professional managers. Yet they remain a powerful, if often mysterious, force in the brewing company. The problems in the company through the last thirty years — and there have been many — have often been laid at their door. The critics say they have diversified unwisely, chosen CEOs badly — one analyst calls them "whimsical choices" — and allowed the company to drift from any clear path. The family looked on almost as spectators as the majority stake in the core brewery business was sold to a couple of foreign beer companies, and then bought back at great cost, both financially and in terms of morale. Once the industry leader, the company has been challenged by archrival Labatt's. Eric himself has been lambasted for abandoning his leadership role through most of the 1990s. He maintains that he does not run the company, that the board and its chosen managers made these choices — although he supported them. But the charges stick to the family like a label on a bottle of Export. Any family that controls a majority of voting shares in a public company must ultimately bear responsibility for that company's fate. Molson Inc. is now back to focusing on beer and hockey — its traditional businesses — and some analysts say it's a sign that the Molson family has become engaged again. Eric, a trained brewmaster, is more comfortable with the current lineup and sees a strategic role for himself.

He has been sensitive to criticism in the media about his leadership — particularly to Peter C. Newman's dismissive conclusion, in his book *Titans*, that Eric "looks like he came from central casting in response to the call for someone who would be believable as the fumbling heir to a 212-year line of brewers." ("He didn't even interview me," Eric contends.) Of course, it is said that the Molsons believe that a family member's name should appear in the newspaper only three times — when he is born, when he gets married, and when he dies.

Perhaps it is time to reflect a moment on what the Molsons have done right. Find another company that has survived under the same owners for 212 or so years, maintaining and even expanding its original franchise. And find another big family company whose members are not tearing one another apart in courtroom conflicts, or making embarrassing headlines. As Eric says, "I don't think we [the Molsons] could survive a dunce. You can't have a dunce, a bozo in charge today." Asked to explain why the Molson dynasty has survived, Eric searches for words. Always the brewer, he falls back on characteristics that make a fine vat of beer. "It's hard work, it's disciplined, meticulous, a lot of detail to get it right. You have to do that to make a great glass of beer, you cannot monkey around. If you follow that into normal business patterns, you work hard, you stay disciplined, you take advantage of competition to get tougher."

For a man who professes no interest in family business, he is unusually well versed in the tribulations of other, more fractious clans — the McCains, the Péladeaus, and even his friends, the beer-making Olands of Moosehead fame, whose Halifax and Saint John branches once competed against each other in the brewing business. Why no noisy Molson feuds, at least in the public eye? "Cool heads prevail," is Eric's simple answer. "You have little squabbles going on and cool heads prevail."

It's also clear that the Molsons have been lucky — it's the only way you get to six generations, with a seventh waiting in the wings and an eighth just entering the world. Early in their history in Montreal, the Molsons got into a lot of businesses — banking, transportation, lumber — and this allowed plenty of room for various siblings and cousins to do their own things. When times got tough in the core brewing business, someone talented was always willing to step up and take command. Eric's grandfather Herbert seized the reins in the early years of this century; his father Tom and uncle Hartland, now ninety-two, led the post–Second World War growth; now it's Ian, sprung from a once-discredited branch of the family, who is puffing new life into the creaking old company. Perhaps the Molsons should be credited with flexibility — with the ability to recruit the smartest of the next generation and somehow persuade them that making beer is some kind of great and glorious crusade.

The big challenge for multigenerational family owners such as the Molsons is the proliferation of cousins with conflicting interests. Some cousins are deeply involved in the company and want to invest in its future. Others are outside the company but draw dividends from it. Still others may be working in the company, but hold few shares and want more direct say in its direction. The Molsons have avoided the latter problem — only one of Eric's sons is actually working at the company. And the chairman says the Molsons have "branched" well, meaning that when the family tree has sprouted new branches, there has been a willingness to cede authority and ownership to the familial group that is truly interested and engaged in the business. Eric's great-grandfather and his brother "branched" the company to his grandfather Herbert; his father's two sisters "branched" their shares to his father Tom and uncle Hartland, who became the standard bearers for "the brewery line," the family branch that owns and controls the brewery. And now Ian, whose father and uncles once left the beer company to buy the Montreal Canadiens, is coming to the fore, buying shares and taking an active role on the board. (Observers say that Ian is also the one pushing his cousin Eric to take a stronger leadership role.) Eric says there are now three family lines seriously involved in the ownership of Molson Inc.: Tom's line (himself, his brother Stephen, and sisters Cynthia and Dierdre), uncle Hartland's line, and Ian's line. As in hockey, every family team needs three good lines.

He has no idea how many Molsons actually own shares, but the controlling group, led by him, is small enough that interaction is quite easy and informal. There is no regular forum for the brewery Molsons to meet and talk about the company, although they meet often. He refers to the group he represents as "my gang." "We branched successfully and put together a small crew of people who communicate well together in order to do what ought to be done — what the company wants us to do — to stay alive as an independent Canadian company for another couple of centuries. But we'll see how it goes. You need a certain amount of luck."

Eric says the family has always enjoyed a knowledge of the core business, beer, and has interacted well with the professional managers in that business. "They seem to appreciate having knowledgeable shareholders in the business. We've had that all this time and still have it." Also, he insists there has been little nepotism. "If you impose yourself too much on an organization, you can't get good people to work for you. Why would they? They're never going to get ahead if their name's not Molson. So we haven't imposed on this public company. We just nurtured it along."

The first nurturer was John Molson, who was born to a lesser landholding family in Lincolnshire, England, in 1763, and orphaned at an early age. When he was seventeen John was stricken with a severe illness, and was prescribed a sea voyage to restore his health. He chose British North America as a destination. His arrival in Montreal coincided with the dark years of the American Revolution, when the continent was rife with intrigue. In 1783, through contacts from Lincolnshire, the young Molson became a partner in a brewery. From this humble partnership, a great beer company was born.

Any history of the Molsons is strikingly free of references to women. There is a good reason: women were barred from any decision-making or consultative role, at least until the current, sixth generation. Another factor is that the Molsons seem to have bred a disproportionately large number of males. (Eric says his own father has eight grandsons, no granddaughters.) The pattern of male centredness started with the first John Molson, who in the 1780s took up with a young British immigrant named Sarah Vaughan, who lived with him as his common law wife. He did not marry Sarah until 1801, eight years after the birth of their third child.

John Molson became a pillar of his community, yet for many years he was tainted by his common law relationship with Sarah. That no doubt prompted their legal marriage in 1801, which finally conferred legitimacy on his three children. It is significant that John took pains to prevent Sarah from participating in the growth of the business. The marriage contract stipulated that John and Sarah were to be separate regarding property, and that control of the brewery would remain with John's estate — even though Sarah seems to have worked hard in the business. According to *The Molson Saga*, one of two official histories of the clan, John provided for Sarah to receive an annuity of 60 pounds a year and living accommodations after his death.

Sombre, solid John Molson the Elder laid the foundation for the company, and the following generations built on that base. The Molsons weren't content to be just brewers — they also became distillers, landowners, shipping magnates, and bankers. Under the guidance of Robert Fulton, the American pioneer of steam transportation, the Molsons built a steam-powered vessel to ply the St. Lawrence between Montreal and Quebec City. In 1854 the family founded their own Molson's Bank, which eventually issued its own bank notes. They survived rebellions, temperance movements, recessions, and occasional outbreaks of family conflict.

In wartime the Molson men resembled the British gentry in their willingness to step up and serve their motherland. According to *The Molson Saga* at least twenty-five descendants of John the Elder, including five women, served in the First World War. Two brothers, Percy and Herbert, were awarded the Military Cross for their bravery in the fighting around the Belgian city of Ypres. Both were wounded and sent home to Canada. Percy's wound was particularly painful — a bullet passed through both his cheeks, shattering his teeth, lacerating his tongue, and damaging his jaw bone. Back in Montreal, a metal plate was fitted in his jaw. Herbert, who still had a piece of shrapnel in his head, was told he could not return to the front. But Percy, damaged jaw and all, was deemed fit for service and rejoined his regiment in France in 1917. One day he stopped in a small French town to discuss the battlefield situation with another officer. A single mortar shell fell among the group, killing him. Herbert survived the war, inherited the brewery, and became the progenitor for the "brewery line" of the family.

Eric Molson claims he is not good at family history, yet he is clearly in the grip of family myth and legend. In many ways he exemplifies the Molson men's style as handed down through the generations — work hard, don't flaunt your wealth, be prudent. He acknowledges that it is tough to instill that attitude in future generations, because they have been born to wealth. He has no magic formula. "You do the best you can, you make decisions in bringing up your children. They're going to work? They're not going to work?" They learn to understand that the Molson wealth buys a nice home and an education, but it doesn't automatically buy a lot of luxuries until they can afford it themselves. "If they're dreaming of having a Porsche [pause] they'll get one some day, but the wealth they see around them has gone into nice homes and education. They get encouragement and support, not giving them jobs and giving them Porsches — they know that."

The rules were all written down in a deathbed message to future generations dictated by John Henry Robinson Molson in 1897:

> The Molson Family has maintained and preserved its position and influence by steady, patient industry, and every member should be a real worker and not rely on what it has been. All that is good and great of the family should not be underground.

> Your private life should be pure. Make no compromise with vice, be able to say no in a firm manly manner.

> Character is the real test of manhood. Live within your income no matter how small it may be. Permanent wealth is maintained and preserved by vigilance and prudence and not by speculation.

> Be just and generous when you have the means.

> Wealth will not take care of itself if not vigilantly cared for.

Perhaps driven by this ethic, the Molsons were energetic builders who at an early stage pushed beyond their core brewing business. Yet they were not always successful in new areas, and ultimately the family would always retrench to beer. For example, the 1920s were a period of instability among Canada's smaller banks — a situation that presaged the deeper problems of the 1930s. Molson's Bank was concerned about the security of some of its large loans, and earnings were falling sharply. In 1924 the company sought a merger with the much larger Bank of Montreal, to which the family had strong historical ties. The merger, which took effect in 1925, took the Molson family out of banking for good. Years later, Eric Molson, a director of the Bank of Montreal, would attend board meetings of the bank, now a very powerful institution. Once, surveying the boardroom, he quipped to the bank's chairman Mathew Barrett that the Molsons had clearly made one big mistake: "We should have sold the brewery and kept the bank." Clearly he was joking, for Eric loves the brewery.

As one of several brewers in the Quebec market, Molson's rode a roller coaster in the early decades of the twentieth century. The company weathered the Prohibition Era fairly well — it had to make a weaker temperance beer, but its market expanded to include more consumers, including women. However, in the late 1920s, the company suffered a sharp reduction in market share, about the time it was rocked by a price war with rivals Dow & Co. and National Breweries. In 1930, Herbert Molson, then the president, hired an advertising firm to undertake an in-depth market study. The research showed that the public was moving toward lighter, sweeter beers. Molson's developed fresh formulas and a flashy ad campaign and was able to recapture market share.

During the Second World War the younger cousins got involved in the defence effort. The company was managed by a highly competent caretaker, a fastidious bachelor named Bert Molson. After the war, Herbert's sons Tom and Hartland returned to take control, ushering in the most exciting period in the company's history as Molsons found themselves swept up in the postwar economic boom. The central character in the postwar period was Hartland Molson, a dashingly handsome figure whose flair ran against the solemn Molson grain. As a young man, Hartland had attended Royal Military College in Kingston, Ontario, where he distinguished himself both as a scholar and as an athlete, excelling at football and hockey. He was never really inclined to enter the brewery business, and trained as an accountant. But like many other Molsons, he was lured into the family firm, largely on the quiet urging of his dying father. The Second World War beckoned, and Hartland, who was mad about flying, signed up as a fighter pilot with the RCAF. He had a great war: he logged sixty-two fighter missions before he was ambushed by a posse of German fighters, badly wounded in the leg, and forced to bail out of his Hurricane fighter. Unable to continue in the war, he returned to Canada as a hero.

Tom had been trained as a brewer and engineer, but socially he was shy; Hartland was the natural leader. Bert called in Walter Gordon, scion of the Woods Gordon accounting firm, to help him choose a successor. Gordon, later a federal finance minister, recommended to Bert that Hartland succeed him as president and CEO, and the Molson board unanimously agreed. Tom settled into the role of chairman, a position now occupied by his own son Eric.

Hartland's national expansion included the company's first foray into Toronto, where Molson's snapped up prime land near the waterfront right under the nose of archrival E.P. Taylor, who owned Canadian Breweries. In 1957, Hartland and Tom bought the Montreal Canadiens hockey team, which the family had partly owned as far back as 1924. Ever since, the brewery line of Molsons have deemed the Canadiens a "legacy asset" that transcends mere business, even though sports franchises can also be effective marketing tools. "We hold the team in trust for the people," Eric says simply. The television image of Les Canadiens in the 1950s and 1960s was of Rocket Richard driving for the net, defensemen hanging on to him like ill-fitting suits — and of a Senator Hartland Molson smiling as his team chalked up another goal.

One chapter of the Molson story is more tragic than glorious. Hartland knew when he assumed the presidency that he would have to start grooming his own successor. He immediately set his sights on a brilliant young cousin named Percival Talbot Molson. Driven to succeed, P.T. captured almost every academic and athletic prize he encountered, including a Rhodes Scholarship. His great ambition was to be a diplomat, and after the Second World War he joined the Foreign Service, in which he rose to become executive assistant to Lester B. Pearson, the minister of external affairs in the Liberal government of the 1950s.

Tapped by Hartland to join the brewery, P.T. was torn — he loved external affairs, but he felt a duty to serve the family business as his father Walter had. When Walter died in 1953, P.T. made his sentimental choice — he joined the company as Hartland's assistant. P.T. Molson was one of those great could-have-beens: he could have been a great diplomat; the family felt he could be a great senior executive. In 1966 he rose to president of the company, succeeding Hartland, who moved into the chairman's role. But P.T.'s marriage was crumbling, and he was suffering severe depression. Two months after he was elected president, he drove up to the Molsons' family retreat in the Laurentians after an exhausting week at the office. That Sunday, alone at his country home, P.T. took a shotgun and shot himself through the mouth. The following day, when he did not arrive at work, Hartland called an employee of the Molson estate to determine his whereabouts. He was found lying on the floor of the solarium. P.T. was the last Molson to serve as president of the parent company.

Eric sees the loss of P.T. Molson as a terrible personal tragedy but also as a great loss to the company. "The death of P.T. was a disaster for us. It was a case of a guy who made the wrong decision, who was a wonderful foreign service officer." Eric says P.T. was a natural "service guy" who was not inclined to make decisions in a hurry, who was more cerebral and deliberate. It was not a style that was conducive to business, where there was a lot of on-the-fly thinking. "But he was good, brilliant — I wish he were around today. It would have been nice to go through this whole process with his brilliant mind."

With the death of P.T., the company turned to Dave Chenoweth, a senior vice-president who had joined the company from Pepsi Cola, bringing with him a strong consumer goods and marketing background. Chenoweth had earlier been considered for the presidency, but he felt that a Molson should be appointed. Now it was his show, and according to Eric "he really put us onto the modern map." It was Chenoweth who took Molson's right across Canada as a brewer, and who pushed the company to diversify. Amid the tragedy of P.T.'s death, the family had done what it needed to do, and turned to outside professional management.

The Molsons' diversification program began with the purchase of Vilas, a Quebec furniture company, in 1967. The next move was more dramatic: in 1968 the company acquired a St. Catharines–based conglomerate named Anthes Industries, headed by a respected manager named Bud Wilmott. There are some who feel that Molson's bought Anthes just to get hold of Bud Wilmott and his vaunted abilities at acquiring and building companies. Indeed, Wilmott, who became Molson's president, did prove to be the best part of the deal: almost every Anthes holding was eventually sold at a loss. In 1978 the company added the Diversey cleaning company, which manufactured cleaning and sanitation materials used by companies around the world.

The period 1968 to 1998 was the conglomerate era, when the family ceded management to people who better knew how to run retailing, furniture, and other businesses. Eric clearly has mixed feelings about it. Few of the acquisitions really panned out. Off the top of his head, he can think of only one adventure that ended happily, the development of the Aikenheads hardware chain in the 1980s and 1990s under CEO Mickey Cohen. Molson's built the chain, then sold out to American box retailer Home Depot when it realized it could not fight the inevitable.

Yet Eric insists that diversification was a smart move, at least in the beginning. "We diversified for the right reasons in 1968," he says. The brewery had spun off some nice cash reserves, but the beer business was maturing in

Canada. Also, it was facing heavy regulatory barriers in its home country and was being barred from expansion into the United States by a protective U.S. government. Other brewers moved into Europe, but in retrospect that wasn't entirely successful either. "You have these resources and you're trying to do more for the shareholders," Eric explains in his choppy manner of speaking. "[There's] crummy growth in the beer business. Government regulators breathing down your neck in every province. You can't go to the States. It's stupidity to go to France or Italy or England." Rather than merely ramp up the dividends, he says, the company chose to use its resources to grow. If Molson's had simply paid out its cash to shareholders, it would have gone down a different track — "and you end up selling the brewery some day."

The move away from a pure focus on beer effectively removed the Molsons from active management in the parent company. Eric's career reflects that transition. He was a born brewer, not a conglomerate manager. As a child he was gripped by the inner workings of the beer business and by the chemistry that underlay it. "I was a scientist. I was fascinated by the periodic table. I got into it and then I got more and more [involved], wondering what was going on in the fermentation cups." That interest took him to Princeton, where he studied yeast fermentation using the new technique of electron microscopy.

He says he could easily have become a doctor or a scientist; but looking back, he is certain he made the wisest choice, although for a strange reason: "I can do a lot for a lot of people as opposed to being a teacher or a doctor." The way Eric sees it, becoming a truly influential researcher or scientist was a bit of a long shot. Back home at the brewery, he has been able to help people — consumers, employees, and others who depend on Molson's for a livelihood — in a tangible way.

Out of Princeton, Eric trained to become a qualified brewmaster. He never worked much outside the family company, except for a year spent at Moosehead Breweries, the Oland family business in Saint John. Philip Oland and Tom Molson were beer makers and good friends, and both had sons who were poised to enter the family business — Eric at Molson's, Derek at Moosehead. So the two scions switched places, learning the beer business at a safe distance from each other's head office. "It's hard to work here, if the family influences are strong around the plant," Eric says. "It makes things more difficult, we've never worked for our fathers. That may be one of the rules of family businesses." (Derek Oland, now Moosehead's chairman, has a slightly different memory of the exchange. He says he originally wanted to be a farmer, but flunked out of McGill University's Macdonald Agricultural College at Christmas in his first year. Still in Montreal, he applied at Molson's and got a job in the lab for eight months. "They were very kind," he recalls, and he learned a lot. Later, Eric Molson would serve at Moosehead for a year.)

At Molson's, Eric worked his way up on the beer side of the business as a chemist, and then as an assistant brewmaster, and still later as Hartland's executive assistant. He insists that he deserved every job he took. In many family companies, new positions are created for children. But in each case, Eric was succeeding someone else in the position, which gave him a chance to measure his performance against an established standard. When he became Hartland's assistant, his uncle was a senator as well as president of the company. "He needed a head office bagman — that's what they used to call me — the guy who sets up and writes the speeches, takes the notes, has his shirts prepared, puts him to bed, wakes him up, gets him breakfast, tips the waiters. I got that job because I was well educated and they needed a general well-educated guy. It was also a damn good spot to get to know Molson's across the country."

But he couldn't see his future as a "professional aide de camp," and when a manager got sick in the production area, Eric was keen to help out. When that manager died, he took the job and never looked back. "I'd been complaining about the foreign part of the company, and a guy taps me on the shoulder and says, 'Okay we're putting you in there to do it.' I fired some losers, rearranged things. I've had these challenges and I've always been measured up. Measured in the same way as other managers. I've made some errors and I've made some smart moves. I could write a book on them." He rose to the presidency of Molson Breweries — the beer division of the company — in 1980, and in 1982 he joined the parent company's board as vice-chairman. In 1988, when chairman James Black was ready for retirement, the two decided it was Eric's turn. As Tom Molson's older son, he owned the most shares, and he had the most experience in the company.

So why didn't he take the jobs of president and CEO? It would have meant bringing the Molsons back into senior management. "I'm a brewer," Eric explains. "I had been president of Molson Breweries but it was part of a conglomerate. I don't believe that anyone can be that good in a lot of businesses. I'm only good at beer so I wouldn't dream of trying to manage a diversified business. It's very very complicated and very very tricky."

Eric, who often speaks in unfinished sentences, gets positively eloquent on the subject of his true calling. "I know the beer business, I'm experienced, I used to make it, sell it, research it. And when I walk into a tavern, I know exactly what's going on. I walk into a brewery and I know exactly what's going on — anywhere in the world — so I know that business real well. But I don't know lumber, retailing, stationery, cleaning, and sanitizing, even though I pick up a little bit. But I never had a real feel for it."

He believes that the Eatons, despite their calamities, probably knew retailing, the measures and methods that make retail work. "You measure yourself in sales per square foot. In our business you measure yourself by market share, because if you don't [have it] then the other guy's got it. We measure ourselves by various efficiencies, quality of products — but in retail, I'm not sure what it is. How does a retailer know that you have to change your stock, or you gotta remerchandise, you need a new set of fittings, new lights or ... I don't know."

Eric's years as chairman have been tumultuous. Two years after he became chairman, the company hired a flashy outsider as CEO — Mickey Cohen, the former federal bureaucrat and Bay Street lawyer. Cohen came in just as Molson's was completing its purchase of Carling's Breweries, E.P. Taylor's old company — a move that cemented its control over the beer market in Canada. But Molson's also ended up selling 60 percent of the brewery business to Australia's Fosters and the United States' Miller Brewing, creating a partnership that would last for a number of years. Again, Eric says, it made sense at the time, because it freed resources for diversification. According to Eric, Cohen's great contribution was to focus the company narrowly on three lines of business — beer, cleaning and sanitizing (under its Diversey organization), and retailing (Aikenheads, Beaver Lumber, and others). But Diversey failed to perform as projected, even though Molson's had made acquisitions to strengthen its market share. By the time Cohen left in 1996, the company was perceived as a weak underperformer, burdened by debt and losing beer market share to an onrushing Labatt's.

Clearly the family has been frustrated by the poor results of conglomeration. "It doesn't seem to work," Eric says. "You study the world of conglomerates and I don't think you'll find many successful." So like repentent sinners, the family and the board decided the company should be born again as a pure brewer. Noncore assets were sold, and the brewery was bought back from its partners in two stages for more than $1 billion. Then began a strange dance of CEOs. In came Norman Seagram, a brewery type who had left Molson for a while. But he lasted only eight months, and was replaced by corporate lawyer James Arnett, a mergers and acquisitions specialist who is close to Eric. Yet the chairman insists that his family does not anoint the CEOs. "People write that, but it's not true — the board selects the CEO. The family can be part of the discussion but it is the board that does the selection — Mickey Cohen, Norm Seagram, Jim Arnett. It will be the board that selects the CEO, not the family. Naturally, the family gets involved in that, at least I do. I'm on the human resources committee, which has a role to play to make sure we have the right resources."

At the same time that Arnett became president, Ian Molson emerged as a power in the company. His rise is viewed by Molson watchers as a significant shift within the clan. Ian is a former managing director in London for Credit Suisse First Boston, a respected international merchant banking concern. In personality he's a sharp contrast to Eric — more outgoing, more confident, clearly someone who's made it on his own terms. He is the son of Billy Molson, who spent his career in the stock brokerage business and played a role in one of the most serious ruptures in the family's history. In the late 1960s, Billy and his brothers Peter and David bought majority control of the Canadiens from the brewery line led by cousin Hartland. The family history says it was a sweetheart deal, and in Hartland's view it was justified: it was among family, and it gave his three younger cousins a chance to establish themselves in a business they wanted to own. The three sold all their Molson shares to buy the hockey team.

As often happens, the new owners had a different view of the business. Instead of ploughing profits back into building the company, the three brothers went after larger dividends, *The Molson Saga* relates. The company listed itself on the Montreal Stock Exchange. Then came the big blow to family unity — in December 1971, just before the launch of a new capital gains tax, David, Peter, and Billy sold the Canadiens to a consortium headed by Edward and Peter Bronfman. Hartland's group didn't even have the opportunity to bid on this "legacy asset," which they had nurtured through the years. Hartland and Tom were crushed. According to *The Molson Saga*, "neither Tom nor Hartland said anything to their cousins, but after the sale they took pains to avoid social contact with them. When Hartland returned from Jamaica, the first thing he did was to have a photograph, which showed him with David, Billy and Peter on the day they purchased the Canadiens, removed from his office."

But seven years later, in 1978, the brewing Molsons discovered that there *are* second acts, or at least second periods. Rumours began circulating in Montreal that the Habs were for sale again, and this time the Molsons' arch-rival Labatt's appeared intent on buying the company. That would imperil Molson's major advertising venue, the television show *Hockey Night in Canada*. The company bid $20 million for the Canadiens and its franchises, plus additional sums for the thirty-year lease on the Forum. On September 1, 1978, the Bronfman consortium sold the hockey team to the brewing Molsons, who resumed their long-term love affair with the Canadiens.

Time seems to heal all wounds. Ian's re-emergence suggests that the family has moved well beyond the divisive sale of the Canadiens to outsiders. "Ian is a very important member of our board, very very good," says Eric in his choppy way. "He has beer in his blood. While he was a merchant banker with Credit Suisse First Boston, he knows brewers all over the world. He's up to his neck in Molson shares, and he's extremely skilled, a world-class merchant banker, and I'm an experienced brewer type. We make a pretty good team."

Ian is now deputy chairman of Molson's and seems destined to take Eric's place as chairman. Some observers speculate that he could be the first family member in many years to become CEO, but Eric scoffs at that suggestion. Will any Molson ever again be president and CEO? Eric doesn't totally rule it out, but the possibilitry seems increasingly remote, even though the company is back to being a pure-beer play. The family now operates as a major share-holder, not as hands-on, day-to-day managers.

What would make the Molson family sell the company? Eric gets almost mystical on this point. He says he always has to make sure that the company — its managers, employees, and various stakeholders — wants the family owner-ship. "You know, no corporation wants to have a bunch of idiots as controlling shareholders." And how do you find out what the company wants? "We can ask once in a while. We find out. The company does not dislike the Molson family." Eric says the brewery employees are welcoming the Molsons back on more of a full-time basis after years under a more remote partnership structure.

Eric says that having family ownership means the focus of the company has always been on the long term, rather than on delivering short-term earnings spikes. That has hurt its image in terms of Bay Street, but he insists that share-holders — A and B holders alike — have been loyal. There have been no share-holder revolts, although some analysts are derisive about the Molson family's stewardship. The chairman votes the proxy for the family group's shares, and according to Eric this group is satisfied with his conduct of those duties. "I could lose that role, but they want me to continue. We'd talk about it and do whatever has to be done." At this point, however, it's a small group repre-senting some trusts and family corporations, plus his own shares and those of his three siblings and his father's estate.

Share performance is obviously a concern, "but it's a healthy company in our terms. It's not a great maker of wealth for shareholders in total, but it will be — and it's seen some tough times. And we think it's better for share-holders [for the company] to do it this way, and we think shareholders will bless us for it rather than just bail out of the thing. There is some value to our country, to our society, to our stakeholders, to stay an independent Canadian company." One of the advantages of significant shareholders, such as the family, he says, is that they can think longer term. "And if the board of directors also wish to think longer term, then we have an ability to ride these waves."

What about the future? Eric concedes that as the family moves into seven and now eight generations, the ownership group could splinter even more radically. He can see the day when the Molson family shareholders could number more than 200 people. The choice of chairman and spokesman is not going to be easy. Already, he and his family are talking about preparing for that day, thirty to fifty years down the road. "We always talk long term in our family, we've been around so long," the chairman says. "And in the next fifty years we gotta have a way of saying that before you [the chairman] start foaming at the mouth, the time has come for 200 people to get together and pick some person to represent them on the board, two or three people." He sees other families who do it that way, and he's been asking them how they function. Many of these are brewing organizations. Before it was sold in the early 1980s, Schlitz had 215 family shareholders, who elected a chairman from among their ranks. Eric promises that a similar mechanism will be in place by 2030 or so. "We have an eighth generation being born and by then we'll have a ninth. If the company thrives, then if we want to keep the shares, we want to stay together."

Eric and his wife Jane have three sons, but only the youngest, Jeff, a former marketer at Coca-Cola, is employed at Molson's. The oldest, Andrew, is a lawyer who works for National Public Relations, which also does public relations work for Molson Inc. The middle son Justin is employed by an environmental foundation.

Eric has been working with senior managers and the board to craft a future for the company, which has been reduced to a Canadian brewing company, a once-great hockey team that failed to make the playoffs in 1998–99, and a collection of sports and entertainment assets. If Molson's is not going to be a diversified company, it will have to grow as a brewery through geographical expansion, and that will require more aggressive moves in the United States and internationally. Eric shies away from saying "acquisition," but that's certainly on the mind of a lot of analysts.

But analysts have questioned the company's continuing ownership of the Canadiens, who have been underperforming both on the ice and on the bottom line. Molson's in mid-1999 hired a New York investment bank to determine how its money-losing sports and entertainment group could be overhauled. Besides the hockey club, this division includes the $265 million Molson Centre arena in Montreal, a 50 percent stake in Universal Concerts Canada, a 20 percent ownership in CTV Sportsnet, and Molstar TV Productions. In September 1999 the company announced that it would entertain purchase offers for the sports and entertainment assets, with the exception of the hockey team, which was deemed a strategic asset. The company's determination to retain the Canadiens exposes Eric Molson's contradiction. If this were not a "family company," surely the hockey team would be a saleable asset instead of a cherished and untouchable legacy — a kind of private heirloom locked away inside a public company. Eric, meanwhile, argues that the marketing synergies between the brewery and the hockey team must be better managed.

While Eric protests that his family does not "run" the company, it becomes clear that even he doesn't entirely buy this. He speaks admiringly of the Ford family and how it has played a powerful role in the continuing success of founder Henry Ford's car company. It is pointed out to him that Henry Ford II, the founder's grandson, actually saved the company in the 1940s and 1950s, when things looked bleak. Eric says his family has saved Molson's, too. "We've had to make gutsy decisions as a family over the centuries — sell the bank, expand across Canada, sell this, buy that — gutsy, tough decisions. This has been a gutsy, tough decision — to de-diversify, get that other half of the partnership back, focus on North America. [It was a] gutsy decision to go into the United States. Gutsy. It's a tough, tough business. It's tough enough here — we're the only Canadian [big brewer] left."

That sounds suspiciously like a man who runs a family company.

ELEVEN

THE SMITHS —
HOW TO SAVE A FAMILY BUSINESS

Geoff, left, and Don Smith, of London, Ontario-based Ellis-Don Construction Ltd.

THE FIRST THING YOU NOTICE when you walk in the door are the pictures. A giant photo of Toronto's Skydome dominates the lobby of Ellis-Don Construction Ltd.'s head office in London, Ontario. Across the room, another wall displays a collage of Ellis-Don's greatest hits, the Skydome again and various other buildings and projects, all framing a smiling portrait of the company founder, Don Smith. The lobby is infused with the spirit, energy, and drive of Don Smith. The only problem with this picture is that Don Smith isn't allowed to come to Ellis-Don anymore. His seven children won't let him walk in those front doors without permission. They own the company now, and one of the stipulations is that their father can't enter the office building on Oxford Street, in an industrial area near London's airport. He now has an office downtown, where he can look after his personal business. But he can't visit and chat with the workers, or check over the numbers, or berate and fire underperforming employees, which he used to do ruthlessly and decisively in building a great construction company.

"They just told me I wasn't welcome," grumbles Don, seventy-five, who still sits on the board of directors and is still owed a bunch of money by his offspring. "I used to go out there and ask for figures and they wouldn't give them to me. 'Just go to the board meetings,' they said. I think that's stupid." And who are the "they" preventing Don Smith from visiting the company he founded fifty years ago with a few thousand dollars? They are Geoff Smith, one of his seven children and now president of the company, and Jack Adams, one of Don's oldest friends and now chairman of Ellis-Don. "Adams said I couldn't come out," Don Smith snorts again. Jack Adams, interviewed in the spartan boardroom at Ellis-Don, says that's too bad, but having Don Smith around the office would send out the wrong signals about who was in charge. "He'd like to see all the [construction] jobs, and he'd like to pick out those jobs that are underperforming and he'd like to visit the site and tell the supers either to perform or else he was going to can them," says the crusty, gravel-voiced Adams. But he can't do that anymore, and if it makes him mad, so be it.

In fact, the attempts to bar the father have at times verged on comical. Consider the athletic room incident. At one point during his stewardship of Ellis-Don, Don Smith built a fitness room inside the head office, and he loved to use it almost every day. One day, shortly after Don had left the company, son Geoff got a call from his father asking if he could come out to use the athletic room. Geoff could see the problem — Don in the office, Don watching over things, Don hanging around, Don confusing people by his presence. He quickly called Adams, who sounded out the other Smith children. He then relayed a message to Don: no, he couldn't use the athletic facilities. However, if he wished, Ellis-Don would buy him a membership at the YMCA around the corner from his downtown office. "I don't think he ever took us up on that, but that was our response," says Adams, who has known Don Smith for almost sixty years. "I admit it's difficult for a person like Don Smith, who has built this business from nothing to accept that kind of treatment, but it had to be."

It's possible that Don would only take such humiliating treatment from a trusted friend. Adams, also seventy-five, has had a sterling business career, which includes thirty years running Emco, a London building products company. The Ellis-Don story is interesting for a lot of reasons, but the role of Jack Adams is what makes this succession truly special. He is the outsider who made it happen, who holds it together, who tells the truth, and who is respected by both sides — both the departing parent and the incoming children. "He played a pivotal role at a pivotal moment and really for no obvious reward that I can see," says Geoff Smith. "It was just very important at that moment for that to happen, and it was good luck rather than good planning." There was every reason to believe that if not for Adams, the Ellis-Don succession would never have happened. In fact, it is hard to imagine where the company would be right now — sold off, probably, and possibly broken up into chunks. He respects the father for what he has built, but he also knows that the children, the board, and the managers can never really take control of the company unless Dad is physically absent from the scene. This is the kind of advice that Tom Bata Sr. and Mac Cuddy could have used.

Adams says the role he plays is vital to the continuity of any family firm, of any size. He sees the need for some kind of monitor, referee, honest broker, whether it's an outside chairman, a friend of the family, or a respected professional adviser. "But he must have some authority. I'm the chairman of the board; technically I call board meetings. I'm involved in the preparation of the agenda and satisfy myself that major items are brought to the attention of the board. You need that function performed by somebody and ideally not a member of the family. In my relationships to the Smith family, there are no favourites — everybody is treated equally, everybody gets the same information."

In Canada, Ellis-Don has been an industry leader — its annual revenues are estimated at more than $650 million. But no matter how successful a family company might be, it runs the risk of getting into trouble, or breaking up, during the management succession. According to Peter Drucker, at the point of generational succession what the business needs and what the family wants tend to collide. He adds that there is only one solution to the impasse over succession: "Entrust the succession decision to an outsider who is neither part of the family nor part of the business." Drucker says that British prime minister Benjamin Disraeli played this role for the banking Rothschild family in the 1880s when the third generation began to die off. Disraeli persuaded the family to accept the youngest, but ablest, of the fourth generation, Leopold from Vienna, as the head of the family's banks in London, Paris, and Vienna.

By the time the succession problem becomes acute, it is usually too late to bring in an outsider. By that time, family members have committed themselves to one or another solution. Moreover, succession planning has to be integrated with tax and financial planning. For that reason, family businesses usually try to find an outside arbitrator long before the decision has to be made, and ideally before feelings become hardened. The Smiths were just damn lucky. Their succession planning had all but collapsed, and the company was in danger of being sold off in a kind of emergency dispersal. Then Adams came forward and saved the day, and saved the family, and indeed probably saved the company. He has stuck around to help out as a mentor and financial adviser, to guide Ellis-Don through the bumps as the children of Don Smith take over.

One day in August 1996, Jack Adams got a phone call from his friend and neighbour Don Smith, whose voice betrayed worry and desperation. He had just learned that his plan to sell his construction company to a group of managers had fallen though. At the last moment the buyout group couldn't raise the financing, and Don was left holding the bag. At seventy-two, Don was anxious to retire, to finally leave the highly successful company he had built over almost fifty years. But there were no other buyers on the horizon, and no others likely to emerge. Despite its undoubted successes in the past, the company was still reeling from the recession of the early 1990s, from an unwise investment in the Caribbean, and from uncertainty about its ownership future, which had left employee morale in tatters.

And this was not just any company. This was Ellis-Don, the second-biggest construction company in Canada and one of the best-known brand names in the business — a key player in building the Skydome, Atlanta's Olympic village, Toronto's Metro Convention Centre, Calgary's Bankers Hall, and sections of the massive Canary Wharf project in London, England. No construction company said "Canada" as strongly and clearly as Ellis-Don. Only one, PCL of Edmonton, exceeded it in size.

In many cases the solution would have been a slam dunk — just pass the company on to the children, six of whom had served in the company at various times and in various roles. But Don Smith had an uneasy business relationship with his children, which was to be expected considering his driven, no-holds-barred personality. Relations were especially tense with his former heir apparent, his smart and ambitious son Geoff. The young man had been a company lawyer, then head of the Alberta division, then president of whole business, but he had left Ellis-Don in a rage over his father's domineering nature and what he saw as the board's unhelpful attitude in pushing the process of succession. The two were not talking. "From the time I'd left the company, I'd spoken to him once," says Geoff, who had bought a small telecommunications outfit in nearby St. Thomas. The children had become onlookers as their father prepared to sell Ellis-Don to a management-led group.

Adams, a chartered accountant and a smart numbers guy, looked closely at the situation. Any outside buyer who performed a due diligence on the company was likely to pass on the purchase, he figured. The company had suffered a number of financial shocks and badly needed someone who was committed to Ellis-Don — who would wade in and rebuild its still viable but wobbling business. "Don came to me and said, 'Jack, I want your help,'" Adams recalls. "He explained the circumstances — he wanted to retire. I looked at the situation and had discussions with senior people here and concluded that the logical buyers were his family." The children already effectively owned more than than half of the company as trust beneficiaries, and they would need to strike a deal to buy their father's stake. Spread seven ways, the deal might work. Four of the sons and one daughter still worked in some capacity at Ellis-Don. Geoff was out but still had a keen interest. Only one daughter, a social worker, had not been involved directly, but she was sympathetic to the idea.

Adams got on the phone with Geoff and his siblings to test the waters. He also phoned Don's wife Joan, a powerful person in her own right, a former London municipal politician who rose to become an Ontario provincial cabinet minister. "She thought it was a wonderful idea," Adams remembers, and that pushed him onward. Then he hastily convened a family meeting at the Smith cottage, near the resort town of Grand Bend on Lake Huron, about fifty minutes west of London. The first meeting took place without Don, as Jack led the family through the agreement. All seven, it turned out, were onside. Within weeks, the deal was hammered out with Don, and the company was sold to the children. Even Don was impressed with how his children had finally embraced the idea.

For Jack Adams and Don Smith, it was one of the high points in a friendship that went back to the early 1940s, when they spent a year together at De La Salle Oaklands School, a respected Catholic boys' school in Toronto. Jack Adams became an accountant with Peat Marwick; then in 1950 he moved out to London to join Empire Brass Co. (later Emco), where he was controller at age twenty-four. Within six months, Don Smith had also moved to London with his brother Ellis (hence Ellis-Don) to build a construction company. Adams says that Don started with a capitalization of $20,000, including $5,000 of his own and $5,000 of his mother's money. (His father had died when he was very young.) Adams knows the dollars involved, for he was Don's informal adviser, and even set up the books for the new company on the Smiths' kitchen table. "Our paths crossed early and we renewed our friendship and have been friends ever since. From time to time, business issues would develop that Don would like advice on. He would often consult me." Adams would also become the executor of Don's will and a trustee of Don's family trust. All of this gave him an insight into the Smith family's dynamics that would prove highly valuable.

Both men have had great business careers, though dramatically different ones. Don is as entrepreneurial as they come, wilful and often mercurial. He thinks of accountants as nothing more than necessary evils. Adams is the accountants' accountant, and fashioned impressive credits as a corporate number cruncher. When he joined Emco as controller in 1950, its sales were $15 million a year. Thirty years later, when he retired as president, they had hit $650 million, and today they're over $1 billion.

In the 1970s, Adams headed a committee of the Canadian Institute of Chartered Accountants that prepared a ground-breaking report on the accounting profession. He was also the consummate corporate director, prominent in the unglamorous yet essential role of serving on audit committees. Canada Trust, an exceedingly well-run trust company based in London, recruited him for its board. He was a director of Toronto-based Canada Malting, where he helped extract an extra $20 million for shareholders in a takeover bid. In the early 1980s he was invited to join the board of the Canadian subsidiary of the Woolworth Co. The board was made up half of Americans and half of Canadians, he recalls, and it had been a rubber stamp board. "I left it be known early that I wasn't going to be a rubber stamp."

He wasn't, and it led to bigger things. The chairman of the American parent invited Adams to join the big company's board as an independent director. It was a huge coup for the guy from London; it was also the beginning of a strange adventure. One day in 1994, he got a tip from a senior officer inside Woolworth: "Jack, they're cooking the books." Adams couldn't believe it: "I figured, 'This guy's gotta be on a trip.' But it turned out to be true." Certain officers in the corporation were alleged to have misrepresented the retail company's financial statements. In the wake of the scandal, the CEO was forced to step aside temporarily and the chief financial officer was fired. Woolworth needed someone of complete probity to move in and run the company while the accounting scandal was being investigated. Adams stepped forward as chairman and temporary CEO, and moved down to New York for a year. He remembers it as "a great experience. They were always very kind to me and very appreciative." After the results of the investigation into the scandal were released, Adams went back home.

While Adams was forging a corporate career, Don was building the company — when he wasn't helping raise big bags of money for his other passion, the Liberal Party. His partner, his brother Ellis, had left the business after a few years. Ellis-Don was a good place to learn the business, but supervisors did not stay long. Don's compulsive personality was hard on people. In some ways, he was a great delegator — he would let his people bet big-time on a single project. But if they failed, he could be merciless. He was always firing somebody, but the construction business is famously confrontational: projects are bid on, projects are completed, suits are filed over deadlines and dollars. In a bare-knuckle business, Don's knuckles were well calloused. "He was very tough, he'd fire his mother," Adams says. "The history is that it's not a company where senior people stay for years — it's a tough business."

Construction is also among the most viciously cyclical of businesses: one moment you're riding a building boom; then, with a twitch of interest rates or the first signs of oversupply, the well of projects dries up. Don has kept graphs of the life of his company, and it shows massive swings in fortunes every six to seven years. When times were good, he says, he would take all the business he could get because he knew it would change. His motto was, "There will be shitty years ahead right after that, so go out and grab it today." The company was propelled by some big projects. In 1980 it built a large IBM plant in Toronto's Don Mills area. The Skydome, of course, was a $550 million megaproject that won the company huge attention. (The grandiose vision of the project's owners would result in vast cost overruns.) Ellis-Don built a fair bit of the General Motors presence in Ontario — GM has accounted for $700 million to $800 million worth of work for the company, he estimates. "They knew we could live up to their schedule," he says. And he insists that Canary Wharf in London's docklands was a winner for the firm, even though the massive project hit financial snags, which contributed to the collapse of its developer, the Reichmanns' Olympia & York Developments Ltd. The trouble for Ellis-Don was that the Reichmanns had too many project managers, and it had to take a secondary role, but Smith is happy overall with the results.

Six children — five boys and one girl — were involved in the company early. It quickly became clear that Geoff, the fourth-oldest child and second son, was the most likely to succeed his father. As a young lawyer he articled at a London firm, Lerner & Associates, where he was offered a position in matrimonial law. Geoff wasn't that interested, and there was also a job available at Ellis-Don. "One of the advantages of family business is that you get all sorts of experience really quickly," Geoff says. He started out cleaning up the welter of legal claims the company was facing. Then his father needed someone out in Alberta, where the Ellis-Don operation was in some trouble. Geoff agreed to move out, and he did an outstanding job turning the division around. That performance convinced Don and his board of directors that Geoff had what it took. He returned to the company in 1989, bucking for a promotion, and was appointed president in 1990.

It was not a great time to be heading the company. The Smiths were being reminded the hard way that business and family affairs can make a disastrous mix. The company developed Windjammer Landing, a $40 million luxury resort in St. Lucia, described by one newspaper as "114 Mediterranean-style villas ... nestled in the lush hills surrounding a secluded bay on the northwest corner of the island." The Caribbean project was initially a family investment, the inspiration of Don Smith's daughter Lynne and her landscape architect husband David Cram. Don loved the concept — Windjammer would sell the units to private investors, who could spend their holidays there and rent the villas out the rest of the time. Windjammer would take 25 percent of the proceeds, and the investor-owners 75 percent. But the project was laden with debt and came onstream just at the beginning of the recession. Then the Gulf War knocked the stuffing out of the vacation property market.

Ellis-Don ended up providing guarantees for some $25 million in financing. At one point Don told a reporter from the *Financial Post*: "It has wiped out everything I made in my first 30 years of business" — a statement that Geoff insists was somewhat of an exaggeration. But there was no exaggerating the serious impact on Ellis-Don at a time when it was coping with one of the worst of Don Smith's carefully charted industry recessions. At one point a senior company official, who chose to remain anonymous, told *Post* reporter Eric Reguly that Windjammer was "knocking the hell out of our earnings. Without Windjammer, and the management time we're devoting to it, we'd be doing a lot better." In the middle of this crisis, Lynne and her husband split up (they would eventually divorce). The resort was transferred to Ellis-Don's books in 1991.

According to the *Financial Post* report, in June 1992, Don wrote a letter to one American villa owner painting a dismal picture: "I have either directly, or through Ellis-Don, invested more than US$50 million in the Windjammer Project. I have personally paid the banks US$9 million of my own money, some of which I had to borrow, and Ellis-Don has had to inject US$16 million of its money to keep the project afloat. This has meant a loss of US$25 million this year to myself and the company. Obviously, this cannot continue."

Windjammer, Geoff says, was "one of the great lessons, just a wild and painful story. It was difficult. At least we stuck with it — if we didn't, we would be in a more serious problem. It's a great resort and somebody else will take it to that greatness." When he became president, his role was to run the business and not get involved in Windjammer's travails. But by 1990 it had become a management issue. He skates away from the issue of whether the company should have offered security for a personal family investment: "It's just something that looked good that got out of hand." But at another point he admits that it shook up family harmony: "I was not too diplomatic and I was too loud." As of late 1999, Windjammer, now profitable, was still owned by the company, and a search was continuing for a buyer to take it off Ellis-Don's hands.

Geoff was having his own problems. Like many young heirs, he was growing impatient with the process of change. His father, still chairman and a very hands-on operator, kept dangling succession in front of him. "Dad is always two years away from retirement," he smiles. "I'm sure he believes it." He remembers going to his father a few days before the older man's seventieth birthday. He observed to Don that they were both approaching milestones — the father was seventy and the son nearing forty. These are ages when decisions are made about the future:

"You make yours and I'll make mine," Geoff said. And for a few months the younger man actually thought it was going to happen — that Don would retire and move out. He felt he had a clear commitment. Geoff feels that at this point his father's hand-picked board should have seen the opportunity and pushed for a succession plan. "When the founder can't solve it, it has to be the board ... You need some kind of weight brought to bear on people. I said, 'Do something.' I think some of the board thought I was outside my area of responsibility."

Don felt that Geoff did not appreciate that criticism from certain board members, just as the company was trying to weather the property downturn. "They came down a little heavy on him," he says. Adams's recollection is that Don simply remained highly controlling, and that Geoff couldn't take it any more. As for the board, its members were in Don's hands in any case. It soon became clear to Geoff that the patriarch had no intention of stepping aside for him, no matter what he had been told. It hit home to Geoff one day when his father gave a little speech at the office to commemorate his birthday. Don noted the problems of the Royal Family, and particularly the impatience of Prince Charles to take over from his mother. But he suggested with some sympathy that the Queen had no intention of getting out of the prince's way. There was clearly a message in that, Geoff believed. His father advised Geoff not to worry about such matters as succession — he had a good job so why not get on with it? Frustrated, Geoff quit the company in July 1995 and struck out on his own. His father bought out his shares.

Geoff has a better sense nowadays of what his father was going through. "He was the CEO and owned the goddamn company and he was entitled to do that and I don't object one damn bit. You can't argue with those apples. If you'd have interviewed me four or five years ago while this was going on, I'd have had a different view. [But now] I think Don was acting in entirely good faith and was wrestling with the issue, had been wrestling with it for a while. I was entitled to press him for a decision and he was entitled to make it, which he finally did. I'd never suggest he was screwing up. He was just wrestling with whether he wanted to retire and wrestling with whether I could do the job or not."

Could his mother have played a more constructive role? Clearly, Joan Smith is a smart, clear-thinking person. But Geoff says his father was very careful to separate the business from his personal life. "When the succession issues got heated, Don was determined not to let them become a broader family issue, which was right. So I don't want to say she had no role. She was ready to do anything she could to ease the transistion, but I think Don was very careful to keep the business issues separate. She did play a buffering role but was not in the middle of things."

Rebounding from the unpleasant split with his son, Don brought in a new president, an ambitious American named Jim Boocher, who had his own aspirations. A year after Geoff left, Boocher and a group of eight senior executives began negotiating with Don to buy majority ownership in the company. Right up to the deal-closing deadline in late August, everyone assumed the transaction would be done — Don would stay on as chairman and retain a one-third interest in Ellis-Don. The managers would buy the rest. Employees, anxious about the company's future, were hopeful that a solution would finally be found. On the day the deal was to close, Don was waiting in his office for a call from his lawyer. Boocher and his team were huddled elsewhere in the building. The lawyer did call: the buyers couldn't nail down their financing. The deal was off.

That was when Don turned to Jack Adams. According to Geoff, the issue on the table was quite clear: there was a family trust in place to which the children were beneficiaries. The trust held 60 percent of the company, which had a total book value of $37 million. "I emphasized to my brothers and sisters that walking away from the company meant that we were probably kissing goodbye to about $23 million, which required serious thinking," Geoff says now. One result of the children buying the company would be to protect that value.

When I asked Geoff why he came back to Ellis-Don, he couldn't answer immediately. Months later, he faxed me a two-page reply, in which he stated that protection of the family's investment was a big factor but not the dominant one. He could see that Ellis-Don, with its brand name and expertise in building and technical matters, constituted a large business opportunity, "and I had learned that these are not necessarily that easy to come by." He also felt affection for many of the company's people, with whom he had weathered some hard times. These people had helped create a unique corporate culture that would have been lost if the company were dissolved.

He also said that "if the company was lost, I believed that the family would be destroyed." He admits that at the time of the purchase, he felt less loyalty toward his own family than he did to the other people in the company. However, "I also believed that the ensuing fallout would engulf and harm us all, no matter where we were."

Having decided to buy the company, the siblings turned their attention to rebuilding the business. "The only way is to break the back of nepotism, to bring in proper governance," Geoff says. All the children bought that. That day at the cottage, the seven siblings agreed to a basic rule of governance — the family may own Ellis-Don as a unit, but the family could not manage the company as a unit. The ownership would be clearly separate from administration. The siblings met again a week later. In the meantime Geoff had written up some governance rules, which his brothers and sisters accepted:

1. The majority of board members were not to be Smiths or people affiliated with the Smiths. The children were determined to gain fresh views, and not to rely on a rubber stamp board.
2. The criteria for selection to the board were to include the ability to bring a broad and effective governance perspective, to provide work opportunities for the company, and as existing directors to advise and guide new members of the board. The board was to be a working board that would make a real difference in the business, not just a nest of cronies.
3. The president would report to the directors. This would impose a degree of discipline and performance expectations.
4. Family members would not report to other family members. This would eliminate a major conflict that often emerges in family companies. (Geoff later conceded that he had some problems with this one, because it might block deserving family members from advancement.)
5. The issues of promotion or demotion of family members would be decided by the compensation committee of the board, which would be composed entirely of outside directors. This would ensure that mediocrity was not rewarded, as in many family companies.

Geoff says that the rules have caused some stress but were necessary if the company was to prosper and survive. It is intended that Ellis-Don look and feel like a public company, even though it is privately owned. Jack Adams points out that family members have to be meticulous about filing expenses — for example, those involving travel costs and car mileage. They have to be above suspicion. The children also face the discipline of debt. To buy the company — price undisclosed — they borrowed on their own; the deal was not financed through Ellis-Don's cash flow. And their bank debt was substantial — well over $1 million a person, a considerable sum for people who do not carry big jobs in the company. In fact, one daughter, Cathy, toils as a social worker. "They're very much aware of the fact they're on the hook at the bank and they've pledged everything," Adams says. "When you've pledged everything you own, you're going to work pretty hard."

As the children took command, some things changed at Ellis-Don. The board was overhauled, from a group loyal to Don Smith to a group that could work with the new management through the transition. There were four outsiders, including Adams, plus three Smiths: Don, Geoff, and Geoff's brother Michael, a marketing manager. Michael has been commissioned by the board to keep the family informed of the directors' deliberations. But Geoff's expectation is that over the years, the board will become entirely independent. Certainly, Don Smith will leave as soon as he is paid off, and Michael's and Geoff's roles on the board will ultimately wane.

When the children took over the company, it was in chaos. Morale had plunged to new lows, and rivals had been cherry-picking key employees. Why work for Ellis-Don when its future was so uncertain and its earnings had been so badly battered? "There was an utter state of disarray because Don was retiring and the Boocher deal fell through," Adams says. The family was determined to raise morale, retain key people, and provide real incentives for employees to believe in the company and work for it. That is hard to do in a company where equity is controlled by a single family. The only real answer was to provide meaningful employee share ownership. Fortunately, this idea was not new to Ellis-Don. The children's father had always encouraged a certain degree of staff shareholding, but in the various stabs at succession planning, employee shares had reverted to the Smith family. The children wanted to set aside a meaningful amount for the most deserving and valuable people. The idea was that "the company prospers, the employees eventually assume ownership, and if you run it properly, you've got a real asset here," Adams says.

The family and Adams worked hard and long on a plan they thought would work. They didn't want the employees to have to go to a bank to borrow to buy shares. Yet they wanted them to come in as real common shareholders, not as owners of hypothetical phantom shares, as in many private companies. So they froze the current equity in the company, and issued dividend-paying preferred shares to the family in the amount of that equity. Then they issued new common shares, valued at zero, that would capture all of the future growth of the company. Of these free common shares, 55 percent would be retained by the family and 45 percent would be set aside for employees. "It was a more profound thing than I had thought at the time," Geoff says. "My brothers and sisters came to the realization that in order to maximize the 100 percent investment they had, it was a good idea to give up 45 percent of the growth; so now they have 100 percent of the downside and only 55 percent of the upside."

The employees' shares — the full 45 percent — were set aside in early 1998. In essence, the company gives high-achieving employees an option to pick up the free shares if they meet the qualifications: they have to stay with the company for two years and live up to certain performance criteria. The share options were offered to more than 100 of the 450 salaried employees. "We said to them, okay, you've got, say, a hundred shares set aside. You get none now;

in two years if still with us, you get half of them; after another year, if you meet performance objectives, you get the other half." For Geoff this is perhaps the most important thing the company has done. "To me it's crucially important to get as attractive as we can — and our competitors have [employee shares]. You've got to do it to get the best people. The employees had expressed lots of interest ... We owe it to them; they stayed with us. That was part of the reason — to reward them." The employees can sell the shares back to the company according to a formula based on book value and years of service. In essence, the formula rewards long service, providing a kind of golden handcuff.

Ellis-Don's leaders expect that in the future, the employee group and the family group will collaborate to select the board. But no employees and no Smiths will sit on the board — it will consist entirely of independent people who have no relationships with either shareholding group. Again, the separation of ownership and administration will be maintained, with no conflicts of interest. If there is a stalemate between the family and the employee group, after a suitable lapse of time the board itself will move to break the impasse.

The Smith succession is also quite unusual when it comes to the roles of the children. Geoff is the president, but his siblings are clearly not all big wheels in the company. They all have bosses who are not Smiths and who have not been shareholders — another reason, perhaps, to allow broader employee ownership. The oldest brother Bob once ran the Eastern Canadian operation, and is currently based in Toronto, where he manages Ellis-Don's large account with Famous Players theatres. But he reports to two other senior non-Smith managers. Lynne is still looking after St. Lucia and Windjammer. Michael works in the Ontario marketing operations, and Donald and David are project managers in Calgary and Toronto. Adams insists that absolutely no favouritism is shown to the children. In fact, recently the senior group actually discussed, and rejected, firing one of the family members.

Everyone concedes that the Smith children work very hard in the company. Even their demanding father admits to this: "There are no slackers." And there's not a lot of ostentation. "Great displays of wealth are demoralizing," says Adams. "These kids live modestly; they scramble — well, after all, Don had to scramble. He'd look after them at appropriate times but right now they're on their own."

Instead of hoisting members of the Smith family into top positions, Ellis-Don has plucked its key people from the outside, with the exception of Geoff. Adams is adamant about the need for strong outsiders in the top few management jobs. He says the greatest danger in any new generation of family managers is for them to assume they have business skills in their blood. "The fact of the matter is, they're very vulnerable — they're influenced by every article they read in the *Harvard Business Review*; they talk about management by objectives and management by motivation. They need experience in judgment." That means outsiders have to bring a certain balance to the business — for example, if there is already a strong marketing CEO, the company has to recruit a capable financial person.

Geoff says he has a critical role to play as someone who can guide the company through the transition, but he is not wed to the idea of himself, or any Smith, as president. He insists there were any number of people who could have assumed his role as transition leader. "The reality was that at that point in time, these people either weren't available or weren't willing." He finds it hard to describe why he has emerged as the leader among the brothers and sisters. At forty-four, he is the middle child — his social worker sister Cathy is the oldest, followed by Bob and Lynne. Michael, Donald, and David are all younger. Geoff says his emergence is a function of personalities and circumstances. Older brother Bob is considered smart and highly productive but perhaps more low-key. "I'm not sure it's something everybody wants to do," Geoff says of his role. "To my knowledge, there never has been tension on this issue, between Bob and me, and in general [among his siblings]." As a child, he was a bit more aloof because he was not part of a cluster of siblings. The three older ones were born close together, and his parents took a breather before he came along. As a kid he was kind of on his own.

Besides bringing employees into ownership, Geoff wants to change the culture of the company. Ellis-Don is known as an extremely hard-nosed player. Yet the industry is moving away from its confrontational, lawsuit-mad orientation. On big projects, architects, contractors, and clients are working much more closely as teams. It was an adjustment that Ellis-Don had to make to keep up with changing times. On Famous Players projects, for example, everyone is on the team and everything is done on an open-book basis. Still, the old stereotype has been hard to beat down. "When someone hears something like that three or four times, they forget they don't know it first-hand, they just believe it's true."

Now based in the firm's Toronto-area office, Geoff also has his hands full just building the business. Ellis-Don has been active in the United States, but in recent years it has found the competition difficult. Rebuilding the U.S. operation hasn't been easy. "We're just now turning a corner; in fact, we keep turning a corner but there is still another corner." The U.S. operation has been reduced to a manageable level. Ellis-Don has also forged a strategic alliance with a Florida company about one-third of its size.

Looking back on the succession wars, Geoff wishes he had known then what he knows now. Like David Bentall, another property and construction heir, he has learned that the incoming generation cannot control the agenda. The owners — the older generation — will give up the company only when they're ready. There is no question that the timing is absolutely the parents' call. "The big mistake that I made was you're kind of ambitious and you want to move ahead. But there is no point in moving ahead until the first generation is ready. It's stupid and if I had to do it again, I would certainly do that differently."

Yet he is happy with how things were eventually resolved. He has the feeling of being in control of his own life again. Rebuilding the company, after its years of drifting, has been tough on everyone, not the least his young family. "It's just the way life is. I answer to a board and they can fire me tomorrow. But it's important in my life for me to be doing something I'm in reasonable control of. I can screw up but I've got myself to blame."

Jack Adams likes his elder statesman role in the new Ellis-Don. At first, after the family buyout, he worked every day at the company; since then he has cut back to maybe once a week, often for just a half-hour at a time. He'll pop in to see Geoff and discuss any outstanding issues. He has a small office and a computer, all he needs. He feels he still has a role to play in restoring some conservatism to the accounting practices at the company — practices that became quite creative under its entrepreneurial founder.

He still likes to get out of the house and get his hands busy in business. He serves as chairman of London Hydro — once again, he's trying to salvage an organization wracked by conflict and scandal — and sits on the board of another private family company, Sifton Properties. He has made it clear to the Smiths that he is expendable at any time — that he doesn't depend on his role for income. He was getting a nice salary, but he voluntarily cut it by half at the second anniversary of the sale.

Perhaps his hardest work was done in the first six to nine months after the sale, when the children were concerned about their father's ability to actually retire from the company. The fear, Adams says, was that "we would be facing upsetting interference by Don because he's a hands-on fellow. He can't help himself — when he gets exposed to a situation, he wants to offer his comments and tell people how it should be done. We simply couldn't have that. So we expressed that concern to him in pretty strong terms, and with some reluctance he accepted."

Geoff Smith has been going to his father for advice on specific issues, and the two are rebuilding a constructive relationship. "Geoff consults me more often than before," his father concedes — "once or twice a week." Don Smith insists that despite his frustration, he's happy with how things have turned out. "You hate to turn [the business] over, but in the last few years, I was pretty damn tired at night."

TWELVE

THE PRICES —
BROTHERS

The Price family of Sunterra Farms; brothers, back row from left, Glen, Doug, Ray, and Dave, with their parents, Florence and Stan.

Photo by Jeff McIntosh

RAY PRICE, WEARING JEANS and a white golf shirt, sharply yanks the steering wheel of the shiny new four-wheel-drive GMC Jimmy and sends it plunging through a deep mud puddle. Murky water splashes up against the outside door and panels. "What are you doing that for?" his brother Doug, in a "Ken's Electric" baseball hat, yells from the back seat. "I haven't got it dirty yet," replies Ray as he swerves back onto the lane that cuts through the big feedlot, with its network of board fences, drainage ditches, and 12,000 head of beef cattle.

It is a bright May afternoon at the Price brothers' feedlot a mile or two outside Acme, Alberta. The FWD, a lustrous bronze now spattered with grey mud, belongs to Ray and Doug's younger brother Glen, who lives in Calgary and who likes to keep his Jimmy in immaculate condition. Glen has kindly lent his brothers the car, and Ray and Doug feel devilishly inclined on this day to give the vehicle a bit of breaking in, rural Alberta style.

The horsing around is typical of the Prices, who have to be the closest, most un-hung-up family business owners in Canada. Nobody in this clan gets too big for his britches, not even brother Art, the former oil executive and current high-technology maven, who still plays a big role in the company that spawned his fine career. Ray and Doug are giving a visitor a tour of the family's huge pig and beef complex in central Alberta, about forty minutes by car northeast of Calgary. The company, called Sunterra, is an impressive thing to contemplate

— a pig breeding and farrowing operation with 7,500 sows, feedlots for 40,000 beef cattle, a pork-processing plant in nearby Trochu, and a farming operation spanning 13,000 owned acres and many more that are rented. To top it off, the Prices retail their own pork and beef products, plus a lot of other people's fresh, perishable foods. Sunterra Food Markets operates five deli-style outlets — two in Edmonton and three in Calgary (with another on the way) — including a high-volume café, bakery, and deli combo in the Bankers Hall office complex. This is where the Oilpatch picks up sandwiches for lunch, or prepared meals to take home at the end of the day.

The village of Acme is the family's base of operations. The Prices' sprawling collection of businesses rings up annual sales of $150 million and employs more than 500 people. Sunterra's unpretentious offices occupy a long, one-storey building in downtown Acme, right beside Mom's Restaurant and across the road from the grocery store. Acme — population 600 — is a busy town, its front street lined with pickups and FWDs, so many it's hard to find a parking place for lunch on a weekday.

In all, five brothers work in some way at Sunterra. Four of them are in charge of some aspect of the vertically integrated farming, processing, and retail operation. Dave Price, forty-nine, a low-key, amiable man, runs the pig operations; Doug, forty-five, opinionated and colourfully profane, looks after the feedlots; Ray, forty-one, blessed with a sly sense of humour, is the chief financial officer and runs the meat-processing plant in Trochu; Glen, a baby-faced thirty-four, manages the retail business from his Calgary base. Brother Art, forty-eight, is deeply involved in Axia, his own multimedia and marketing company, but he works part-time as Sunterra's chairman. Two Price siblings are not directly involved in the core business — Al, forty-seven, a former high school principal, now works with Art in product development at Axia. The only sister, Joyce, thirty-eight, is a schoolteacher just outside Edmonton.

However well the brothers run Sunterra, they are quick to credit two other people. Parents Stan and Flo Price raised their children to be hard-working and independent, but also solicitous of the needs of their fellow siblings. According to Stan and Flo's credo, there are no big favours at Sunterra: nobody gets a free ride or even a cheap one. And that's what makes this company run better than many family businesses. "You own what you pay for and you get paid for what you do," says Art, summing up how the Prices operate in the world. And that is certainly how Stan and Flo worked it out. If a sibling wants to own part of Sunterra, he has to come in as a buyer of shares — nothing is guaranteed. Shares are bought and sold on a commercial basis — no discounts, no under-the-table deals. After all, somebody is usually selling the shares and doesn't want to take a beating. Although the family owns 80 percent of the company, the shareholders include a handful of non-Prices, who have occasionally sold shares to the sons.

Stan and Flo might help out financially — maybe they would guarantee a loan — but the lending is at commercial rates. It makes no difference whether you work in the business or outside — you can still obtain ownership if you're willing to buy it. "We don't have an environment where if you worked there, you were entitled to something different than if you don't work there," says Art. "No matter what you do, inside or out, that's your choice." And your salary reflects what you do in the company. Art, as the part-time chairman, gets paid as a part-time chairman, no more, no less.

This straightforward rule eliminates a lot of the resentment that afflicts many family firms. All too often, parents believe that the children who work in the company should get more ownership than those who work outside. The thinking is, "Johnny is president so he should be holding the majority of the shares — and we've got to help him out." Conversely, the parents may believe that all the children should have equal ownership, which can be just as damaging in terms of perceptions of fairness. Art says that at Sunterra, the issue of who owns what and who does what is "delinked" from the discretionary power of the parents or anyone else. There is nothing to debate about ownership or succession; there is no competition for Mom and Dad's favour. For that reason, there are fewer grounds for resentment. The brothers insist that this will be the model for any future generations: succession will go to whoever wants to put up his or her money. This rule may be Stan and Flo's most valuable legacy to their seven children and twenty-six grandchildren.

The Prices are the Cuddys without all the nastiness. It is hard to compare families, their dynamics are so different. But the Prices are the one clan in this book that on the surface most resembles the battling Cuddys of southwestern Ontario. Each family owns a food-based business that has extended far beyond its farming base. Like the turkey-breeding Cuddys, the pig-breeding Prices were pioneers in developing an animal genetics program in Canada, thereby contributing to this country's farming and agribusiness base. Each family has a global outlook that transcends the small community where its business was first begun. Yet each has kept its roots in its community. Each company was built by entrepreneurial, far-sighted parents, who had a vision that far outscaled the world they were raised in. Each family has had five sons active in the business, and each son was able to hive off responsibility for his own part of the operations. The Prices and the Cuddys are both "good families" — the kind that would seem to give family business a good name.

But that's where the similarities end. The Cuddys sling mud at each other; the Prices seem to have sprung from a too-good-to-be-true TV series, perhaps *The Waltons* or *Little House on the Prairie*, albeit with a multimillion-dollar business thrown into the plot. Simply put, they get along, they solve problems together, and they leave their differences in the boardroom. Whether this will last is anybody's guess, but it has been the state of the Prices for the past thirty years. Why have the Prices remained friends while the Cuddys have battled one another bitterly? Differences of personality are of course critical, and the Prices are, well, a bit less intense than the Cuddys. Also, their business is not nearly as big — yet. But there are other factors. Right from the start, Stan and Flo Price drew their children into the decision-making and ownership of the business. There was no sense that one son was ahead of the others — they could all come into the business on an unbending commercial basis. The oldest son, Dave, now forty-nine, actually helped persuade his father to diversify into pig breeding, and he started buying shares back in his early twenties, and the others joined in.

And as they aged, Stan and Flo were willing to step back from the business and let their sons run it. Glen says that when Sunterra opened up its retail operations in Calgary in 1990, his father was there to bounce things off, but in the final analysis the boys had to do it themselves — to learn what worked and what didn't. As the shops started to run smoothly, Stan backed even farther away. Glen was frankly surprised at the extent to which his parents retreated from operations and let the boys take over. Today, at seventy-one, Stan and Flo are there for guidance, but they don't intrude. The brothers welcome their parents' intervention when it happens. "Dad is always really good at putting up the stop sign before you engage in something," Dave says. "He understands business at a fundamental level."

The other element at work is family dynamics. Stan and Flo are much more of a team than Mac Cuddy and his first wife. The importance of a strong and independent-minded mother who can smooth the relations between entrepreneurial fathers and their headstrong sons and daughters cannot be underestimated. Dilys Cuddy, who was divorced from Mac and then died relatively young, was not there to perform that important buffer role. Mac's second wife could not or would not fill that role (in fairness to her, it should not have been expected). Also, the Price family contains another important element — a son who left, built his own career, and came back as a kind of consultant and catalyst. Art, the former president and CEO of Husky Oil, a major player in the energy industry, knows the world of banking, boardrooms, and professional management. He is the outsider/insider who returned bearing the gifts of detachment and knowledge of the wider world. "I have the luxury of coming to the table without worrying about the day-to-day issues," he says. He inspires respect from all his siblings as well as his parents. This consultative role is essential in family businesses, which often become too inward-looking. The Price family is fortunate to have a son and brother in that role. Having said all that, the key factor in the Prices' good relations is Stan and Flo, who have shied away from playing trivial power games in building this business and their family. Many parents enjoy pitting their children against one another; they love to pull the strings and watch their progeny dance. There seems to be none of that here.

Stan and Flo live a few miles outside Acme in a twenty-year-old grey flagstone ranch bungalow that they built for their retirement. It is nothing fancy. The yard is sparse and a little unkempt; there's a pond in a gully in the backyard. Inside, the house is all deeply stained wood panelling, very warm, with plush armchairs and sofas and wagonwheels hanging on the walls. Flo is a lively woman who still works at Sunterra, printing newsletters and brochures and helping out with the marketing. The boys consider her the keeper of the culture. She still gives new Sunterra employees a tour and a bit of the Price family lore. Stan has been slowed by a collision with a runaway bull a few years ago. The accident left him with a badly wounded head, from which he has recovered. He's bent by arthritis, but his mind is still supple and his sense of humour crackles.

Stan Price and Florence Landymore met at the high school in nearby Crossfield. They had gone to different one-room elementary schools where grade acceleration was common. Stan and Flo, both smart kids, were always a couple of years younger than their classmates, which seemed to draw them closer together. Asked if Stan was her high school sweetheart, Flo makes it clear that certainly wasn't the case at first — he had to work at it. They both came from homesteading stock — Stan's parents came up from the United States. Flo's grandfather had worked on the big Burns Ranch in Midnapore when Alberta was still part of the Northwest Territories. After Flo left school, she taught for two years as a teenager in a one-room school. She married Stan in 1948 when they were both twenty-one. They moved over to the Acme area where they started farming on a small, sandy acreage — mixed stuff, some cows, pigs, and chickens. They didn't know it at the time but the land was considered sensitive for its high erosion potential. A local agricultural service board had taken the farm under its wing, with a mandate to instruct whoever farmed it on how to wring some crops out of the sandy land. Stan and Flo, always blessed with a sense of humour, call the place Sandy Crest; some unkind neighbours preferred the sobriquet Poverty Flats. When the experts came around to help, the young couple convinced the interlopers that they could manage just fine on their own. The Prices say the farm is now one of the most

productive pieces of land in the municipality, thanks to their determined enrich-
ment of the topsoil through load after load of manure.

Life was not easy for the newlyweds. The first year, their crops were snowed
under; then they got hailed on in each of their first four years. "That was part
of our education," says Stan, who made a little extra digging ditches and helping repair telephone lines around Acme. The family was coming along — four
children were born in five years. To supplement his income, Stan tried Jersey
cows — "the most useless things we've ever had," Flo grimaces. But after
separating the whole milk for cream, the Prices ended up with waste skim
milk, which they couldn't cart away. Hence, the purchase of some pigs to
drink the skim milk. A business was born. Stan knew pigs from growing up
on the farm; he liked the animals and did well with them. He was looking for
something to sink his teeth into, and got interested in the breeding side. He
acquired some of the new Landrace breed once they started working their way
into Canada. He even went down to the States to a Landrace growers' convention, where he won a prize against tough American competition. Impressed
with Stan's pig savvy, a big American company offered him a research job and
a hefty salary, but Stan turned it down. The offer was, if anything, a confirmation of the path he had already chosen. Stan was determined to develop
fine pig-breeding stock in central Alberta, all the while keeping his hand in
the beef business.

Meanwhile, the family was getting older and taking its place on the farm.
Stan, who was becoming involved in pig associations and community groups,
had no fears about leaving Flo and the young kids in charge when he headed
off on trips. He considered these activities essential in both building his business and giving back to his community. The children were expected to take on
heavy responsibility at a young age. In this way, knowledge was transferred
early between generations. Doug remembers that when he was sixteen, the
family was building the first of the barns that would house the nucleus for its
pig-breeding stock. To fill those barns, a load of pigs was being shipped from
Britain. The plane was booked, everything was in place for their arrival. But
at the last moment, the contractor who was building the barn went bankrupt,
leaving the project incomplete. The Prices were desperate. So Doug, at sixteen,
recruited forty-two boys from the Acme High School — total enrolment ninety-
one — to put up the building in a kind of 1960s version of a barn-raising bee.
After the work was done, Doug went to school the next week with a chequebook in his back pocket and his father's authority to pay the entire work gang.
"I was the most popular kid in the school," Doug says. But he is still immensely
proud that his father trusted him with the chequebook.

To some extent that pattern continues with the third generation — the children of the five brothers. For example, Doug's teenaged sons often work long, hard hours cutting, storing, and packing silage in the huge, cement-floored pits near the feedlots. For a stretch of time they work the night shift, from 6 p.m. to 6 a.m. The brothers regret that the kids can't do as much on the farm as they did: the machinery is too complex and expensive and the risks are too large. So they look for ways to involve their own children without exposing their offspring and themselves to much danger. It's a big challenge to replicate the kind of life and responsibilities they had as kids.

At a young age the brothers' roles had already been established. Dave liked the pigs — at ten, he was showing animals at the Calgary Stampede. Doug liked the cattle, and Ray was a whiz with numbers. As for Art, he was the obsessive tinkerer. "Art was always greasy, he was always monkeying around with the equipment," says Flo. He once designed and manufactured an ultra-efficient wagon for loading and unloading baled hay — although today Glen still insists the thing didn't work all that well. Of course, Stan points out, it was little Glen, the youngest boy, who had the thankless task of placing all the bales in the barn. Art also designed the company's first pig-growing units. But when he graduated from high school, Art left for university and an engineering degree — the beginning of a career that would take him to the corridors of power in the energy industry.

Stan and Flo actively encouraged their children to play in team sports, and baseball and basketball were always at the top of the list. It was understood that if one of the children had a game on a certain night, someone else would pitch in to cover his or her farm chores. "I don't think anyone missed a game or a practice, but there were times when it was exceedingly difficult to get off from the combines and the tractors," Flo says. "But they learned that in order for their brothers and sister to participate, they had to help out." The Prices were good baseball players. At one point, Dave, Art, Al, and Doug were all playing on the same team. Al was especially talented, and would soon qualify for Canada's national baseball team as a catcher. This skill, along with his passion for teaching, has taken him to a lot of places in the world as a baseball instructor. At Art's Axia, he helped create a training CD-ROM for young ballplayers that is endorsed by the U.S. Little Leagues. The brothers don't play much anymore, but recently they took a memorable baseball tour, visiting the hallowed grounds of Fenway Park in Boston and Yankee Stadium in New York.

In the 1970s, inspired in part by Dave's consuming interest in pigs, Stan moved more aggressively into the breeding business. He managed to link up with a rising new pig-breeding system based in Britain known as Pig Improvement, run by a man named Ken Wooley. Stan formed Pig Improvement Canada in collaboration with Wooley, a local veterinarian named Jack Greenaway, and a geneticist in Lacombe, Alberta, named Howard Fredeen. For a while this pig breeding, marketing, and distribution company was a joint venture between these Canadian partners and a large British company, Dalgety. There was a shotgun clause that provided a process for one partner to buy out the others. The British partner decided to trigger this process by making an offer for the entire venture. Dalgety assumed that the Prices and friends wouldn't be able to afford a counteroffer, but the Canadian partners could, and bought the entire company. That was a turning point for the family business. Now owned by the Prices and their partners, PIC became the Canadian franchise for the worldwide pig-breeding system; it also had the right to trade and distribute breeding stock in other foreign countries. From the start, the Prices had a global outlook that took them outside the boundaries of Acme and Alberta. "The business always had a global strategic position, a global founding idea in the hog genetic business," Art says, adding that "Father was not a bashful guy."

Buying out Dalgety was a fairly risky investment in the 1970s. But in growing the pig and beef operations — the family always maintained its interest in beef cattle — Stan was never afraid of debt and was always highly leveraged. It was the only way he could take the assets of that first small farm and build them into a fairly significant mid-sized company. "He started with nothing so he had to lever every dollar he had and take on risk," Doug says with some pride. "We had it levered right up to our nuts all the time. We're not afraid of risk."

All this time, Art was developing a career outside the family business. He moved into Husky Oil, where he climbed the ranks to become president of the company in 1983 at a youthful thirty-two. As he rose, his career became tied tightly to an energy megaproject, a heavy-oil upgrader plant at Lloydminster on the Alberta–Saskatchewan border. The $1.3 billion upgrader, operated by Husky and supported by heavy government funding, developed a reputation as an unwieldy white elephant. But Art and Husky stubbornly stuck with it. In the 1990s, after he left the company, the project finally began to show signs of paying off.

Art's years at Husky were tumultuous. In the 1980s the company came under the control of Bob Blair, the ambitious, politically connected engineer who built Nova Corp. into a energy, pipeline, and petrochemical giant. But the Nova years were a period of vast debt accumulation. Eventually, Blair persuaded Hong Kong tycoon Li Ka-shing to buy into Husky as a 40 percent partner; then in 1994, Li took the entire company off Nova's hands. The Hong Kong entrepreneur dispatched a key deputy, John Chin-sung Lau, to Calgary to keep an eye on Husky. According to published reports, Lau, a vice-president, and Price, still the president, conducted a cold war against each other for two years, and employees were caught in the middle. In mid-1993, Art resigned as president, although he maintained an office at Husky for a year and helped Li identify investment opportunities in the Oilpatch.

Freed from Husky, Art rediscovered his roots and started putting more of his time and money into Sunterra. His brothers say he was tired of being a corporate henchman and wanted something of his own. The family business looked awfully appealing. Flo says the reason was more deep-rooted: "I don't think you ever take farming out of the boy or girl. [Art] used to come out and when we were packing silage, he'd run the equipment. He still gives Doug a fair bit of advice on how it should be done." Stan, Flo, and Glen find this very funny — Art apparently likes to micromanage a bit with his farming brothers.

And he remains a tinkerer. "I'm a sucker for machines," he says, "whether it's a tractor, a fast car, a boat, or an airplane." In 1995 he launched his own high-tech company called Axia — a business that sprawls across a range of high-tech, particularly Internet, activities. One part is a company that designs and sells computing networks to corporate customers. Another is a marketing agency that provides conventional print and broadcast campaigns for corporate customers. Then there is the Axia NetMedia group, which turns out CD-ROMs and on-line projects, including baseball and hockey instructional CDs co-developed by brother Al, the baseball instructor. Art's brothers have invested in Axia, just as he has put money in Sunterra. Why take the chance? "We know who's running it — that's why you make the bet," Doug explains with a finality that suggests there is no reason to argue. "Art said it could go a long way or it could sputter out in six months." By 1999, Axia had grown to a company with more than $25 million in annual revenues.

The Prices' hog and beef business expanded throughout the 1980s, but the family was somewhat frustrated. They were breeding and growing fine pigs and good cattle, but as soon as the livestock left their hands, they lost control over the product. They could see an opportunity to process their own meat and provide a fresh, high-quality product right to the customer. They would offer an alternative to the mass-production players that dominated the meat business. They believed there was a market that was willing to pay for this quality. Processing was one link in that chain, retail was the other. They started to think about how to develop a channel that would move the product straight to consumers' hands. "Everybody felt there was a market there where we could make some money," Glen says. One step was buying the processing plant in Trochu, the other was to set up a chain of stores.

The Prices figured they had the right guy to lead this effort. Glen Price had graduated from the University of Alberta with a commerce degree. Through Art, he found a job in Hong Kong with Hutchinson Whampoa, one of Li Ka-shing's companies, where he worked in the consumer food retailing operations of that giant conglomerate. Glen found that doing business in fast-moving, nonstop Hong Kong was an instant education. But after fourteen months he was at a watershed: he would have to either put in a long stint at Hutchinson, or come home. So he came home, in part because he missed the family.

His brothers wanted him to do some exploratory work in their fledgling retail operation. He had his doubts. Although the family dynamic was healthy, he wasn't at all sure how he would fit in. And what if he failed — how would the family deal with that? And was this new division simply being created for him as an elaborate job-making device? His brothers and parents worked to assuage his fears. Glen finally realized that his own family's business was perhaps the best career opportunity he had. First, he worked with his brother Ray in researching the meat retail market and its margins. In 1990, led by twenty-four-year-old Glen, the Prices opened their first retail market, in southern Calgary.

There has been a learning curve. The retail operation hit some resistance from the Prices' long-time bank, the Royal Bank of Canada, so the family had to switch over to the Bank of Montreal. The first store in Calgary did fairly well, but the landowner of the building went under, and the outlet eventually closed. But the second market, in downtown Bankers Hall, was a big success. Still, the Prices have found that the stores have not been as prominent in terms of retailing their own meat products as they expected. At the moment, the retail arm accounts for only about 5 percent of the family's meat sales — much more is exported to Japan, which has become a vigorous pork market. (A representative of a Japanese company actually works with Sunterra at the Trochu plant.) In fact, 65 percent of Sunterra's meat is exported. The brothers have also discovered that their best Canadian market is not "sophisticated" urban-ites, but rural consumers — people who have grown up appreciating quality food off the land. Still, Glen says, the stores are a valuable form of market intel-ligence — intelligence that goes straight to the processing business. Also, differ-ences between the Calgary and Edmonton markets have become apparent. Snack items such as muffins and coffee are much more popular among Edmonton office workers. The Oilpatch types in downtown Calgary tend to work straight through to lunch, and then straight through to dinner, and take less time off for breaks. So the Prices have done well at selling prepared meals that can be taken home by busy people. The family also has its eyes open for other markets, including a downtown Toronto store.

This integrated supply system certainly wasn't what Flo and Stan and Dave had in mind back in 1970 when they helped launch the pig-breeding venture in Canada. "I think it was a big surprise, actually," Flo says. "I'm still surprised when you think of the scope of the company and the way it's integrated now and the skill and dedication of each of the family members to each sector." Stan says that the same basic principles are involved, no matter how big the company has become. "If somebody says, 'How did you go from a section of land to thirty sections?' there isn't much difference if you follow the basic principles."

As the company has grown, the Prices have had to make hard choices about their collection of businesses. Last year they sold one of their landmark companies, PIC, the marketing and distribution operation for the pig-breeding stock. It was felt that this business had to become much more global if it was to thrive, and the family had enough already on its table. Also, says Flo, "it's a changing world now — you had to go more deeply into genetic manipulation and all the technical stuff." The proceeds from the sale achieved one major result — it allowed the Price family's partners to recoup a bit of cash from their long-term investments. The sale of PIC did create a void for some family members, but the continuing pig-breeding and growing operation took up the slack.

At the same time, Sunterra has been greatly expanding its beef feedlot operation. Doug, who had been running his own separate feedlot, folded this business into Sunterra in exchange for shares and cash. (Doug still has his own cow-calf outfit.) And the family bought a much larger feedlot in another community. With so much going on, simply running Sunterra is becoming a more challenging proposition. At the top of the organization chart sits a board of directors consisting of the five brothers and three outsiders who represent the nonfamily shareholders. But much of the decision-making falls to an executive committee — or "Execo" — which consists of the four operating brothers plus Art, the chairman. Stan and Flo sit in on meetings from time to time.

Decision-making among the Prices seems almost too straightforward. Art says they rely on a teamwork model that seems to have developed naturally from the family ethos. Stan and Flo's work ethic and sharing of responsibility set the pattern. But he argues that this teamwork approach goes beyond Sunterra or the family business. Of the companies he is involved in, none operates on a top-down, hierarchical basis: "It's always a team of people." In fact, he insists this model is essential for survival in today's fast-moving, interconnected, and internationally oriented business environment.

The brothers say that when any issue comes to the table, everyone gets to say his piece, but the sibling who runs the particular division has wide discretion to make his own choices. Art, they say, brings a sense of balance and boardroom savvy. The biggest challenge, the brothers say, is deciding which issues should be resolved inside the respective divisions and which should be brought to the Execo level. For example, which problems should Dave keep at the pig division level, and which should he bring to the board? That separation of issues is something they're always working on.

The family members insist that they do not shy away from dissension. In fact, the company could not function without constructive debate. "The riskiest thing is no difference of views," Art says. "A well-run organization has different views and good ways to get to a common view ... A different opinion has to be valued, as opposed to [being viewed as] out of line — and people respect it." The Prices always keep their business differences inside the boardroom, and don't draw them into their personal relationships. "I think everyone in the group knows they can disagree without having any rise to friction level," Flo says. "I used to worry about the potential friction, but I think they've got it [in hand]. It's not for us two to get involved. They're adults — even if you worry a little bit, it's not our business."

The family likes to say that when Execo meets, the company has five CEOs — sometimes seven when Stan and Flo are there. "We've all got the CEO hat on," Glen says. "And at the same time each guy is president of his own division. Whether it will always be that way, we don't know." The brothers concede that at some point there might be outsiders at the table. If they diversify into new areas, they may well hire nonfamily presidents for the new divisions: they will assume the leadership roles themselves only if they are the best for the jobs. They are also quick to credit their supporting staff for the growth of the organization. There is some discussion by employees along the lines of, "I could never be president here." But Dave insists that many on the staff see the benefits of a reliable, long-term direction and philosophy for the company. He feels that leadership will become increasingly fluid, providing more opportunities at the top: "If anyone demonstrates a superior expertise, we'd just move over."

Flo doesn't want the business accomplishments of her five sons to be blown out of proportion. For her, the family is more important than financial achievement or any business legacy. She emphasizes that what Al and Joyce have accomplished as teachers is just as important as what the boys are doing at Sunterra. Joyce, she points out, has made a real difference in children's lives through her championing of outdoor education. "People who work with children, and their own children in particular, probably have more influence in the world than any Pig Improvement Canada or other businesses. Teaching is something you never hear of as success." She can't imagine having a family business where the nonbusiness people are treated any less generously than the siblings working in the company. "I think you have to give credit to people who do something that isn't as public — who volunteer in the school, for example. I think the economy and public as a whole look too much at financial success and not at personal things."

Flo, ever the proud mother, says that the family has succeeded because they have strived to always be a bit ahead of their time. She laughed when a friend in Texas told her that prepackaged, precooked, ready-to-eat food was all the rage — Glen has been selling it in Sunterra's markets for eight years now. Exporting to Japan? The family has long experience in doing that. Art, she says, was perhaps the most adventurous. There were a ton of complaints about the Lloydminster upgrader project, and political controversy still hangs over that megaproject. "But as for the upgrader, now everybody wants one because it is the way to process [heavy oil] in the future." She says it's a family trait to try things that haven't been done before. "I get into trouble in the community for not colouring between the lines myself, but it's more fun that way. I've never been able to stay in a box."

Stan, meanwhile, says the secret has been nothing more than patience and perseverance, which the boys learned when they started out on the farm. The Prices believe that agriculture, being a long-term kind of business, teaches you the value of hanging on and waiting. "In agribusiness, you tend to be a lot more long-range focused," says Dave. "We're thinking about what we're going to do five to ten years down the road."

The model developed by Stan and Flo has clearly worked in the second generation. But what about the third? There has been a fair amount of discussion about how the twenty-six grandchildren might be brought into the business, and how ownership might be continued. So far, no one in the next generation has graduated from university, and no one has betrayed any interest in taking on Sunterra as a lifetime career. What everyone agrees on is that the next wave of Prices will have to work their way into the business — if they want ownership, they will have to buy their way in like their fathers and uncles.

Glen, who has no children so far, says that a lot of families fail at business because the children receive something without earning or paying for it. "But for us, it's totally understood by everybody that if you're entering the business as an employee, you have to perform as good as or better than any other employee." He says it's the same when it comes to being a shareholder. "If you want ownership in this, you buy it on the same basis that any other outsider would buy it. And yes, there is some benefit to having the knowledge and the background and comfort level [of a family member]. But in terms of payment, each individual put the money up to buy ownership. It makes it totally equitable and it makes everyone appreciate their ownership that much more."

Does the business really need to be passed on? It could be sold. The brothers are somewhat divided on that. Doug says seeing the company continue in the family would be a great thing — no matter whose children take the reins — but he also admits that "that's a rancher talking." Later he adds: "I just don't want a farm sale." For Ray, it's no big deal. He just wants his five girls to do what they want to. Dave's goal is to have the company remain strong into the future, and it would be "an extra bounce" if the family were involved in making that happen. Doug emphasizes that there will be no free lunches. The five brothers have had to work hard and sacrifice, and the children won't be treated any differently. He recalls that when he was renting land, Stan was tougher to deal with than any of the neighbours. "[Our children] are not going to get any breaks from us guys because that's why we are what we are. Someone can't be allowed to come in and just piss it away."

If there's any apprehension on the horizon, that's where it lies — in what the next wave of kids will do with this sprawling business. To better understand the options, Stan, Flo, and the brothers have been involved in the Canadian Association of Family Enterprise. In fact, in 1995 the Prices won CAFE's Jaguar Achievement Award for Family Enterprise of the Year. But the brothers admit they're just a tad uncomfortable with CAFE meetings, with their unbridled candour and encounter group confessionals. Everyone is so open and talkative about how bad family business is, how painful it can be. The brothers couldn't believe how much people wanted to talk about their tortured feelings. They couldn't relate to all this, because their experience has been almost totally positive.

THIRTEEN

WORKING IN THE FAMILY BUSINESS

I T'S HARD TO WORK WITH YOUR HUSBAND. Just ask Joan Berta, who says that the leap from corporate life to join her husband's market research venture almost ruined their marriage. These days Joan, sixty, is national executive director of the Mississauga-based Canadian Association of Family Enterprise (CAFE), an organization that tries to keep family businesses alive and thriving. Five years ago she took a golden handshake from her job in sales at Stelco Inc., in Hamilton, to join husband Ray at his company, Applied Consumer & Clinical Evaluations, in Mississauga, Ontario. Ray had founded the consumer research company in 1986 and had been urging his wife to join. They would be "copreneurs" — the trendy appellation for married couples who go into business together. She agreed in 1993 to take over Canadian operations while Ray was building up the company's American business.

"I understood that to mean I could do anything with [the Canadian operation] I wanted to," Joan told *Globe and Mail* reporter Dawn Walton. "That wasn't what he really meant. What he meant was, I could run it the way *he* had been running it." The responsibilities of each spouse were never specified: "My husband and I were absolutely maudlin about it: 'Our relationship is so good and so strong, this is going to be absolutely wonderful.' A couple of people said, 'Look out.' We just said, 'They don't know us. We can do this with our eyes closed.'"

242] IN THE BLOOD

In truth, their eyes were closed, to the dangers of couples — in fact, any family members — going into business together. Within about nine months Joan and Ray were butting heads. They finally set out job descriptions, but once their roles were defined, Joan didn't like what she saw. At Stelco she was used to having a lot of responsibility, and she wasn't prepared for the superior-subordinate relationship. The Bertas, who have four adult children, none of whom works in the family company, sought CAFE's help in separating family issues from business dilemmas. In December 1997, Joan left the company, although she still holds shares. She now runs the national office of CAFE out of an office at Applied Consumer & Clinical Evaluations. "I say this publicly without shame, [CAFE] saved our marriage," she says now.

Joan's experience underlines the challenges facing families in business — the problems inherent in reconciling roles in the family with roles in the business. Sometimes the resulting conflict may be more than the family relationship can bear. Joan learned to understand that Ray's business was "his baby," and that no matter what role she established for herself, he would always see himself as the superior player in the company. It is to the credit of both of them that they broke up the management relationship once they realized it wasn't working, and before it destroyed their personal relationship.

Joan now dispenses wisdom and counsel as the full-time national director of Canada's leading family business counselling and self-help group. Her observation on couples who think they can work together is this: "They bring their loving relationship into the business expecting that it's going to work for them. In some cases, it absolutely does, and in some cases, it absolutely does not." The answer, she says, is to get the business relationship worked out in advance, and put it in writing. That may sidestep any monstrous collision, but nothing is absolutely guaranteed. The truth is that many entrepreneurs lure family members into the business with the promise of challenge and responsibility, but all they really want is another beast of burden — someone who will work hard and loyally in the company name.

Joan's travails underline the biggest challenge that faces family businesses — managing the crucial area where family, ownership, and management roles intersect. It is one thing to be a wife and mother, and even a part-owner, but taking on a management role can complicate matters terribly. There is the sheer claustrophobia of the people you live with at home being the same ones you work with at the office. How can you ever escape them?

Business consultants and academics have developed a tool to help understand these complex and conflicted relationships. They call it the three-circle model of the family business. Think of three big intersecting circles that overlap in sections but are independent in others. These circles represent the three subsystems of the family business: the family, the business, and the ownership. Each person connected with a family business sits somewhere within the realm of those intersected circles. Where they are precisely located defines their relationship to the issues, challenges, conflicts, and potential solutions to family business problems. The 1997 book *Generation to Generation*, written by four of the leading American family business consultants, describes the relationship: "Any individual in a family business can be placed in one of the seven sectors formed by the overlapping circles of the subsystems. And people who have more than one relationship to the business are found in the overlapping systems."

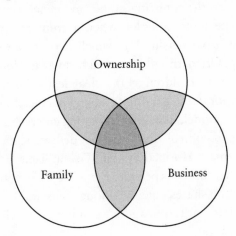

When she worked for Stelco, Joan found herself in two of the intersecting circles. She was a member of the family and she held some ownership in what was essentially her husband's business. Her problems began when she tried to move into active management of the business — the third circle — which changed her relationship with the company and brought her into conflict with her husband's view of their roles. Of course, the Berta situation is fairly simple as these things go, and it was fairly easily resolved. The true power of the model becomes apparent when we start looking at companies that have been around for generations, where siblings, children, and eventually cousins get involved in ownership and administration.

Once you define where you are within those circles, and where your colleagues and relatives are, you can figure out what's driving both them and you. Mind you, the model won't automatically solve any problems for you: it is just a visual definition of the various roles that intersect in a family business. It is particularly useful when, as in Joan's case, people move among the circles, establishing new roles in the dynamic.

The first rule of family business is that no single rule works for every company. Geoff Smith of Ellis-Don makes that point: "What we did worked, but it probably will not work in your situation." Every situation is different, and companies do not stand still. The problems arise when family members don't see that the company has changed and that its rules, structures, and principles have to shift with the times. Most companies begin with a controlling owner, a single entrepreneur who dreams up a business idea and pushes it — with a Charles Bentall or Don Smith in construction, or a Mac Cuddy in turkey production. This stage usually involves a relatively simple form of family ownership. It is clear that a single owner is in charge, and the real challenge is deciding who will lead the company in the next generation.

The issues become more complex when a company moves into a phase referred to as "sibling partnership," in which two or more brothers or sisters share the ownership. Often, this phase is reached when a founder cannot or will not designate one of his children as the clear leader in the next generation. According to *Generation to Generation*, sibling partnerships may operate on a "first among equals" model, in which one sibling emerges as a leader, but without a clear mandate of control. This creates a delicate situation, as reflected in the balancing act being performed by Joan Fisk at Tiger Brand. Joan Fisk has been designated by her father as president, but she lacks voting control because her father has split the shares equally among Joan and her two brothers. It's been a tense partnership at times, and it's still not clear whether these siblings will be able to work it out.

An even more complex model is the cousin consortium, as exemplified by multigenerational companies such as Molson Inc. and Oshawa Group. This is a monstrously difficult group to manage, because some cousins are family members, owners, and managers; while others are just owners; and still others are just managers. Tensions between those roles can destroy a company, as they brought down the family ownership of the Oshawa Group.

For a mature business that is owned by a vast number of family members, one key to survival is to instill a powerful sense of family traditions, symbols, and folklore. This can be done in a number of ways — for example, by maintaining artifacts from the family's past. The Molsons own a huge collection of paintings and objects from the family's glorious six-generation history. Family members can quote the dying testament of their late-nineteenth-century ancestor John H.R. Molson, who instructed future generations to live frugally and humbly and to work hard. The secretive Mannix family of Calgary, owners of a resource and construction empire, maintain a museum at their head office. Another Calgary family company, Atco, also has a museum, which describes how the company was founded by the Southern family, who started out as suppliers of trailers to Alberta's fast-growing construction and resource industries. It is also essential to hold family gatherings at least annually, to reinforce the far-flung cousins' identification with the company and its history.

Generation to Generation describes how one unidentified family — which sounds very similar to the Molsons — has held on to its beer company for more than 200 years. To motivate each generation to recommit to the business, the book notes, many companies hold clan meetings or retreats at which elders tell stories of the family's values or traditions. "The seniors in one Canadian enterprise that has 200 cousins in the fifth generation talk at such events of the family's dogged efforts to succeed — captured in its motto, 'Perseverance Pays.' The retreats feature ritual retelling of core myths about the family and the business: How the founders tried many beer recipes before hitting on one that became a best-seller, and how the family decided to tough out a province-wide labour crisis when other beer-makers sold their plants or moved away because of the threat of violence and sabotage. These heroic stories inspire younger family members to carry on the legacy."

It is difficult to carry a company into the cousin consortium stage, because it means keeping the business intact for three generations or more. Few companies survive that long, although such longevity is more common in Europe, where family traditions are stronger and career opportunities are more limited. As *Generation to Generation* points out, the United States and Canada place a stronger emphasis on entrepreneurship, independence, and mobility, and focus on the nuclear rather than the extended family. Peter Green, a consultant who has advised many family firms, says that alliances of cousins run against basic human nature. One reason you get along with your extended family, he says, is that you don't have to live with each other. "There's not a family where we don't bitch about someone else in the family," he says. So imagine when members are thrown into the pressure cooker of a business, where there is intense competition, and where people are judged day in and day out for what they do. "Any hope of a common goal goes out the window when there is competition among clan members to be noticed and to excel," Green says.

Of course, it's not just the ownership model that changes with time — it's the very nature of the evolving company itself. Leon Danco, the pioneer of family business consulting in the United States, offers a light-hearted model for the different stages of business evolution: first, the wonder period; then, the blunder period; next, the thunder period; and finally, the sunder or plunder period, which often ends with the death of the company. A common problem facing family companies is how to align the business phase with the right kind of ownership/management structure. In the startup period, the lone owner-manager is the appropriate management model. But as the startup company moves into the expansion phase, new pressures come to the fore. Often, the strengths of the entrepreneur — drive, creativity, single-mindedness — have to be blended with the discipline and expertise of professional managers — people who are specialists in finance, human resources, operations, and marketing. It is not that the entrepreneur's talents are no longer needed; rather, they must be mixed with the skills of specialists, whether those people are family members or recruited from outside. Often, a professionally trained son or daughter, educated as an MBA, an accountant, or a lawyer, propels the company forward in a period of expansion. That is when the founder's vision finally pays off in spades.

After a period of high growth, there follows a stage of consolidation and reinforcement, when the company's business model generates nicely rising sales and profits. But inevitably, the company moves into slower mature growth and finally, a plateauing of sales and profits. Competitors leap in, often with new technologies, new products, or new business models — the Internet, direct sales, one-to-one marketing, whatever. This mature phase is where the Wilsons of Nova Scotia find themselves now. Will they be able to fashion a rebirth of the core business? Will they watch over its decline? Or will they move into something entirely different? Fortunately, a new generation of owners is coming on, who may be able to lend dynamism and energy to the process.

Peter Drucker, the most prominent management guru alive, has some ideas on how companies can survive and even thrive as they move into this more mature phase. Drucker is that rare management theorist who takes the family-owned company very seriously. (Most management textbooks don't even deal with the particular characteristics of family companies.) He sees tremendous potential in these companies — they tend to be more horizontal in structure, more team-based in approach, and more flexible than large public companies. Also, there is often a fiercely held belief in the values and mission of the company. But Drucker worries about the ability of these companies to transcend the family's personal needs for wealth and prominence. In his book *Managing in a Time of Great Change*, he identifies three basic attributes of successful family companies:

First, family members do not work in the business unless they are at least as able as any nonfamily employee and work at least as hard. Drucker points out that it is much cheaper to pay a lazy nephew not to come to work than to keep him on the payroll. This issue was prominent in the case of Oshawa Group, which retained family members as top managers even though a number lacked the confidence of the employees or even the board. You know you're in trouble when directors use that faint-praise description of family members: "He's a nice guy but ..." Drucker writes that "if mediocre or lazy family members are kept on the payroll, respect for top management and for the business altogether rapidly erodes within the entire workforce. Capable nonfamily people will not stay. And the ones who do soon become courtiers and toadies."

The best family companies are those that assess family members as stringently as they assess nonfamily managers: the same performance standards apply to sons and daughters as to anyone else in the company. Some children of owners find that the bar is raised even higher for them, because their parents desperately want to avoid the nepotism label. This can be rough on family members who don't achieve the standards.

Second, no matter how many family members are in the company's management and how effective they are, at least one top job is always filled by an outsider. This position is typically the chief financial officer or head of research, which are the two posts where technical qualifications count most heavily. Drucker points out that the world's oldest "family business," the Mafia, follows this rule faithfully, in its native Sicily as well as in the United States. "As anyone knows who has seen a *Godfather* movie or read a *Godfather* book, in a Mafia family, the consigliere, the lawyer, who is the second most powerful person, might even be a non-Sicilian." Tom Hagen, the lawyer played by Robert Duvall in the movie version, epitomizes this type of trusted outsider.

But this is a difficult and often fragile role, especially when branches of the family are fighting with each other. The family consigliere often ends up having to choose between one side or the other. Also, the consigliere must often sublimate his or her ego and take a background role as younger, less able family members advance in the company. Archie McLean, a loyal and skilled food industry manager, was the McCain brothers' trusted helper for years. When the two brothers split bitterly over succession, he made a hard choice. Although he admired Harrison, he joined Wallace, who had offered him the president's job in another large business he had acquired, Maple Leaf Foods. Then McLean was thrust aside at Maple Leaf to make way for Wallace's younger son Michael. McLean felt that the timing of Michael's ascension was premature, so he quit the company. "There's a baseball cliché which says you win some and you lose some and some get rained out," he told *Report on Business Magazine*. "In the case of Maple Leaf Foods, the relationship got rained out." Like Tom Hagen, the family lawyer and trusted lieutenant in *The Godfather*, Archie McLean learned that in the end, blood always runs deeper than business relationships.

Third, family-managed businesses, except for the very smallest ones, increasingly need to staff key positions with nonfamily professionals. Writes Drucker: "The knowledge and expertise needed, whether in manufacturing or in marketing, in finance, in research, in human resource management, have become too great to be satisfied by any but the most competent family member, no matter how well intentioned he might be." And these nonfamily professionals have to be treated as equals, or they will not stay.

This need for an outsider with strong technical skills was a highlight in the case of BC Bearing. Once the company reached the $100 million mark in sales, its board of directors advised Wendy McDonald and her children that a highly skilled financial specialist was needed. BC Bearing was forced to reach outside the company to hire a well-respected chief financial officer who could help take the company to the next level.

When Peter Green was a young management consultant in Britain, he found himself working on a project for a family company. "I didn't realize what the hell was going on. There were huge relationship problems and I didn't see how these were continously affecting the company. I once witnessed a fistfight, cousins fell out, and they were being egged on by the elderly patriarch." That nasty initiation somehow didn't put off Green. He has spent more than thirty years as a professional manager, over half that time working for families in Britain and Canada.

This experience has led him to conclude that a family business is like no other business and, it follows, that being a manager in one of them is like no other managerial experience. It has given him a certain perspective that he would like to pass on to other professional managers who find themselves in similar situations. They need to be prepared for those "other issues," says Green, who has been president of two Canadian family companies — Andres Wines of Winona, Ontario, controlled by the Peller family, and most famously, Cuddy International, the strife-torn poultry breeding and processing company.

Those "other issues" — that is, family issues — are very much part of the decision-making process in such companies, Green warns. "Unless you understand something about what those tensions are, you are going to fail miserably, even if you try as an outsider to direct such a company." As a young consultant, his recommendations were totally sterile because he didn't understand the family dynamics. Surprisingly, this didn't turn him off. He promptly left management consulting to join another family company. In his early thirties, Green found himself trying to move some male family members out of jobs that were totally inappropriate for them and into positions where they and the company could benefit. "There are horses for courses and they weren't suited," he explains.

Still, those are the kinds of issues that outsiders can perhaps deal with. Green warns that nonfamily managers can never hope to solve the family's personal problems or issues that involve their own human relationships. "If you do try, you're screwed because you will soon be seen as being on the side of Jimmy and not Billy, even though that's not your intention. You get burdened with issues you cannot solve. You've got to be very clear about this: you're not there to be a counsellor. The difficult thing is even though you may say that, you're often ignored because that's precisely what the old man wants — some kind of super family counsellor, somebody who can undo all the problems that have built up in the family." Such a task is difficult if not impossible to accomplish because the tensions often go back to childhood, to the relationship between the mother and the father.

Another danger is isolation — the tendency that family businesses have to cut themselves off from the rest of the world. Even more than other corporations, these companies often turn inward, away from the ideas and trends sweeping the world. Often it's a sole proprietor who is caught in the snare of his own ego, or a couple of brothers, or a cast of cousins. Too often, such businesses look only to the family for counsel and ideas. In rural areas these family companies may dominate small towns, but they are divorced from wider realities: they have been big wheels for too long in Cambridge, or Truro, or Sept-Îles. Even urban families tend to close in on themselves. The challenge is to tap knowledge and expertise wherever it can be found and to encourage a free flow of information.

As Joan Berta found, one way to meet this challenge is to join CAFE, which has chapters across the country. The membership fee, about $600 a year, is low enough to make CAFE accessible to most medium-sized companies and many small ones, although the very smallest family businesses might find membership hard to justify. What CAFE does is tie people in with a network of like-minded people who share the same objectives and concerns. One of the most popular features of CAFE is its personal advisory groups (PAGs), which bring together about a dozen family business people from different industries to talk about their companies and their experiences. PAG members can gather practical advice — for example, how to hire a lawyer, or how to fire an underperforming cousin. But often these meetings turn into no-holds-barred encounter groups, and not everyone is comfortable with the candour. Other companies have worked with the de Gaspé Beaubiens' Business Families Foundation, which provides immersion courses on family issues — for a fairly high price tag. CAFE and the Business Families Foundation are now undertaking a joint venture to try to deliver these courses to a smaller scale of business.

One of the greatest challenges facing family businesses is how to establish proper governance. Too often such businesses are run as playthings of the family. The problem is that companies governed in this way do not survive — they are killed off by nepotism, incompetence, and constant bickering. So how do they develop concepts, rules, and structures to govern themselves in a way that provides some competitive advantage? More and more private family companies are adopting the mechanisms of widely held publicly traded companies, which ideally remove governance from the realm of the personal, the arbitrary, and the nepotistic. Most family firms of any size have shareholder agreements that set out what is to happen when someone wants to leave the business and sell his or her shares. They also have mission statements that set out the company's goals and values and codes of conduct to establish rules of behaviour for family members.

Most important, companies are making increasing use of boards of directors with a majority of independent members; these can exert important influence over promotions, compensation, selection of managers, and performance standards. Too often, the mediocrity of family businesses can be traced to the lack of a strong board, and to the presence on it of family cronies, long-time legal advisers, and "trusted" retired managers. This is not to say that public companies are pristine examples of objectivity and fair dealing — often they have been hijacked by the company's professional managers or become pawns of a controlling shareholder — but at least the standards are more clearly defined.

And it's not just a matter of what's good for the individual company. Some observers contend that the lack of skilled, well-trained boards of directors is a major flaw in many of Canada's family-owned manufacturing companies, and has led to wide productivity gaps vis-à-vis larger companies and small to medium-sized counterparts in the United States. Only strong, independent boards ask the right questions and choose the right CEOs. In this regard, the record of family companies has not been good. Owners have spun nice stories about independent boards, but they have not really followed through. When he ran Seagram, Sam Bronfman installed a board of directors, but he had little respect for it. When his son Edgar joined the Seagram board, he asked his father what the directors did. "Why, declare a dividend and have a drink," said Sam.

Some business clans have benefited enormously from their willingness to cede command to a strong board. For all the problems of the Bata family, the shoe company has at times drawn strength from a strong complement of outside directors. The painful resignation of Tom Bata Jr. as president can be attributed partly to Frans van den Hoven, the no-nonsense chairman of the Bata parent company and a former president of the consumer products giant Unilever. (Of course, given the problems at Bata since then, once might wonder whether it was a good idea.) That's why the aspirations of Geoff Smith are so encouraging — his goal is to remove himself and his brothers and sisters from the governance of Ellis-Don, and to lodge governing authority with an independent board selected by the shareholders, which include company employees. Under Ellis-Don's new operating rules, the pay and job status of family members employed by the company is determined by a committee of independent directors. Of course, all this implies a certain risk: What will happen if the board decides Geoff should not be president? These issues haven't been tested. But the risk is far greater that the company could die from an overdose of nepotism. Also, some companies may be too small to sustain or afford a full-fledged board. So how about a more informal advisory council? Or even a couple of mentors that the family company can turn to? The principle is the same: to remove governance from the whims of the family owners.

Parents of teenagers know this all too well — communication problems can destroy a family. This is equally true for a family business, especially as the family branches out and various levels of interest evolve. It is fashionable now to talk about family forums or assemblies, at which all family members have the chance to learn about the company's performance and strategy from senior family members and top executives, and to offer their feedback. Some organizations also have family councils — smaller groups of a half-dozen family members that meet regularly with board members and senior managers and act as intermediaries with the broader family. The terminology is not as important as the aim, which is to keep the more peripheral relatives informed about the company's direction.

Joan Berta and her husband Ray say that their family council consists of all direct family members — namely Ray, Joan, and their four children, none of whom actually works in the company. The council meets in Mississauga three to four times a year, bringing together a daughter from the Toronto area, another daughter in Hamilton, a son in Chicago, and a son at university in Buffalo. It's an opportunity to discuss the business, including its struggles to crack the American market. But the council is also a way to keep up to date on purely family matters, such as the arrivals and progress of grandchildren. Joan explains that the children come from two marriages, so communication of some kind can be extremely valuable.

In other situations, these mechanisms can be quite complex. The Finnish manufacturing conglomerate Ahlstrom has 200 family members with a stake in the parent firm, which is now in its fifth generation. To bring these disparate interests together, there is an annual assembly of all family members involved in ownership, as well as their spouses. It's an informal gathering that serves as a forum for family members to discuss anything, explained chief executive

Krister Ahlstrom in an interview in the *Harvard Business Review*. The Ahlstroms also have a family council of five members elected by the assembly. It serves as a communication link between the family, the board, and the CEO, and as a casual sounding board for the CEO and the directors. "Because there are 200 of us — and the family is growing — we had to put our values and practices in writing," explained Ahlstrom. "The family council drafted a document — the Ahlstrom Family Values and Policies — that was extensively discussed."

If they work well, these assemblies can be critical intermediaries between the senior family members in the business and the rest of the clan. But they don't always click. The Wolfes of Oshawa Group tried family councils, but the meetings were often ineffectual because they lacked the commitment of some key family members. Councils or forums can also be rendered irrelevant if all the time is spent gossiping or bragging about the kids. Another risk is that the meetings will be hijacked by someone with a strong personal agenda. It is often a good idea to hire a proper facilitator who is independent from the company and its players.

Howard Book, a Toronto psychiatrist who counsels family businesses, is a big advocate of family forums as a mechanism for disseminating information to the broader family. "If you're a family member, you're kept in the loop and feel allied with the business, and it offsets any feelings among the family that they're being taken advantage of, that they're getting screwed." Not everyone would bring spouses into the deliberations of the family council, but Dr. Book certainly would: if left outside the process, they may feel excluded and cheated in some way. The spouses of family members have a powerful effect on how the business functions. If they don't understand the business, there is a greater danger that they will make waves. "You get wives who are envious of each other and one will say to her husband, one of the siblings, 'How come your brother gets all this money?' which translates into 'How come your brother spends more money on his wife than you spend on me?'" Of course, this left-out feeling can work the same way with male spouses.

To deal with their problems, business families have traditionally drawn on the expertise of professional advisers, usually lawyers and accountants. The tax and legal issues are often complex, especially around the issue of succession. These experts are helpful in a technical way but not necessarily for solving all family crises. One problem is that their expertise is narrow — it is hard to find one person who can meet all personal, business, and taxation needs. Also, these paid experts are always in danger of being co-opted by the family — most often by the founder or the heir. More wealthy families take a team approach, and call on an accountant, a lawyer, and a family business adviser who handles the softer issues of relationships and human dynamics.

The best of these family business advisers have strong training in organizational development, or a background in therapy or psychology. They combine a sense of how organizations work and are run with a perception of family dynamics and personal needs. Some of these consultants do very well financially, particularly the superstars of the profession, who are based in the United States. At the high end, US$5,000 a day is not an unusual fee. Clearly, these people are not panaceas; often, the family divisions are already too entrenched for any solution to work. Boston innovation consultant Cavas Gobhai worked with the Cuddys, but probably he arrived too late to do much good. A number of Canadian companies, including the Chaplins of Canadian General Tower, have received help from David Bork of the Aspen Institute in Colorado. Pioneering family business counsellors John Ward and Leon Danco spent time with the McCain family, but to no avail. Closer to home, Jonathan Kovacheff, a lawyer and organizational consultant in Toronto, has worked for Joan Fisk and Tiger Brand; he also helped the Canadian General Tower heirs with their career plans. University of Calgary professor emeritus Joe Lischeron has developed a practice with a number of clients in the Oilpatch. The Wilsons of Halifax reached out as far as Minnesota to find consultant David Chapman. Distance, they say, is not an obstacle when you have found someone you are comfortable with.

In the late 1980s, Toronto psychiatrist Howard Book developed a lucrative sideline to his individual practice. He saw how many of his private patients were having difficulty juggling their business and family lives: "In a family-owned business, people are at one and the same time owner, executive, and employee, and unless these spheres are kept separate, you have a problem." Also, he could see family patterns repeating themselves in the company — for example, the president son who could not talk to his mother, the chairperson, which was causing paralysis in the business.

Dr. Book says he provides a forum for talking about smouldering, hidden issues in a constructive way. "I'm a facilitator, I'm a referee. I don't allow them to shout or throw things or insult each other. I try to keep the focus on how people feel in order to allow them to talk about issues they have not felt free to talk about. And how the family belief system inhibits talking openly about very important issues."

Often he is approached by the mother and son in a family company where there is a strong male founder who does not want to retire. The two have no authority to hire the psychiatrist, but they ask Dr. Book to approach the father to start a dialogue. If the father resists this invasion of his space, Dr. Book appeals to his basic desire to continue a legacy. "Even though he might die, the business has the opportunity of living on," he explains. He sees mothers as wielding a strong informal influence in male-led companies. "This is someone with a lot of informal power and influence on the husband CEO, and she has concerns. Mothers are brokers, in effect. They are very helpful to powerful husbands, who often rely on their wives for help and advice. In one case, a mother who had no equity in the company was invited by the father to come and sit beside him for the interviews. With her beside him, he was more open, more pensive. It was really helpful in allowing us to go forward."

Management literature indicates that the mother's main priority usually is not the success of the business, but keeping the family together. In some cases, says Harvey Levinson, a distinguished Harvard psychologist and expert on organizations, she can actually play a negative part. For the sake of family peace, she often wants to keep all the children in the business — in other words, to keep them happy, even though they may not deserve such treatment. She often wants to override performance expectations and rules. "In her concern for preserving the family, the mother often contributes to the corruption of the business," Levinson has written in the journal *Family Business Review*. "A business has to be managed as a business, and if it's not managed as a business, it's not going to survive."

Dr. Book admits that he cannot perform miracles. Often he is running up against age-old resentments. He looks on the families he meets as a continuum, with healthy, well-functioning families at one end, and on the other end families that "can't ask each other to pass the pencil without getting into an enraged, destructive battle. Those kinds need family therapy first because they are highly dysfunctional."

He says that well-functioning clans are able to get along in a business sense, but even they run into particular tasks that stir up emotional difficulties. Perhaps the biggest of these tasks involves determining succession. "The dysfunctional families will not be able to even look at succession because they are so dysfunctional," he says. Adaptive, healthy families will be able to manage that difficult task — at most, they may need a facilitator to help them through the bumpy spots.

But succession is such a difficult issue that it deserves a chapter of its own.

FOURTEEN

PASSING IT ON

Pity THE POOR FAMILY BUSINESS HEIR. Surely not, you scoff — not those spoiled brats, the ungrateful beneficiaries of nepotism and wealth. Yet the children of family companies may be the most misunderstood figures in the business world. They are often the product of dysfunctional families. As the offspring of driven entrepreneurs, they are frequently lonely as children. When they succeed, their victories are attributed to luck and a silver spoon; when they fail, their critics crow at their misfortunes. They are cursed by their family's success — by high expectations and comfortable lifestyles. They can't leave the business because they won't earn so much anywhere else; yet they find little joy in staying around, only to be ignored by a stubborn and authoritarian parent.

Too often the father or mother stays on long after the normal retirement age, and the children get bored, impatient, or rebellious — or all three. Those children who are deemed wanting and are cast out of the family company end up wandering the hills and valleys of modern business, looking for some sense of purpose. Tom Bata Jr., David Bentall, Jonathan Wolfe, and Bruce Cuddy, all of whom are oldest or only sons, were suddenly rejected by the companies their fathers or grandfathers had founded. They probably should never have set foot in the family business, and it took each of them more than forty years to understand that.

Peter Green certainly sympathizes. Working for or consulting to families, he has had to fire young heirs or usher them quietly out of the company. He has had to intercede on behalf of the children with a hard-nosed, demanding father. He has seen history and expectations weigh heavily on their shoulders. He says that dissuading a young person from working in the family company is one of the trickiest jobs around: "First, he thinks his only career option is inside the company, and second, if he were to opt out, he would really lose his face within the family."

Part of the problem is the inflated expectations of the company's leader, who thinks he is creating a dynasty that will last forever. "The old man, even when he's not the founder — he believes a family member has to lead this company into the distant horizon. But that's not necessarily true," Green says. "Today, things are more complex and a great deal more professionalism and training are required to be successful."

Succession is the challenge most likely to make or break a family company. How does one transfer ownership and management in a way that serves the needs of both the family and the business? In this book, succession has been the one issue that has consistently thrown successful companies and families off track. The Cuddys, the Mitchells, the Bentalls, and the McCains — all were torn apart by succession issues. Yet a succession that is carried out wisely can lift a company into a new growth phase. Why are some companies so good at it, and others so tragically incompetent?

Succession was easier in earlier times, when primogeniture ruled: the oldest son always took over the company. This system still exists in parts of Europe, which may explain why business succession often seems so seamless on that continent and why companies are sometimes hundreds of years old. It may also explain why European businesses so often lack dynamism — these old, protected companies are run by old, protected male heirs. This uninspired approach seems to work best when the company has a strong franchise based in land or agriculture. Example: Italian and French wineries. But in the highly competitive, knowledge-based economies of the 1990s, the valuable assets of companies are found between their employees' ears, and these mechanisms don't work as well.

Edgar Bronfman Sr., in his memoirs *Good Spirits*, describes how in the 1960s his father Sam elevated him to be the next-generation leader of the Seagram liquor company: "My father was an empire builder, and true to the customs of his times, the emperor wanted a male heir. As the first son among four children born to my parents, I was destined to be that heir." To show how times have changed, when Edgar chose his own successor, he bypassed his older son, also named Sam, to pick the younger sibling, Edgar Jr., whom he saw as the more instinctive businessman.

The problem is that many of these patriarchs are conflicted, frustrated men. They yearn for their sons or daughters to take over, yet they are impatient with them or feel they aren't quite up to it. Unfortunately, many of the people around them — directors and senior managers — come to the same conclusion, often simply because the children are not like the father. But then who is? No one will tell the founder anything different from what he wants to believe. "What these people don't really understand is that they themselves are very forceful personalities and that's where their success lies," says Green. "They don't understand the extent to which they have sycophants around them — that it takes a lot to stand up and say to the founder, 'You're full of bullshit.' If you said that as a director, you'd be gone before the next board meeting. That's the Achilles' heel of such people, and you see so many of them."

It's almost as tragic when the son or daughter does have real skills but is constantly demeaned by a controlling parent. Often, the attitude is expressed as, "My son can't replace me, he lacks my guts and drive." As the fathers become sceptical of their children's abilities, they become susceptible to the next pretty face that comes along — often a bright manager recruited from the outside. So the child is thrust aside in favour of a "professional manager," leaving the kid to sulk and rage and become a worrisome distraction to the business. Says Green: "I've seen situations where the children are reviled, publicly just put down, while some young guy is picked off the street with a decent background. Somehow the old man expects him to fit in with these guys [the children] who have been kicked around all the time."

Harry Levinson, the psychologist and Harvard Business School professor, sketches the problem in sharper relief. In an interview in the *Family Business Review*, he explains why parents are so reluctant to let go and why their children feel so inadequate: "In some cases, the father dominates so much that he psychologically castrates the son. In other cases, the father just doesn't want to let go and provide the son or daughter with the opportunity to succeed him. Another thing that goes wrong is that most of the time in family businesses, the CEO doesn't do an adequate job of evaluating the competence of the children or the different competencies of the different children."

Howard Book, a Toronto psychiatrist who counsels family companies, says that many fathers are wrenched by an internal conflict. The father wants his name to endure through his company, but he's torn because he doesn't think his son or daughter has what it takes. Meanwhile, he worries about whether he will still be considered successful if he stops owning and managing the business. What's he going to do when he's no longer the CEO, when he's just Joe Ordinary? Without the title of CEO or owner, he may feel he will have trouble even introducing himself to strangers. "It makes him feel like a has-been, and for some it affects feelings of self-sufficiency and self-worth," says Dr. Book.

Many parents become manipulative — they love to keep on pulling the strings, even at times pitting child against child. In *Good Spirits*, Edgar Bronfman Sr. writes that his father Sam applied the strategy of divide and conquer to the succession competition between Edgar and his brother Charles. "While Charles was in Canada and I was in the United States he told each of us uncomplimentary things about the other and deliberately kept us apart. His insecurity was such that he had a fear that we might combine and throw him out. Our friendship survived, thank the Lord." Edgar was determined that this form of torture would not be replayed in his own succession.

Faced with a manipulative parent, the children may roll over and take it, or they may react in extreme ways, proclaiming their independence while frantically trying to emulate their larger-than-life parents. Pierre Péladeau, the Quebec printing entrepreneur who died in 1998, left huge shoes to fill both as a businessman and as a personality. A reformed alcoholic, he built Québecor Inc. into one of the continent's major printing companies. He constantly demeaned his younger son Pierre Karl Péladeau. "Pierre Karl would say, 'Look Dad, I saved $5 million on this deal,' and the father would say, 'Well, you should have saved $10 million,'" said Andre Gourd, former head of Quebecor's newspaper and media group, now a management consultant, in an interview with *Forbes Magazine* in April 1999. And yet the father clearly admired the son's ability — early on, he designated Pierre Karl as his successor over his older brother Erik.

Even so, the public bullying continued. At one point the father exiled the son to Europe, where Pierre Karl worked mightily to build Québecor into one of that continent's largest printers. When Pierre died, the younger son, at thirty-seven, assumed the CEO's mantle after a brief transition. While his father could be a delegator and conciliator — with unions and other companies, if not with his children — Pierre Karl's style is that of an angry young man who has something to prove. He is a radical centralizer and perfectionist who chews out staff regularly and drives executives out of the company. Pierre Karl is also demonstrating a desire to outdo his father in the big-deal department; he won the newspaper chain Sun Media in a $1.3 billion transaction, making Québecor the country's second-largest newspaper group. He has now set his sights on expansion into the United States, where his father failed abysmally. Says Gourd in his *Forbes* interview: "You just want to say, 'Look Pierre Karl, your father's dead. You can set the bar anywhere. Relax. Try to enjoy life. Don't be so mad at the world.'"

Pierre Karl, like his father, is a compulsive personality, although his vices seem fairly normal in comparison. He gulps coffee constantly and has battled a cigarette habit. The family has clearly been damaged by the father's lifestyle — seven children by three wives, a disruptive home life — and the early death of Pierre Péladeau's first wife and Pierre Karl's mother. Even as the heir was taking command at Québecor, Pierre Karl and his brother Erik were battling in court with their sister Anne-Marie, an admitted cocaine addict. The brothers had cut off their sister's $10,000 monthly income in a bid to force her to undergo treatment for drug addiction at an élite Montreal clinic. In turn, Anne-Marie was seeking a court injunction to force the brothers to free up the money from the family holding company. Anne-Marie was also alleging that $21 million worth of shares that she owned had been sold by her brothers without her permission. Eventually an out-of-court settlement was reached.

The Péladeau succession has degenerated into a series of legal battles; at one point there were four lawsuits before the courts at the same time. Here, a strong-willed, tempestuous founder has continued to pull his children's strings beyond the grave. At one point Erik and Pierre-Karl Péladeau sued a retired judge, Jean-Paul Saint-Louis, a trusted adviser whom their father had appointed to oversee the one-third stake in Québecor's voting shares that was not controlled directly by the two brothers. The brothers accused their father's friend of leaking secrets to the media, charging huge fees for his services, and fomenting conflict among the children. Ironically, Pierre Péladeau had entrusted Saint-Louis with the voting control of the one-third interest because he feared conflict among his sons.

Not all family situations are as extreme as the Péladeau fiasco, and not all parents are manipulative. Even so, the Péladeau story underlines the perils of the succession adventure. Not all families end up suing each other, but inevitably there are hurt feelings, pain, and misunderstanding. There are a number of "best practices" that families can follow:

First: Plan early, and set a definite exit plan. Think of succession as a process rather than an event. If the departure date is delayed, the children may not adequately prepare themselves for leadership, and the parents may become too set in their ways. The earlier the parents set an age and time for their exit — and the more resolutely they stand by it — the more likely they are to find other things to do with the rest of their lives. If the succession plan is too ambiguous, the parents may never leave — except when they're carried out — and the children may never acquire any sense of purpose. Rein Peterson, a York University professor who teaches an undergraduate course on family business, likes to tell his students that the real theme is, "What to do about Daddy."

The greatest tragedies arise when the son or daughter waits too long for the mantle of leadership, and finds it denied in the end. Theirs become wasted lives. "What happens with adult children, who are chained to the business, is that they are overpaid, they can't leave and find a job elsewhere that will match their lifestyle," says Dr. Book. Even selling the business is a better outcome than this state of limbo — at least it gives the children a chance to go out on their own with a bit of cash. Early planning can also provide certainty for professional managers, who can better assess their career chances and determine their options.

If succession is left too long, without someone being chosen as the leader in the next generation, the competition between siblings can split a company apart. Edgar Bronfman Sr. was not going to allow a festering rivalry to develop between his two sons, Sam and Edgar Jr. So he moved very early in identifying Edgar as his successor, which caused great pain to Sam. Edgar Sr. blundered badly when he blurted out his choice to a journalist at *Fortune*. As a result, Sam read about it in the press instead of hearing it from his father. Still, Edgar Sr. doesn't regret taking clear and decisive action: "Having my two sons line up supporters as if it were an election was not good for them, for the corporation, for the family, or for me."

Second: Train the owner. Everyone talks about training the kids for leadership, and that is clearly a high priority. But it is equally important to equip the parent for retirement. In his practice, Dr. Book tries to overcome what he calls the parent's "resistances." Instead of simply urging the owner to put together a succession plan, he asks some questions: "How would you feel if you had to sit down now and write a succession plan? What will it be like for you to give up this business? Do you have images of what days will be like when you are no longer involved in the business?" Dr. Book tries to understand the fears that often lie beneath the surface.

"For a CEO, it may be the feeling that asking him to initiate a succession plan is like asking him to arrange his own funeral — it stirs up in people ideas of death, of being put out to pasture, of being worthless and useless." Another possibility is that the owner's marriage is tenuous — in fact, the wife might prefer that the husband spend all his days at work. "To have him home and under foot is something she may want no part of. He may be lionized at work but a pain in the ass at home." The trick, he says, is to get the parent to talk about all the things he can do in the future, such as advisory boards and philanthropic work, and to discuss his marriage and what he might do or not do. Once families deal with these resistances, the actual planning becomes much easier.

It is important for the parent to actually leave the company when he retires — after a suitable transition, of course. There must be hard and fast rules to make sure he doesn't hang around, watching over the kids, second-guessing decisions and confusing employees about who is in charge. The young Smiths who took over Ellis-Don were adamant that Don Smith, the founder, could not have an office at the construction company, or even show up to use the gym. While it sounds cruel, it is actually an attempt to minimize the risk of conflict.

Third: Prepare the heirs. Education is, of course, important. Many families spend a lot of money buying the best possible degrees, so that the children are qualified to assume senior positions in the company and to prepare the organization for the challenges ahead. But the children need to tread carefully as well. They come home with their newly minted MBAs, LLBs, or BComms, and often with fresh ideas about running the old company. Does Dad like that? Not necessarily. No matter how compelling the new ideas, they often clash with how the company has long been run. For example, the heir may want to institute strategic planning, which is often ignored in entrepreneurial, owner-managed companies. There may well be justification for the owner's scepticism: often, the heir's highfaluting management ideas pull the company too far from its natural strengths — its street smarts and its gut feel for the market. In retailing particularly, there is as much art involved as science. Families often find it hard to resolve these two perspectives, both of which are valuable.

Equally important is career planning for the young generation — that is, serious thought about where all the children and cousins will work. Not everyone in the family is going to be groomed as president or a controlling shareholder. Children may be expected to grow up with an instinctive feel for the trade, when what they really need is to be mentored and guided. Family background can actually be a disadvantage in the career stakes. The lucky ones go off to work someplace else where they can learn to be managers, and can develop confidence on their own terms.

This raises another key requirement for business heirs: They should work outside the company for at least five years. Time outside is essential if heirs are to gain some self-respect and confidence. They develop the sense that they are not getting ahead just because they are Molsons, Batas, Olands, or Péladeaus. Those who rejoin the family business do so with some personal credibility, especially if they have done well in the outside world. Almost every family company spouts this rule, but not all of them put it to good use.

David Bentall spent two years at Toronto's Cadillac Fairview before returning to the family company as a manager. Eventually, his uncle blocked his rise to the presidency of Bentall Corp. Today, David says he should have stayed away longer and then waited for the company to approach him. He should not have assumed that his old job would be waiting for him. Too often, children work outside for a number of years but are not carefully tested and reviewed when they come back in: it is simply assumed that they have picked up all the skills. It is also critical that they be given a job that already exists, not some *erzatz* position that has been created for them. When they take on a real position, they are less likely to be tarred with nepotism, and performance standards are already in place by which to assess the young heir.

A board of directors or advisory board can be critical in establishing a performance assessment process that applies to both family and nonfamily personnel. When a company doesn't assess family members with rigour, it loses on two counts: it will be badly led, and no one with any talent will want to work for it. Consultants suggest applying a battery of psychological tests to the younger generation, including assessments that judge the person's appropriateness for various positions. Also, mentoring relationships should be established inside the company. It is critical for an heir (or any other family member) to have a knowledgeable and influential teacher who is not a parent.

Fourth: Separate ownership from management. This is a critically important mindset, yet it is often the toughest to instill. It is an absolutely necessary condition for a family firm to continue. Family members must reject the long-held notion that they must not only own the company but also actively manage it. This new way of thinking opens up opportunities to nonfamily professionals who can do it better. It also brings a hard-headedness to family deliberations. The family company can then be considered as a store of wealth and value, rather than as some sacred trust or great emotional legacy. As the Eaton family discovered, legacies often turn out to be chains that shackle both the family and the company.

The ability to own a family business often gets short shrift as a skill or talent. For many family members, the real pride comes with being a senior manager, a hands-on operator, the great benefactor who glides across the factory floor to the adulation of loyal long-time employees. Yet that should not be the case. Strong and wise ownership is a real talent — some people do it well, others don't. These days, families can evolve into good owners, leaving the management to professional outsiders. "A great family company is a combination of the ownership and wisdom of the family, and of professional management," says Derek Oland, fifty-nine, the fifth-generation owner of Moosehead Breweries of Saint John, New Brunswick, who recently hired the first non-Oland ever as president of the beer company. "Ownership isn't worth a damn if the company is going down the tubes," he adds.

Fifth: Ask, "Would you buy this company?" This is the big question for both successors and existing owners, for it helps them understand why they are holding on to the family company. Owners who understand their own motivations can make better decisions about the future. Jonathan Kovacheff, a Toronto management consultant who works with family businesses, says he likes to ask entrepreneurs whether they would actually want to buy this particular company on an arm's-length basis. And if they wouldn't, why are they involved in it at all? He asks them to compare the business's returns to what they'd get from investing cash in a stock index such as the Toronto Stock Exchange 300. Could they sell the family legacy and more profitably invest the returns in the stock market?

How this question is answered is a dependable guide to whether the person is getting involved for business reasons or (more likely) for emotional and continuity reasons. Even when it is for the latter reasons, the owners may still opt to keep the company. At least they now understand the forces that are driving them.

René Hétu has practised this sane approach to ownership. He and his family founded and built Interweb, a highly successful Montreal-based printing company that reached sales of $120 million a year under their guidance. But the Hétus sold the business in 1998 to a much bigger printing company, GTC Transcontinental, also of Montreal and also a family business. René had two sons in the company, both highly regarded managers in the printing industry. Yet the entire family was prepared to sell because they saw Interweb as a valuable asset — not as an untouchable family legacy.

The family had examined the company in the early 1990s and decided that if within five years it had hit $100 million in sales, they would consider their options — to sell or to build. Five years later, they concluded it would be better to sell out to a bigger company that was on a growth path. The industry was consolidating, and only the consolidators — the companies that were buying smaller firms — were likely to flourish. After the sale to GTC, René joined the new owner's board, and the sons, thirty-two and thirty-five, negotiated five-year employment contracts with the new owner. They now think they can bring something of their own culture to the new parent company.

Sixth: Match different managers to different times. A family company often chooses for a successor the son or daughter who most resembles the existing owner-manager in style and skills. Bata employees and managers were clearly looking forward to a successor who would be as charismatic as the ruling couple, Tom Sr. and Sonja; instead, they ended up with a smart but unexciting son. Tom Jr. might in fact have been the best choice for the times, but he was considered "a poor people person." That image did not help when he clashed with the board over the direction of the company. And so he departed — a tremendous waste of management resources and human capability.

Different skills are needed for different stages in a company's history. "What makes a great entrepreneur, what makes a great startup leader, does not necessarily make a great professional leader," Dr. Book says. More mature companies need people who are stronger on organization, strategy, and management discipline. "It will be a different organization ten to twenty years down the road, and [the owner's] style may in fact not fit the organization's needs." Unfortunately, the hard-driving founders often feel less secure, less confident with the style of leadership that is needed in the future. "Often these companies don't have a structure to prepare for the entire life cycle of the business — a strategic plan and a mission. The CEO father, because of his own style, may be pressured to pick someone who is like him, which is not what the company needs at this stage."

Seventh: Consider everybody. No one should be overlooked as a candidate for key leadership roles — and that includes younger sons, daughters, sons-in-law, and daughters-in-law. (Of course, it is even better to consider nonfamily members as well.) It is becoming more common to choose a daughter as the next leader. One advantage is that it releases reluctant sons from the burden of leadership and opens the company up to what may well be its most committed, most talented people. However, male entrepreneurs often have trouble seeing their daughters as successors. In their minds' eye, daughters stand for something gentler and more feminine than being a hard-nosed boss. Also, a number of company founders are selecting their daughters as heirs, but then exerting such repressive control over them that they appear to have no will of their own.

Conversely, some owners embrace the daughters as future leaders because they are less threatening than the sons. Often, male owners have had an easier relationship with their daughters, with less rivalry and less posturing. The choice of a daughter over a son may promise a smoother, less rancorous transition. The choice, of course, should be made on the basis of leadership potential and ability to carry the company to the next phase. That was the thinking of Jim Warnock, the tough-minded head of Tiger Brand, when he chose his daughter Joan Fisk as president because he felt she had the marketing skills so badly needed if the garment company was to survive and grow.

Don't forget the potential value of in-laws, male or female (although few companies seem to have tapped the daughter-in-law pool yet). The most successful in-law in Canadian business history is Laurent Beaudoin, who married the daughter of Armand Bombardier, the snowmobile inventor, and built Bombardier Inc. into a diversified international manufacturing company.

Surveys show that the idea of male primogeniture has been laid to rest in many

Canadian companies. At least, that's what they're saying for the record. If it exists at all, it's not being admitted, or it's being practised in very traditional families — perhaps among new Canadians recently arrived from countries where primogeniture still thrives. In a recent survey of 485 family-owned companies in Canada, the owners ranked integrity and commitment to the business as the most important attributes of a successor. Surprisingly, birth order and gender were rated the least important among the thirty characteristics cited by the owners.

"The family business managers in our survey recognized that for the good of the business and the good of the family, an evaluation of a potential successor's integrity, commitment to the business, respect of employees and decision making and interpersonal skills must guide the selection process. If the best candidate is not the first-born male, so be it," the survey authors James Chrisman and Jess Chua of the University of Calgary and Pramodita Sharma of Dalhousie University concluded in an article in the *Family Business Review*.

Eighth: Prune the family tree. Fewer shareholders makes it generally easier on everyone. The great danger is to have many small chunks of ownership held by people who are not involved in or committed to the enterprise. Family shareholders who do not work in the business are often more concerned with personal wealth than with reinvestment or growth of the company. Also, they are vulnerable to being bought out by other companies, which increases the possibility of a creeping takeover. In any case, the company has to spend a lot of time and energy making these people happy — time that could be devoted to developing the company.

Many family leaders try to restrict the number of shareholders in any generation, often by paying people off in cash instead of shares in the company. This is a challenge for a parent whose entire wealth is contained in one business. If he wants to be fair to all the children, he may want to leave them equivalent amounts; yet he lacks liquid or near-liquid assets that can be dispersed to pay cash to the nonbusiness heirs. This is a good argument for early preparation and for sound financial planning advice. It's one reason why financial consultants urge owners not to tie up their wealth entirely in the family company.

Ninth: Teamwork, teamwork. It used to be the prevailing wisdom that family businesses should be managed by one all-powerful leader. That's quickly changing. In the next generation, many family businesses will be led by more than one successor. Partly this is a reflection of parents' desire to be fair to all the kids. But it also signals a new attitude toward leadership — a recognition that all the necessary skills cannot be found in a single person. Several of the families profiled in this book are preparing for their children to work together as teams. This trend is nowhere more striking than at Telemedia, where the three children of Philippe and Nan-b de Gaspé Beaubien have established an office of the chief executive, rather than naming one single CEO. Dad is sceptical, but what can he do?

This trend is borne out by the massive U.S. study of 3,000 family firms conducted by Arthur Anderson and MassMutual in 1997. Of the family companies surveyed, 42 percent believed that more than one family member would serve as co-CEO in the next generation. The survey sponsors issued a warning, however: "Decision-making can be more difficult when a consensus is required. These families would be well-advised to include independent outsiders on their boards of directors to assist in decision-making and the special challenges of co-leadership." Team leadership makes it imperative to have strong governance practices captured in written documents.

Large, diversified companies have an advantage here. If the owners cannot make up their minds between two or more children, they may simply allocate different parts of their holdings to different siblings. That is what the late New Brunswick billionaire K.C. Irving did so brilliantly — each of his three sons runs a different part of the business. Paul Desmarais, the shrewd owner of Power Corp., has taken a similar route. It's even better when the children can be involved in geographically separated entities.

Tenth: Bring on the reinforcements. "To choose your own successor is likely to be a guarantee for failure," says the Harvard Business School's Harvey Levinson. Owners of any mid-sized or larger company should rely on an independent panel to choose the successor. Preferably, that panel should be a board of directors that has monitored the next generation in action. This is probably a board of directors' most important duty. Levinson says that if you don't have an independent board, you will find it hard to judge the comparative abilities of the children, especially if you don't have psychological test data and you don't have any experience outside the company to go on.

In a Deloitte Touche study, almost two-thirds of Canadian family businesses surveyed did not have any nonfamily members on a formal or advisory board. However, the most surprising result of that study may be that 35 percent of the companies *did* have nonfamily board members, which suggests this idea may be catching on. Also, the higher its sales, the more likely the company was to have independent board members. When a company does not have a board with independent directors, it often puts together a more informal advisory council.

Family businesses also need lawyers and accountants. If a company is large enough and its problems sufficiently complex, it may also require family business consultants or facilitators. The owner in the current generation may be comfortable with his current coterie of advisers, but what about the next generation?

Successors usually want their own people around them. Thus, advisory firms should also have succession plans, so that the senior practitioners can hand over the files to more junior people. If the advisers' companies are smart, they'll start grooming their own people and moving younger people into position to work with the sons and daughters of their clients.

Eleventh: Show me the money. This book is not about financial planning, but you can't avoid it. It's another reason why succession planning should start early. Let's say you want to get out of the business but you need enough money to live in retirement. The classic approach is the estate freeze, in which the owner converts his common shares into income-paying preferred shares worth the current value of the company. Hence, the term "estate freeze." The parent gets dividends to live on. The children are issued common shares that will capture only the future value of the company, thereby deferring capital gains taxes to a future date. The owner, if he wants to continue to call the shots — alas, many of them do — can retain voting control through his holding of the preferred shares.

Some parents just want the cash out right away, which means the kids have to come up with financing for the purchase. That can be a difficult challenge for still struggling successors. Lenders are coming up with increasingly sophisticated borrowing options to allow business succession. In fact, one merchant banker, Roynat Inc., a unit of the Bank of Nova Scotia, has targeted family businesses as a growth market for its services. These lenders offer secured financing for companies with tangible assets, but Roynat, for one, is even willing to lend against a company's goodwill. Also, a number of family companies — particularly if they are short on tangible assets as security — are turning to mezzanine financing, a form of unsecured debt backed only by the company's cash flow. For this to work, the company has to be a solid, profit-earning company — what Toronto investment banker Gordon Sharwood calls "a foundation business." The interest rates may be high relative to asset-based loans, but if the company has a consistent earnings base, it can meet the repayment schedule.

Twelfth: Meet the buffer manager. The parents may be ready to move out of day-to-day management, but the children may be too young to take control. That raises the opportunity for a transition manager, who can hold the fort until the kids are ready. Derek Oland, chairman of Moosehead Breweries, has two sons in their early thirties, with graduate degrees from the Harvard Business School and from INSEAD, an international business school based in France. Both sons worked outside the company for a couple of years before joining it. They're clearly not ready to assume the most senior management positions.

Enter Bruce McCubbin, a fifty-seven-year-old professional manager whose tours of duty include senior executive positions with Imasco, the big tobacco and retail conglomerate. McCubbin's steady hand on the daily business has freed Derek, fifty-nine, to think more strategically, and to perform his various duties outside the company, and has provided his sons with time to season. Derek is careful not to tip his hand as to whether one of the sons is a president-in-waiting. He is perfectly comfortable having a nonfamily manager in the president's role for as long as it makes sense. He also doesn't want to put a lot of pressure on his sons. "I don't believe anything should be preordained," he insists.

These days, Sharwood, the investment banker, is seeing a lot more of these transition or buffer managers. It's all in the demographics. When he went into business, parents had their babies when they were still in their early to middle twenties. The result was that when the father or mother hit retirement age, the children were in their forties, old enough to take over the family company. But now couples are waiting longer — often much longer — to have children. As a result, "the old man and lady are sixty-five and the kid is twenty-five. It's got to put a lot more focus on this issue of the buffer manager." That's creating a seller's market for savvy interim managers who can guide the family company for ten or fifteen years until the offspring are deemed ready to take over. It's a tough job, because you have to balance the parents' need for a comforting exit with the child's impatience for power. But if you're that patient sort, you'll find lots of work over the next twenty years.

FIFTEEN

THE FUTURE OF THE FAMILY BUSINESS

F RAN'S IS A LEGENDARY TORONTO restaurant chain, known for its retro 1950s ambience and its basic fare of western sandwiches, coffee, and rice pudding. Such unpretentiousness made it an appropriate venue for meetings aimed at saving family businesses from extinction. For several months in 1983, three men — an investment banker, a university professor, and a management consultant — would get together at the Fran's outlet on St. Clair Avenue in midtown Toronto, and plot their strategy for how to give more clout to the family business. In late 1983 they unfolded their plan — they convened the first meeting of the Canadian Association of Family Enterprise.

A varied crew of business owners and managers attended that first gathering: the president of a jam company, the son-in-law of a newspaper owner, and the boss of a trucking firm. Also, the owners of a starch manufacturer, a printing shop, a paper products supplier, and a gas bar chain. Among the dozen or so businesspeople gathered that day, no high-tech company was represented. Perhaps that shouldn't be too surprising: it was 1983, and personal computers had not yet arrived on the world stage in a big way, and Bill Gates was not yet the wealthiest man in the world.

Seventeen years later, CAFE, the organization that arose from that meeting at Fran's, has grown to a membership of nearly 1,000 companies from coast to coast, but one thing hasn't changed: there are still very few high-tech companies on the list. In fact, you'd be hard-pressed to find many high-tech companies today that consider themselves family enterprises. It's possible that back in the 1950s, IBM considered itself a family company under the father-and-son team of Thomas Watson Sr. and Jr. — but certainly not the IBM of today.

"So will Microsoft become a family company?" asks Gordon Sharwood, the Toronto investment banker, during an interview in his downtown Toronto office. Sharwood was one of the founders of CAFE and has been one of its guiding lights over the years. Along with York University business professor Rein Peterson and management consultant Dave Gallagher, he envisioned an association that would speak for the hitherto unrepresented. Family companies, usually small to medium-sized operations, lacked a voice in public life, yet they were an important economic force in Canada. His vision has been realized: CAFE is a national organization and is strong and growing. But today, Sharwood wonders aloud whether his vision of 1983 will have much relevance for the twenty-first century. He questions whether the fast-growing information technology companies will adopt the family business model that has powered industry in the nineteenth and twentieth centuries.

Sharwood, an irrepressible type who seems to know just about everybody in Canadian business, thinks that may not happen. As a financier with his own company, Sharwood & Associates, he helps provide funding for many of the surging information technology companies that are driving the new economy. But these companies' founders are not thinking about getting their kids working in the business or passing anything on to the next generation. Their business model works in another way: you have an idea, you raise money from friends and relatives, you develop your idea, and you tap venture capital to advance your idea. Then you launch a public offering to raise more financing, and if you and your early shareholders are lucky, you cash in — if not from the IPO, then when you sell out to a big company for big bucks. Your dream is to lever a bit of knowledge, a handful of employees, and proprietary rights over some lines of software code into a huge payday.

Typically, high-tech entrepreneurs don't build a company to pass it on; they build it to sell it. If they're ambitious and smart, they may found and sell several companies before they retire to the golf game and the Florida condo. At the end of the day, they may have some wealth but certainly no factory, no mills, no tangible assets to bequeath to an heir. "In knowledge-based businesses, when you have a entrepreneur, can you move it to the next generation?" wonders Jonathan Kovacheff, a Toronto consultant to family companies. He says he knows of only one technology company that could be called a family company, in the sense that two generations are active in the business and the founder plans to hand the business over to his offspring. That is a scientific firm in Halifax involved in developing ocean-based plants for food.

At the same time, the family business model dominates the so-called old economy of manufacturing, resources, construction, and traditional retailing (i.e., not the Internet kind). A recent Deloitte Touche survey of 766 Canadian family businesses illustrated this: more than 25 percent of the companies surveyed were retailers; just over 20 percent were manufacturers; 12 percent were wholesalers; and 5 percent were transportation and warehousing firms. The largest "high-tech" component was professional, scientific, and technical services firms, which accounted for just 4 percent.

So are we seeing the beginning of the end of the family business? Will it erode as a model of business because it lacks the capacity to generate innovation and wealth in a knowledge era? Will family companies be relegated to no-growth areas, or to backwaters such as mom-and-pop retailing? (My apologies to small shopkeepers, some of whom are remarkably high-tech in their methods.) Of course, concern about the future of family enterprise is nothing new: entrepreneurial smarts have always been devilishly hard to pass on from one generation to the next. That is why the expression "shirtsleeves to shirtsleeves in three generations" still carries so much resonance. There is little certainty that the father's or mother's drive, persistence, and abilities will be inherited by the children. But in the knowledge-based company, where creativity and innovation are so critical, the likelihood is even less.

As Sharwood looks over the lists of companies that have survived for generations, he sees a lot of what he calls hard-asset companies — beef packers, beer companies, resource companies, and a few service providers. Consider the family companies profiled in this book: two meat packers, a turkey breeder and processor, a brewer, a bearings distributor, a clothing manufacturer, a supermarket retailer, and a heating oil and gas station company. However successful these individual companies may be, they are hardly standard bearers for your high-growth gazelle industries of tomorrow.

It's not that asset-based companies will disappear in the twenty-first century — there will still be a need for factories and breweries and farmland. It's just that their share of the country's wealth is in decline. Many of them operate in mature industries in which growth is limited and the best any company can do is steal some market share from its rivals. There is never much hope of a breakthrough product or technology that will seize industry dominance — as Microsoft did with its PC operating system — or carry the industry to a higher plateau. In mature industries, business is an incremental game.

As technology changes more and more rapidly — who could have predicted the impact of the Internet? — the life cycles of the companies that are creating and commercializing technology have become compressed. In the life of a high-tech company, one year is a long time, ten years is an eternity, and no company thinks about hanging around for 100 years.

This is not to say there are no high-tech family companies — only that there are precious few of them. The one that comes most readily to mind is Motorola, the communications equipment maker based in Schaumburg, Illinois. CEO Christopher Galvin represents the third generation of his family to lead the seventy-two-year-old company, following in the footsteps of his father Robert and his grandfather Paul, the company founder. Galvin is widely considered highly qualified to run Motorola, but there is always the whiff of nepotism, even though the Galvin family owns just 3 percent of Motorola's shares. Clearly, he was not directly anointed by the family, but the weight of his name, and, the high regard in which the Galvins are held, in addition to his undoubted talent, have obviously swayed the board of directors.

So Motorola is an anomaly — a high-tech firm in which the imprint of a brilliant and forceful founder is still palpable, and in which the founder's heirs still command a significant amount of loyalty. And Motorola, while an innovative company, is not a technology leader: it is better known for applying technology than for breaking new ground. Microsoft is the more classic story of the late twentieth century. It did not exist thirty years ago, yet it has emerged as the greatest generator of stock market value in the world and as a dominant force in the computer revolution. And it's all built on sequences of computer code — not a machine, or a mill, or a new robotic cutting arm. Bill Gates, the controlling shareholder of Microsoft, has never seen himself as building a family company. Even before his first child was born, he announced that he did not intend to bequeath his fortune or his company to his progeny: "I believe that to be a dangerous practice. [My children] will have enough to be comfortable with. The rest I plan on donating to charities." In 1999, in a single donation, Gates gave $5 billion in stocks to his own foundation.

Some sceptics suggest that he may change his mind as his children grow. Many people in the early stages of forming a company do not think of legacies. Sharwood heard one young founder of a company admit that he never thought of it as a family enterprise until his children entered their teenage years. "My thirteen-year-old said, 'Dad can I have a job in my family company? For the summer?' All of a sudden, I said, 'This is *my* company.' 'But dad,' the kid asked, 'aren't we part of your company?'" Suddenly, a family company was born.

So Gates may yet soften his opposition to family enterprise. But it is fair to ask: does Gates really "own" the company and hence have the ability to pass on its significant assets? Certainly, he and co-founder Paul Allen saw the commercial possibilities of the personal computer, and Gates himself drove the Microsoft operating system to industry dominance. But surely the software engineers who write the code and brainstorm the products are as much the owners as Gates, who holds the largest block of shares. One can argue that if the engineers were to walk out the door, the "ownership" of the company's critical intellectual assets would leave with them. The hard physical assets — head office, land, even the patents — would stay with Gates and his team, and those assets have some short-term value, but the key ownership of intellectual capital would be gone.

As much as anything else, Microsoft and other software companies offer a distinctive package of culture and compensation that allows innovation to take place. Their competitive advantage consists of an amalgam of factors: a creative environment, a flexible if sometimes stressful worklife, casual dress, volleyball courts, and huge potential payoffs through the realization of stock options. That is their "edge," and it isn't something that resides in a particular family or individual. The Microsoft model says that everyone who works at the company gets a chance to own shares. Gates is one of thousands of Microsoft employee shareholders, many of them millionaires and billionaires.

The family company has difficulty finding a place in this shareholder and incentive culture. The family company is usually privately held. The shares are controlled by the ruling family and are often tied up in trusts that extend back for generations. That means there is no real opportunity to dispense stock options based on publicly traded shares — a limitation that can pose a significant challenge for companies that want to spur their people to great things. How do you instill incentives without losing family control? There are phantom share plans that try to replicate the share ownership of a public company, but they lack the medium of a real marketplace. Thus, working in a family business, as opposed to a high-growth technology company, involves some material sacrifices, even though the psychic and emotional benefits may be considerable.

The seven Smith children who now own Ellis-Don Construction have allocated 45 percent of the company's common shares to its employees, to be distributed according to years of service and ability to meet performance objectives. The shares are distributed for free, and the company is committed to buying out shareholders under a formula based on book value when they depart. Will this fire up Ellis-Don's workforce? The Smiths hope so — that is the reason for the program, which is their response to the incentive challenge facing family firms.

Of course, family companies can and do go public, thus providing an open marketplace for employees to buy and sell their shares. Some go public largely for that purpose. Or they are compelled by their need for capital to finance growth, R&D, and acquisitions. An initial public offering can also be an estate planning tool for the owners, or a way to solve a succession impasse. If you can't settle on a successor, or if choosing a successor could rip the company apart, one option is to sell off the company (or parts of it) to public shareholders.

Families wrestle with going public because it often leads to reporting requirements, regulatory demands, and — perhaps most worrisome — a loss of privacy. Also, business kin argue that going public works against the key strength of their business model — the ability to take the long view and to evade the short-termism of markets and quarterly reports, the whims of analysts and fly-by-night public investors. Family companies offer the option of working for someone who has a consistent long-term view. For example, the chief executives of family firms tend to stay around much longer than those at public companies.

Certainly, the stock market is a great disciplinarian, forcing management to zealously pursue profit instead of coasting on past glories. But some large companies have thrived for years as private family concerns, with no shortage of profits or innovation. They have relied on amenable bankers for capital. "When you go public, you get two things — money and trouble — and Cargill has enough of both," snorts Jim Cargill, the former CEO of the giant family-owned commodities company based in Minneapolis. Cargill Ltd. has remained resolutely private throughout its 135-year history.

In Canada, family companies that want to hang on to ownership control, and to satisfy their appetite for expansion capital, can have their cake and eat it too: they can tap public markets without surrendering their stranglehold on the company. The Molson family sold shares in its brewing concern as early as 1945 but has retained effective control. And capital-hungry businesses such as Ted Rogers's high-growth communications empire have managed to combine public financing with family ownership. In Canada there exists a wondrous mechanism that allows companies to issue nonvoting shares to the public, while the family holds on to the majority of the voting shares. This can seem vastly unfair to the hordes of public shareholders, who are prevented from exerting much influence over the composition of the board and the direction of the company. This model has been sharply criticized by shareholder rights advocates. In response to stock exchange guidelines, many companies have put in place "coattails provisions" that require any takeover bidder for the company's voting shares to make the same offer to the nonvoting shareholders, thus cutting them in on the action. Like them or not, nonvoting shares enable family companies to tap public financing while maintaining effective control.

Not everyone is pessimistic about the future of the family company in a knowledge society. Rein Peterson, the York University business professor and CAFE co-founder, sees a parallel between family businesses and today's knowledge companies — in each milieu, the defining aspect is personal relationships. Knowledge companies, he says, are people-type businesses, just like family companies. Surely, he postulates, there is a great deal of compatibility. Both offer an alternative to the large, inhuman corporate bureaucracies.

Peter Drucker insists that the family business should have a great future, because it naturally breeds the same culture of teamwork, values, and flat hierarchy as today's high-tech companies. In the best of these companies, entrepreneurs create a climate of collegiality and teamwork. That is, in fact, what many large, publicly traded companies are trying to do today. But creating this climate in a public company can cost millions of dollars in consultants' fees; family companies often achieve this atmosphere simply because the family members are all striving for the overall good of the company. If you ask a family business owner for his competitive advantage, he or she will usually say it's the culture — the atmosphere that allows employees to be treated like members of an extended family. Call it old-style paternalism, if you like. These days, the trendy labels are *empowerment* and *bottom-up management*. "If you had to do the same thing in a professionally run company, you'd have to bring in the consultants, like Tom Peters and Stephen Covey, to create that same kind of feeling," Sharwood explains. "But it kind of explodes naturally out of the family atmosphere."

One thing that struck me as I interviewed families in business across the country was the informality and candour of their management groups, both family and nonfamily members. In some firms I was able to move easily from office to office, talking to parents, brothers, and sisters. I encountered no sense of pulling rank, no inhibition or stuffiness. These companies are actually run like the families that own them. They are not always terribly democratic, but you get the sense that all members get to say their piece, just as they do at the dinner table. Try this in the most uptight, bureaucratic, professionally managed companies — any of the major banks, for example.

In some ways a family company — particularly in the first or second generation — is remarkably well suited to the new economy. It tends to be highly flexible. While its perspective is often long-term, it is capable of fast decision-making.

There is often a deeper sense of commitment to the business, to the *idea* of the company, than is found in large, bureaucratic public companies. While the potential for flareups always exists, family members can be more trusting with one another than corporate managers who are not related. Also, these enterprises often have closer relationships with customers — which is, after all, the mantra of today's service economy. The challenge is how to instill these values in every member of the family who is active in the company — and in the generations that follow. Can this commitment be kept fresh in every generation? That is why succession is more than just an internal issue — it is something that society has a stake in.

Can Canadian family companies, which in past decades were protected by tariffs and trade restrictions, remain vital and strong in the global economy? Is our economy too heavily dominated by small and mid-size companies controlled by sleepy, uninspired family managers? Don't ask those questions of David Lam, a forty-eight-year-old Toronto businessman who represents a new model of global family business. Lam owns Tai Foong International, an $80 million company based in Scarborough, Ontario, that buys and sells fish, mainly shrimp, around the world. Lam, who emigrated from Hong Kong in 1969 to go to university, is now the hub of an international network of associated companies. Older brother Sherman runs the Hong Kong operation, which provides financing and fish sourcing. David is a trader and distributor to wholesalers, groceries, and restaurants in four Canadian cities. Younger brother Davy (that's right, David and Davy) split his business off from David's about a decade ago and now operates a separate fish-trading business in Seattle. In the future, Davy will be marketing his brother's processed fish products in the United States.

The inspiration for this network is the brothers' father, eighty-eight-year-old Ming Hui Lam, who ran a trading business in Laos before the conflict in Southeast Asia drove the family to Hong Kong in the early 1960s. David says his father was not terribly successful in Hong Kong, mainly because of language barriers — he did not speak Cantonese or English well. But he held on to his business, which included a fish-processing plant (since closed), until his sons were ready to take over. When he moved to Canada in the mid-1970s, Ming Hui Lam found his middle son David labouring unhappily as an accountant for a big Toronto firm. He reminded his son that accounting was no profession for making money, and urged him to go into the fish-trading business — after all, brother Sherman could supply products from Hong Kong. David agreed and built a walk-in freezer in his backyard in suburban Scarborough. The business was born.

Since then, he has moved up a few notches. Tai Foong, which started out selling to Chinese wholesalers and groceries, has tackled "the Caucasian market," and has won supply contracts for Loblaw's, Fortino's, Sobey's, and other large retailers. David now estimates that its business is split 50-50 between the Chinese-Canadian and non-Chinese markets. "This is much bigger than my father had in mind," he says. The family business has not been all roses — Davy left the company because he didn't want to live constantly in his brother's shadow. Even so, the family remains close. In fact, David credits much of his success to his relations, and particularly to the complementary skills of the brothers. "Business is trust," he says. "All our brothers are working types. Some brothers in other families are not." He also notes that many Asian immigrants work hard in family businesses only to ensure that their children can be educated as professionals. That is not his story — his father always wanted his sons to go into business, and now David's own son, a commerce student at the University of Toronto, is thinking about joining Tai Foong, perhaps after a couple of years' experience with another employer.

The lesson of the Lams is that family business in the 1990s is extremely diverse. It is no longer just about knitting mills and meat-packing plants and heating oil firms; it can also involve multinational trading companies. The Lam family is a global network which makes Tai Foong admirably equipped to trade in fish on a global scale. It is also an example of how families transfer more than tangible assets across generations: they also pass on trading finesse, savvy, and bits of valuable knowledge, just as Ming Hui Lam has to his three sons. It isn't software code that he is bequeathing, but a subtle feel for business.

We still know too little about family business and why it works — there is a shortage of research, even though the family enterprise is the most widespread form of business in the world. My research took me to the University of Calgary, where business professors Jess Chua and Jim Chrisman are making it their mission to understand family businesses. For this project, they have received more than $1 million in funding from an anonymous Alberta family, widely believed to be the Mannixes of Calgary. These two professors, along with their research partner Pramodita Sharma at Dalhousie University, are part of a growing tide of academics who are starting to pay attention to the family in business. At York University in Toronto, a chair of family business has been endowed, thanks to a donation from Toronto's Tanenbaum family of steel and sports business fame.

Jess Chua says that when the money became available in 1993, he and Jim Chrisman were the only academics in their faculty who expressed much interest in the field. Business academics tend to follow what's hot, and family business is only starting to warm up. Chua admits to a soft spot for the subject: in his native Philippines, all his brothers and sisters work in the family business, which is about to move from the second to the third generation. "My siblings all want me to become an expert in a hurry," he jokes. He also believes that interest in family companies is poised to take off over the next decade. In many countries the great business empires were developed after the Second World War; those empires, like his own family's company, are about to undergo the difficult passage from the second to the third generation. Now everyone will want to know what makes these companies tick.

Chua and Chrisman want to test scientifically many of the assumptions about how to manage a family business. These assumptions are often based on experience or intuition and have not been exposed to empirical study. The researchers intend to collect data, drawing on CAFE's membership lists and other sources. For example, Chua says, there is much hand-wringing that only 30 percent of family businesses are ever passed on from the first generation to the second. "But is that bad or good?" the professor asks. "What if most family businesses don't want succession?" In fact, 30 percent may be a terrific success rate, given the circumstances. But more data are needed before assessments like this can begin. (There is some support for Chua's conjecture: the Deloitte Touche survey of family firms showed that only one-third of family company owners actually believe it is important to keep the business within the family.)

Most academic studies, and most stories in the business media, focus on the family side of the business — relationships, gender, and birth order, for example. These professors want to look at the business side. They note that while there are many academic theories of the modern firm, all of them ignore family businesses, which constitute the vast majority of enterprises, large and small. Chua and Chrisman believe that by putting family businesses under the microscope, they will be able to contribute to the overall theory of the firm.

In the short term, these two pioneers want to find out how being a family business can deliver a competitive advantage in different sectors of the economy. For example, they have observed that the media industry contains many family companies: the Aspers of CanWest Global, the Rogers of Rogers Communications, the de Gaspé Beaubiens of Telemedia, the Shaws of Shaw Communications, and so on. Why is the family model so pervasive in this industry? According to the "agency theory" of the modern firm, certain industries face heavy monitoring costs when the owners and managers of the business are not the same people. In the media industry, for example, there are costs for monitoring such issues as: Are our news stories better than the opposition's? Are good broadcast ideas being hatched? Chua and Chrisman speculate that these monitoring costs may be lower in family companies, in which ownership and management actually overlap.

Succession is another challenge. How can business owners hand down the company in a way that ensures they will also transfer competitive advantage? Chrisman points out that all competitive advantage comes down to knowledge, which is very hard to pass on from one generation of leaders to the next. Perhaps families just do it better. They may contain opportunities for transmitting knowledge that are not available in public companies. Or the advantage may lie in the family's relationships, networks, and ways of thinking and processing information, and in the unique opportunity for would-be successors to become involved in the business at a very young age. "In nonfamily firms, you don't have that opportunity," Chrisman says. And that may be the advantage that David Lam, Geoff Smith, Ray Price, Leslie Wilson, and Bruce Cuddy had over the bright young managers in public companies.

The stuffy University of Calgary seminar room, where I sat listening to the two professors, seemed far away in spirit from the family companies I had visited. Yet in those unprepossessing surroundings I came to realize that the family business may not be on its way out quite yet. It may not be the right model for every flavour-of-the-month Internet startup, but there are many kinds of businesses, low-tech and high-tech, that benefit from long-term thinking, strong core values, and a deeper intuitive knowledge. Family businesses may be repositories of some of the things that confer competitive advantage. The professors should be able to tell us about that some day.

Meanwhile, we are left with only a vague sense of what makes some of these companies great and what makes others self-destruct. In writing this book, I have looked closely at more than twenty organizations, a dozen of them upclose. Some are destroying themselves through jealousy and greed; others have found themselves in difficult situations but are valiantly coping. There is nothing perfect about a family company. The ones that are succeeding tend to be owned by people who believe strongly in a vision, a purpose, and a coherent set of values. The parents and children work to build trust and teamwork. They look after their employees and their communities, not just themselves. They are not passive, faceless owners. So what makes a resilient family company that can successfully be passed on through the generations? This may sound like motherhood, but it is a hard business reality: In the end, it is good families that make great companies.

SOURCES

T<small>HE CONTENT OF THIS BOOK</small> is derived almost entirely from more than eighty interviews I conducted between March 1997 and November 1999. Most people spoke on the record and for attribution. In fact, members of the business families profiled in the book seemed to welcome the opportunity to unburden themselves. Some of the interviews were off the record or not for attribution. In at least two chapters, I relied heavily on the recollections of anonymous sources who were very close to the action but did not want to be identified. I want to thank these people for their trust in me. I hope I have not let them down.

The most extensive individual interviews conducted were those with Eric Molson, chairman of Molson Inc., and Thomas Bata Sr., honorary chairman of the Bata Shoe Organization. Both these men were generous with their time and patience. My longest series of interviews was at BC Bearing, where five members of the family, including chairwoman Wendy MacDonald, sat down for several hours of conversation. Geoff Smith of Ellis-Don was also very open and free with his time. We conducted two extensive interviews, and Geoff also wrote a two-page response to one of my questions. I spent lunch and most of an afternoon with the Chaplins — father Jim, daughter Jan, and son Rick — at a restaurant near Cambridge, Ontario. From them I learned a lot about family dynamics in a mid-sized company. And I spent nearly four hours with Philippe and Nan-b de Gaspé Beaubien, two enthusiastic champions of family business.

I have also relied on some written sources. Professor Rein Peterson of York University generously shared with me his binder of early newsletters from the Canadian Association of Family Enterprise, of which he is a co-founder. For the Bata chapter, I found some interesting observations in *Bata: Shoemaker to the World*, by Thomas J. Bata with Sonja Sinclair. The analysis of family business in Peter Drucker's *Managing in a Time of Change* was extremely insightful. *The Molson Saga* by Shirley E. Woods Jr. delivered important historical information on that beer-making dynasty. I also drew on Edgar M. Bronfman's memoirs, *Good Spirits: The Making of a Businessman*. I read a number of general books on family business management, of which the most useful was *Generation to Generation: Life Cycles of the Family Business*, by four American authorities: Kelin E. Gersick, John A. Davis, Marion McCollum Hampton, and Ivan Landsberg. For pure inspiration, I closely read Paul Waldie's *A House Divided: The Untold Story of the McCain Family*.

As a newspaper editor, I am an inveterate collector of clippings and articles culled from various databases. *The Globe and Mail* has been a rich source of facts and background. I have also drawn information from *The Financial Post*. For the chapter on the Cuddy family, I relied on documents presented by both sides in Peter Cuddy's lawsuit against Cuddy International Corp. In writing about Saskatoon's Mitchell family, I also relied to some extent on court documents — both Fred Mitchell's lawsuit against Intercontinental Foods and Intercontinental's suit against Fred and LuAn Mitchell.

INDEX

INDEX